Critical Responses to Commonwealth Literature

Critical Responses to Commonwealth Literature

Edited by
Dr. K. Balachandran

AUTHORSPRESS
Publishers of Scholarly Books

Worldwide Circulation through Authorspress Global Network
First Published 2010
by
Authorspress
E-35/103, Jawahar Park
Laxmi Nagar, Delhi-110 092
e-mail: authorspress@yahoo.com

Critical Responses to Commonwealth Literature
ISBN 978-81-7273-571-5

Printed in India at Tarun Offset, Delhi.

Preface

Literatures written in English by the writers of Africa, Australia, Bangladesh, Canada, India, Malaysia, New Zealand, Pakistan, Nigeria, Singapore, Sri Lanka and the West Indies can be considered as Commonwealth Literature. The book titled *Critical Essays on Commonwealth Literature,* edited by me had come out in 2006. Again, there is a need for more critical materials on Commonwealth Literature, and that is why this humble book is in your hands.

Dr. (Mrs.) Lily Arul Sharmila's "Wole Soyinka's Poetry: An Epitome of African History and Culture" traces how Africa has contributed to 'Protest Literature'. The oppressive measures of the Whites led the Blacks to protest. Another social factor was the marriage between these two races. What is the duty of a poet? Are not poets concerned with the promotion of social alertness and lively consciousness to resist against the well grounded taboos in the African soil? Did Soyinka feel that he was endowed with God given gift to set things right in his land to uphold traditional and Christian beliefs?

Dr. M. Prabhakar and K. Ram Mohan in their "Black Consciousness in White: A Study of Nadine Gordimer's *A World of Strangers,"* trace the history of the Black Consciousness movement of 1960s in Africa, which has been a source of great inspiration to Nadine Gordimer who is considered to be one of "the guerrillas of the imagination" and the first South African who got the Nobel Prize for literature in 1991. Does the Igbo tribe live in the grip of numerous superstitions and blind beliefs? Do the inhabitants of the Dark Continent of Africa believe in Ogbanje, the presence of an evil spirit in the womb of a woman? Does Gordimer drive home the message through her novel *A World of Stranger* that Whites should realize that the Blacks are also human and the Whites are not superior to the Blacks?

Dr. G. J. Sathyaseelan in his "Wole Soyinka: A Known African voice of the Unknown in *The Road"* asserts that it is a play which can be appreciated while it is enacted on stage as a live presentation—a play about a day in the life of a group of drivers at the side of a Nigerian road. Does it portray their aimless existence, waiting for jobs to turn up, dull routines of talking, drinking, sleeping and dreaming of an exciting future? Is there a quest for the meaning of death? Is there a secret ritual, performed annually on certain festival occasions which includes dance, music, mime, poetry and elaborate costume—for a solemn celebration of the ancestors?

K. Naveenkumar in his "Marginalization in the Select Plays of Wole Soyinka" argues how marginalization prevails in every society. Are we marginalizing others? Are we marginalized by others? Every one has his / her own centre. Does it make others to be in margin from their point of view? Is one's centre other's margin? What are the customs of Yoruban society especially when a king dies? Does the dominant group humiliate the other group? Does it keep them away from important decisions and events of the society? Is there self-marginalization? Is it a psychological problem of an individual?

Dr. V. Sangeetha's "Hurtle as Vivisector and illuminator in Patrick White's *The Vivisector*" asserts that this novel is about the gradual development of Hurtle Duffield as a painter whose spiritual quest is almost satisfied and reaches near perfection towards the end. Does white identify the filth which Hurtle portrays with man's inner spiritual state? Does the filth complicate the search for God? Does White justify Hurtle's approach to God through vivisection? Has he come to terms in some way or other with the moral dimension of the world? Is God the vivisector? Is God the Artist? Is he the God?

Dr. S. Robert Gnanamony's "Aestheticizing Aboriginality in Jack Davis' *No Sugar*" is an attempt to bring out the various struggles and oppressions of the Australian Aboriginal community had to face and their indigenality in the depression years. How the natives of Australia were conquered, then colonised and then turned into the other? Do the white colonisers want the aborigines to be educated? Do the aborigines want to surrender their body and spirit, their land and their possessions to the colonisers? Do the indigenous people of Australia know that Australia is not Europe and any attempt to europeanise Australia may not bear fruit?

Dr. S. Ganesan in his "The Will to Live: A Study of Survivors in the Novels of Mordecai Richler" confirms that Richler's leading characters exhibit great survival ability. Do his characters often fight for survival against all odds? Have they faced the brunt of anti-Semitism and McCarthysim? Have their experiences made them tough, cunning and ruthless? Was Richler concerned with the survival of the Jews in Canada and else where? Do the heroes and villains survive in his novels? Do the heroes save their lives, tradition and humane values? How do the villains survive? By destroying the innocent and the beautiful?

Dr. Raj Kumar Sharma and Mrs. Asra Sultana Mouda in their paper, "Mapping the North as a Female Space in Aritha Van Herk's *Geograpictione Places Far From Ellesmere*" remark that this fiction is a new genré Geografictione, emerged out of the fusion of geography and fiction in the literary panorama. Herk has dexterously interwoven a logical pattern from some unconventional constituents unexplored so far in this remarkable genré. Is it an exploration for a different woman's space distinct from that of male which is symbolically depicted in the exploration of landscape? Does North symbolize an essential source of myth, a convenient place to escape to? Does it represent creativity, charm, invention, space and adventure for the narrator?

Dr. P.K. Patra in his "The Transcendental Power of Love: A Study of Garcia Marquez's *Love in the Time of Cholera*" writes how the novelist shows the contours of love clearly without any pretension and reservation. What is significant in love? Is it not passion for love and its exploration till the protagonist is old? Can old age take away the physical charm and leave the emotion of love? Is the novel an amalgam of two starkly contrasting elements, the sacredness of love and love's embodiment in every day's experience? Is it a portrayal of the conflict between Nature and culture? Which one will win? Is love an eternal fountain which never dries up?

In "Confessionalism in the Poetry of Kamala Das," ***Mrs. Lakshmi Pramod*** observes how Kamala Das's poetry is a recordation of her own experiences and observations; her own unfulfilled love and her own sexual exploitation, frustration, disillusionment she suffered in a male-dominated society. Is she very much a poet of the body, which brings to mind the style of Ezekiel? Is her diction noted for its simplicity and clarity? How is her style? Is it simple? How is her imagery? Familiar and common place? Is her poetry a quest of her woman persona to seek emotional fulfilment within or outside marriage?

S. Kavitha in her "The, Element of Mysticism in the Select Poems of Sri Aurobindo," notices how the seer poet's poetry is a unique blend of the orient and the occident in theme and technique, philosophy and vision. Is mysticism a direct and immediate experience of the sacred or the knowledge derived from such an experience? Does it occur in all the religions of the world? Does its importance vary? Is the experience immediate and overwhelming divorced from the common experience of reality? Is it self-authenticating? Is it ineffable? Does mysticism or mystical experience differ from an individual to another, from one country to another?

Dr. S. John Peter Joseph's "The Poet as Social Chronicler and Reformer: A Study of Basavaraj Naikar's (Trans.) Musings of Sarvajna" is a study of Basavaraj Naikar who popularises Sarvajna, one of the geniuses of Kannada Poetry to the English-speaking world. Naikar's attempt is lauded because of his critical skill of selecting the salient thoughts of Sarvajna's poetry, rejecting the repetitive ones. His analytical approach, clarity of thought and lucidity of style are commendable. Sarvajna's poetry speaks "Friendship with the virtuous is like tasting honey/But the company of the vicious will bring you the excruciating pain of breaking your kidney bones."

Dr. (Mrs.) Thaiyyal Nayaki in her "The Post-Colonial Interpretation of Bharati Mukherjee's *The Tiger's Daughter*" affirms that "bicultural Self" rocks the personality of the heroine of *The Tiger's Daughter*. Is the portrayal autobiographical? Is it a problem of split personality? Do women find their distinctive voices, not before they have battled violently with the images of their own selves as representations of 'otherness'? What is the novelist's message? Is it mongrelization and not just the conflict between two selves?

Dr. V.B. Vinod's "Situations of Incomprehension: Arun Joshi's *The Strange Case of Billy Biswas*" speaks of the why of human intentions and actions. Does family entail commitments and duties? Does it mean submitting oneself to the demands imposed by others? Is Billy a renegade who has to be restrained? Is a

District collector responsible for filing the official report, for, he is in possession of the 'known' facts? Has he to reveal the dark mossy labyrinths of the soul?

Dr. V. Ramesh in his "The Paradoxical Psyche of an Archetypal Indian Woman: Sita in Anita Desai's *Where Shall We Go This Summer*? A Feminist Study" analyses the character of Sita who is an embodiment of intolerance—a hyper-sensitive and out of ordinary character. Does she symbolise a distinct dimension to the image of women in the family and society? Is feminism a worldwide cultural movement to secure a complete equality of women with men in the enjoyment of all human rights—moral, religious, social, political, educational, legal, economic and so on?

Dr. R. Swaminathan's "K.S. Venkataramani as a Pioneer and the Seminal Themes of the Indo-Anglian Fiction" recalls how K.S. Venkataramani was the first Hindu writer in the Madras Presidency, who used the medium of English. Did he observe the simple country folk keenly to hammer all his thoughts into shape? Was he an ardent Gandhian who advised Ahimsa is the noblest rule of conduct that governs our relationships and actions? Are his noels punctuated with the article of non-violence? Did he believe in Gandhiji's vision of Ram Raj—where all are equal socially, economically and morally?

Dr. (Mrs.) Ketaki Goswami in her "Indo-Anglian Drama: Sources, Themes and Techniques" attempts to survey the Indian English contributions of Drama—Mohan Rakesh, Badal Sircar, Girish Karnad, Vijay Tendulkar and Mahesh Dattani. For Rakesh, do non-communication and a tragic sense of life verging on fatalism, matter much? Do the plays of Karnad locate and offer a space for testing out the dichotomies and relative strength of the opposing forces in the society? Are gender issues the most important ingredients in a Dattani play? Does he pose a question, depict a situation or abstain from prescription?

Mrs. V. Anbarasi in her "The Element of Immediate and Enduring Delight in Vijay Tendulkar's *His Fifth Woman*—An Analysis" remarks that there is no unfolding of an absorbing tale of revelatory facts but it is highly dramatic and arresting from the beginning to the end. Did Tendulkar's plays deeply affect the society because of their delineation of stark realities of life? Did his plays jolt the society out of its stupor and was he punished for that? Does his portrayal of women reveal his deep understanding of their problems and feelings? How is his portrayal of life, its various problems and ills? Have his efforts opened fresh awareness?

Prof. Kh. Kunjo Singh's "Basavaraj Naikar's *A Dreamer of Freedom*: A Post-colonial Magic Realism Play" observes how Naikar interweaves, in an ever-shifting pattern, a sharply etched realism in representing ordinary events and descriptive details together with fantastic and dream like elements, as well as with materials derived from myth and fairy tales. Is *A Dreamer of Freedom* a Post-colonial magic realism play, despite its being a historical play about 1857 Indian war of Independence? Does it present the patriotic actions of Bhaskara Rao Bhabe of Naragund Kingdom of Karnataka?

Dr. K. Balachandran in his "Social Problems as Portrayed in Sri Lankan Poetry" asks the same question posed by L. Piyadara, "Can there be peace in Sri Lanka?" One can migrate to any country and settle there. Can it be successful or unsuccessful? To have one's root in one's own country is easy. Will it be so in an alien country? Can one attack any language? Can one be jealous of another language? If God of Death snatches one's life in one's prime years, can it be taken easily? Is unsuitability of horoscopes a problem leading to unexpected death in the war front? Will life in a city fetch happiness? Can one return to one's village for happiness, peace of mind and contentment?

Dr. Basavaraj Naikar's "V.S. Naipaul's *A Million Mutinies Now: A Post-modern Travelogue*" is a fine analysis of the travelogue. Does Naipaul believe in the British values of reason, order and measure? Has he developed a broad humanist vision instead of a parochial brahmanical outlook towards life? Has he exhibited his ability to meet all kinds of people and understand them sympathetically? Is the reader bored when he goes through this travelogue of 520? Does he follow a discursive method of narration or a fictional mode? Does it tend to become minute, protographic and microscopic? Does it help to visualise the whole scene?

The twenty-one critical responses (essays) throw much more light on the various aspects of Commonwealth Literature in a very easy and understandable style. These responses will be very useful to the teachers, researchers and students of Commonwealth Literature for a better understanding and appreciation.

I will be immensely satisfied when these Critical Responses are used and quoted. The success belongs to the valuable contributors, the users and the publisher.

Wish you all a very useful time with this work of literary responses.

—K. Balachandran

Acknowledgements

I sincerely thank Dr. M. Ramanathan, the Vice-Chancellor, and Dr. M. Rathinasabapathi, the Registrar and other Officials of Annamalai University for their gracious permission to edit and publish this book, *Critical Responses to Commonwealth Literature.*

I express my sincere gratitude to all the distinguished contributors who responded readily to my invitation for contributing to and enriching this book.

I would like to record my appreciation and gratitude to the publishers, Authorspress, Delhi who have brought out this book in a very short period and also very attractively.

I like to thank the Indian Association for the Commonwealth Studies, and all those who associate themselves with Commonwealth Literature, for their constant inspiration and encouragement to me.

My sincere gratitude is to Subhiksha Computer, Annamalai Nagar, for preparing the Hard Copy.

I express my heart-felt gratitude to GOD ALMIGHTY for HIS Inspiration and Guidance for ever and ever.

—*K. Balachandran*

List of Contributors

1. *Mrs. Lilly Arul Sharmila,* Lecturer in English, Tagore Arts College, Lawspet, Pondicherry–605 007.
2. *Dr. M. Prabakar,* Associate Professor of English, P.G. Centre, Kakatiya University, Warangal– 504106, Andhra Pradesh.

   Mr. K. Ram Mohan, Ph.D. Research Scholar, Kakatiya University.
3. *Dr. G. Sathyaseela,* Reader in English, Madurai Thiyagarajar College (Autonomous), Madurai–625 009.
4. *K. Naveen Kumar,* Ph.D. Research Scholar, Annamalai University, Annamalai Nagar–608 002.
5. *Dr. V. Sangeetha,* Reader in English, Periyar University, Salem.
6. *Dr. G. Robert Gnanamony,* Prof. of English, Kalasalingam University, Krishnan Koil, Srivilliputhur (via), Virudhu Nagar (Dt.)–626 190
7. *Dr. S. Ganesan,* Asst. Prof. of English, The Rajah's College (Autonomous), Pudukottai 622 001.
8. *Dr. Rajkumar Sharma,* Lecturer and ***Mrs. Asra Sultana Mouda,*** Asst. Prof. , Department of English, Al Margeb University, Lebya.
9. *Dr. P.K. Patra,* Reader & Head, Gauhati University, Kokrajhar Campus, Kokrajhar–783 370. ASSAM
10. *Mrs. Lakshmi Pramod,* Lecturer in English, St. Thomas College, Bhilai, Durg, Chatishgarh.
11. *S. Kavitha,* Lecturer in English, Periyar Govt. Arts College, Cuddalore–608 001.
12. *Dr. John Peter Joseph,* Reader in English, St. Xavier's College, Palayamkottai – 627 002, Tirunelveli (Dist.), Tamil Nadu.

13. *Dr. (Mrs.) Thayyal Nayaki,* Reader in English, TN Arts College, Dindugal, Tamil Nadu.
14. *Dr. V.B. Vinod,* Asst. Prof. of English, National Institute of Technology, Trichy.
15. *Dr. V. Ramesh,* Asst. Prof. of English, Thiyagarajar Polytechnic College, Salem–636 005.
16. *Dr. R. Swaminathan,* Department of English, Kanchi Mamunivar Centre for PG Studies, Pondicherry–605 008.
17. *Dr. (Mrs.) Ketaki Goswami,* Reader in English, East Calcutta Girl's College, Kolkatta Lake Town, West Bengal–700 006.
18. *Mrs. V. Anbarasi,* Lecturer in English, Govt. Arts College, Salem–636 007.
19. *Prof. Kh. Kunjo Singh,* Dept. of English, Manipur University, Canchipur–795 003.
20. *Dr. K. Balachandran,* Prof. of English, Annamalai University, Annamalai Nagar–608 002.
21. *Dr. Basavaraj Naikar,* Prof. & Head, Department of English, Karnatak University, Dharwad, Karnataka.

Contents

1 Wole Soyinka's Poetry: An Epitome of African History and Culture

— Dr. Lily Arul Sharmila

Post-colonial panorama becomes the major focus of the writings that fall into the division of Commonwealth Literature. The poetic muse confers creative yeast on the literary minds to portray the issues of black people. Africa has a lengthy history of occidental profession, settlement and modernization by the way of industrialization leading to the detribalization of Africans. The suffocated Africans, sustaining colonial scars yield to the formation of texture termed 'protest literature.' The oppressive measures approbated by the whites to the large extent offensive against the African victims have been presented realistically as they are. The prohibition of mixed marriage between white and other colours and boundary that segregates the races in accordance with separate areas are some of the examples of different forms of ordeals experienced by the native Africans.

The post-colonial hazards and havoc wreaked by the fair community of South Africa under white administration lend the poets subjects of social issues with varied moods. The poets are concerned with the promotion of social alertness and lively consciousness to resist against well-grounded taboos in African soil. The poems make an enormous spectrum of anti-colonial and imperialist battle to be complete. They evoke the picture of cultural struggle objectifying the restoration of rationality in the African citizens in history, and advocating the dignity and decorum of all kinds in human life. The pen portraits elucidate a sharp contrast between imperialist might on the victims and the contending forces (*Research in African Literatures*).

The poetic subjects selected for evaluation here display variegated impulses pertaining to the upgradation of the victims in the state of patriarchy and imperialism. The subject on the psychological complexities of man calls for the exercise of humanistic directives under the pretext of African struggle for freedom. A permanent oasis is visible through the corner of Africa with her plentitude by way of yielding opulence to the universe in the possible means. The intention of the poet is to witness socio-economic and culture-based human society.

Imperialism has ever been the common historical bane since the genesis of human race on earth. It is the phase of reasoning that most of the countries in the world have been caught in the diabolical imperialism. The nations outside Britain and America have experienced painful hours, and got suffocated through and through in the heat of social injustice at the hands of British and European imperialists. The challenges between colonizers and colonized worlds have been portrayed in multifarious dimensions and shades of archetypal experience (*African Literature Today*).

The subjects poetically handled are well grounded on solid veracity of African phenomena but treated with poetic fantasy. The poetic vigour imbued with the shades of experience from history and politics have combined with the basic features of human world. The complete subjects from African history by virtue of heightened imaginative power have been introduced in lucid forms. The prime object of African enlightened few was to rebuild history through mechanics of fantasy in the context of the illiterates, labourers, tireless strivings during the former and the later phases of their independence. (*Introduction to African Literature*).

A series of ordeals has impacts on the native minds. A timely revival expostulating itself in their urge for writing and revolt against imperial rule could awaken up the people from the slumberous state. The feeling of oneness had not been evolved yet and it was at the point of upspringing in them. There was no concept of a nation, the absence of which dampened their vitality and power of rationality. To reduce to be a mere race and tribe was very disgusting and disgracing, and so the independence of all kinds is indispensable for man to rise up to be a complete being of potentiality which is impeded by certain taboos and shackles of the foreign rule. Being inspired by the patriotic tempo and gusto, the literary geniuses of South Africa submit conspicuously the records of confrontation between the contending powers. (*Yearning: Race, Gender and Culture*).

Africa unfolds a creative space owing to the mighty mimetic impulses of her masses. There are umpteen illustrations covering a vast range of literary texture, modes of expression highlighting the locale, atmosphere, African environment conveyed through means of theory and concepts suggestive of linguistic and social diversity. African verses act as a tool to represent society with recreating means and images perhaps to activate it, to construct and to upbuild. African verses enlighten the track of social sphere and illumine it towards state of righteousness. African poetry is a splendorous form to target at transformation within the realm where the system exercises unscrupulously a sense of bias in terms of community and race. The poems display a picture gallery delineating the severe system of racial legislation in South Africa since the World War. Poems as a reproving rod lash at the predatory disposition of politically and economically strong imperialists. The revolt and ethical standard instituted by the poems brought transition upon the foibles of South African locale into a upgraded platform of perpetual implication.

African poetry undoubtedly holds the mirror up to nature and presents history and culture of the nation as they are. A careful reading of the poems helps one apprehend the spectacle that engaged the Africans most. Imperialism gave rise to the notion of nationhood advocated by the patriotic fervour in the native Africans who began to cherish national aspirations as they could comprehend the glory of their motherland. A sense of suffering led them to human wisdom and spiritual awakening. It was a binding force for the African writers to explore, investigate and gain the grasp over their mighty land, its history and predicament. The ordeals and adverse forces sustained and encountered in the colonial period are contemplated upon so as to impart geniuses a novel creative scape. The flavour of American poetry sprang forth from unfathomable depth of their national mindset. The laughter, gloom and sigh offered the poets the sublimated poetic credentials envigorating them to assert that Black is a Charm *(Poems of Black Africa).*

The Africans collectively endured racist oppression. Racial integration has modified in a basic manner the general source that once acted as prerequisites for winning independence. The black people sustained the holocaust of slavery. But soon the prophetic voices resounded everywhere targeting at the transformation through obsessive interest for racial integration, indispensable to enhance the stature of black life. After the seventies, a phase of reformation in the concept of social identity dawned upon the black community. The major motto was to seek profession for black folks in the industrial sphere. Cultural critique had a particular bearing on black artists. The enlightened intellectuals took upon themselves a greater responsibility of not only promulgating through their artistic forms but also partaking in the black liberation struggle.

The man who waged a crusade against the black oppression and autocratic white was Wole Soyinka, a writer, poet, much remembered as a playwright, UNESCO Ambassador, for the promotion of Nigerian culture, human right, freedom of expression and all kinds. He was the first African to bag the Nobel Prize for Literature in 1986. Being a son of a clergy, he founded the anti-corruption organization in order to seek justice for the students of the university. He was enriched with varied experiences and multifarious skills. He played a vital role in African political history. Much of his portraits of his literary composition throws light on the exploitation of the oppressive boots, and he was very contemptuous about the Nigerian military dictators and political despotism worldwide. His mother was a respected activist of Women's Movement in the regional community. Her adherence to the staunch Anglican faith imparted Wole Soyinka spiritual sustenance and the sense of veneration to the African tradition and values of past.

Soyinka felt that he was endowed with God given gift to set things aright on his land on upholding traditional and Christian beliefs. His literary achievements act as an eye opener to the African community. He has related the current affairs with negrophiles and in umpteen occasions he revolted against government censorship. His feature film 'Culture in Transition,' his famous novel, *The Interpreter*, his dramatic pieces '*Before the Black Out*' and his political speeches sneer at the cult of personality and the corrupt government in African dictatorship. When his nation grapples with the grip of civil war, he worked with patriotic gusto enduring imprisonment for several times. During much of his imprisonment, creativity set a flame and he persisted upon producing more number of work of art..

In 1976, he published a collection of verse under the major title *Ogun Abibiman* which is an accurate analysis of the practical problems and distress of the masses. His collection of poems incessantly rails at the misgovernment in the midst of aggressive despotic African regimes. He designs the drama of existence with his expanded cultural perspectives and visions, entwined with the poetic beauty. His verses are characteristically the outspoken criticism of apartheid and the politics of racial segregation *(Wole Soyinka Biography)*.

His achievements in the sphere of literature and philosophy are outstanding and extraordinary. As a contemporary creative genius of Africa, he has raised a huge cathedral of literary culture, tradition, social order and systems. He was brought under the colonial English speaking background and Yoruba ethnic heritage. Most phase of his writings rested upon the creative yeast offered by the African world and its varied features. His autobiographical works exemplify the intensified political plague of colonial past spread during his lifetime. Thus the entire body of his literature, whether poems, essays, dramatic pieces, make a panoramic view of black African's recurrent cycle of stupidity the portraits framed to alert African community of the chronic fraudulence and abuse of power corruption the imperialists indulged in.

The crippling legacy of European imperialism advocated patriotic feelings in Soyinka. He envisioned a liberated scenario of Africa that could escape its degradation by virtue of technical progress of the present. The African tradition accommodating contemporary reality and obdurate facts lays a firm base for the days to come with the windows open and fresh breeze of self-retrieval, cultural reminiscence and cultural preservation blows. Not only did much of his huge literary compendium openly challenge African authorities but also engage Soyinka in political realism. His heroic deeds led him to a detention, tribulation, acquittal, and he suffered imprisonment and seclusion. He has related his trauma in his works and he has entered into the next phase of intense literary productivity with the publication of *A Shuttle in the Crypt*. The poems in this collection are the fine expressions of his scornful memories and embittered feelings on the hours of imprisonment.

Soyinka's emotional outburst featuring the nature of his art and authenticating the roots of Yoruba tradition certainly identifies his aesthetic codes and practice with other European and African writers. The political history and cultural thoughts manifested in his writings explicate Africa's decline into brutal military government. His literary service to mankind lies in the notion of organic revolution which heightens the intense communal revival during the hours of well integrated cultural self-apprehension, a virtue appropriated to the African society.

The critics of Soyinka can do in a concise foreword like this to quote a few passages substantiating with comments. The unique flavour of this poetry is a subtle unification of simplification and actuality. The supreme nature of his poetic renderings aided Soyinka a writer of eminence to bag the Nobel Prize. A Roscoe in his essay on "Soyinka as poet" in William Walsh's *Readings in Commonwealth Literature* says about what forms the basis of Soyinka's poetry and drama. The universality, the contemporary relevance, adoptability and flexibility are the determinants that annex meaning to his work. Roscoe cites a Christian spokesman to authenticate the hold of Ifa, the traditional religion of the Yoruba people.

> If a will not die; because it is the
> Africanised agesless wisdom and
> Like the phoenix, it will always arise
> From its own ashes, fresh, young invigorated,
> Dynamic, instinct with new life and vitality
> To run another course. With reference to
> Yoruba Traditional Religion, one single
> Aspect of a system embracing all of
> Yoruba Tradition of Life.
>
> (William Walsh)

The tradition of Soyinka is a lively tradition, which he invested to the large extent for creative use unlike other compatriots. There is in his poetry absorption of the past and present, an ideal fusion.

In the poem 'Death in the Dawn', the poet muses on Lagos; one morning a white cockerel flew out of the dusk and dashed against windscreen. A mile further, he witnessed a motor accident and a freshly dead man in the smash. The cock is a sacrificial offering to propitiate the deity and it is so common for the Yoruba practice. The death of a man by accident on the road is associated to the belief that Yoruba owed to Ogun, the God of the roads. The poet asks: "Is this mock grimace/This closed contortion-II." Here cock smashed against the windscreen foretells the death of the man on the road. 'Kill a cock in one's mouth' is a Yoruba saying for mockery.

The information on the tradition of Yoruba is quite essential for a reader of Soyinka's poetry to apprehend the packed poem, 'Rust is Ripeness'. His ambitious poem 'Idanre' holds universal appeal due to its tremendous appeal to the human conditions. This poem is an outcome of a practical experience. It has been written in romantic vein, promoted by sharpened sensitivity and heightened imaginative power. There is a final postscript image:

> And no one speaks of secrets in this land
> Only that the skin be bared to welcome rain and
> Earth prepare that seeds may smell.
> And roots take flash within her and men
> Wake naked into harvest tide.
> The rainstorm, of the first season.

Yet the first thunder clap lent the breath of harvest. A series of pictorial elements—sun rising over a tarmac hill, rich yielding of the year, with the picture of extravagance, abundance, plentitude, glorious throbbing for life in fullness—enhance the charm of Soyinka's verse *(Idanre and other Poems).*

Idanre makes a philosophical speculation with the revelation of the metaphysical mind of Soyinka. "Let all wait for the circulation of time's acrobat." The poem transcends the tension and complexity of the tormenting decades. It achieves universality and holds many implications to all people irrespective of caste, creed and nationality. The symbols used in this poem are evocative, transcending the inner mystery of the poet. To modern world the poem connotes the state of human life related in literary studies by many great masterminds. One is strongly reminded of Eliot's East Coker, "In my beginning is my end in my end is my beginning." While reading Idanre, the concise expressions of Soyinka, "The chronicle abides in clay texts and fossil textures" refers to the notion of absurdism (existential belief) that everything under the sun of human life, turns to dusts and ashes. It is suggestive of human life, fleeing and fleeting with its alternatives of happiness and sadness, poverty and abundance, life and death in cyclic motion. Behind his philosophical contemplation, there run an undercurrent of vigour and a torrential vitality for life, as there is always a sense of veneration in the poet for the objects of nature (earth, rain, seeds, roots, tree, sky, leaves and so). Thematically speaking, this poem is an outstanding piece of composition, which vindicates Soyinka's splendorous poetic attainment.

The substance of the poem Idanre constituted by the poet's variegated practical experiences and accounted from the hours of his walk organizes panoramic renderings so well. The poet visited the rock hills of that name; a God suffused gazing of primal gigant and mastodons, "petrified through some strange history, suckled by mists and clouds." Idanre is a record of that walk through wet woods and sublimated the essence of the night of the poet. The poem abounds in narrative passages, tells of the Yoruba view of the seasons and cyclical movement. It also explicates human life everywhere with its binary opposites, duality, alternatives of melancholy and ecstasy, plenty and paucity, life and mortality following one another in their cycle.

> This road have I trodden in a time beyond
> Memory of fallen leaves beyond
> Thread of fossil on the slate, yet I must
> This way again, let all wait the circulation
> Of time's acrobat, who pray
> For dissolution: the chronicle abides in clay text
> And fossil textures

For a complete understanding of the African poetic scene, one needs to delve deep into the poems of Soyinka. His poems 'Agbor Drancer', 'Dedication', 'To My First White Hairs' and 'Telephone Conversation' display the enormous richness of details in a very accurate and coherent fashion.

The poem 'Agbor Drancer' presents a sharp and daring personal insight into the inert matter, pulsating waves of awakening marked with complexities and upheavals in African political scenario. The whole poem is a metaphorical representation of Africa and her people, the oppressive features that crippled the African phenomena. His exposition and expressions of valuable ideas demonstrate what he saw and felt around African society. The poet seeks to survey Africa caught in the throb of a drum, treading the intricate pattern rippling to meet the green clouds of the forest. The poet casts over a sense of weariness of African world in this line, "tan limbs like fresh foliage in the sun."

He represents propensities, aspiration, ideals, hopes and anxieties, joys and sorrows of the black citizens awaiting independence. The poet says that he should answer Africa's communal call and he loses himself in her warm caress. He expresses his heart-felt feelings to her having confined to the spot. This poem is an envisionment of the poet on the awaiting triumph over diabolical forces of imperialists. *(Perspectives on African Literature*).

The poem 'Telephone Conversation' has been woven around the subject of racial prejudice of the white people. It is an imaginary telephone conversation between the poet and an English landlady about renting a house. It conspicuously offers a scene of oppression faced by the black in renting a house in London. In order to fix the house, he revealed his identity and she queries about his physical features

> How dark?.... I had not misheard Are you light or very
> dark?Brown like plain chocolate or Milk chocolate.....

The black tenant was filled with remorse when the English landlady persisted upon knowing his skin colour, and so he asked her to come and see his complexion instead of listening to his description over the phone. A practical situation described in the poem bears a strong testimony for the sense of discrimination the black in their living environment suffered. This poem is an epitome of twentieth century Africa and a sombre criticism on the African social, political and economic life. In respect of poetic technique, Soyinka never showed a distinct liking for high sounding and impressive diction, but evolved a principle of simple living and high thinking.

The poem 'Dedication' displays faith and hope amidst suffering. It expresses powerfully Soyinka's yearning for future want of change of state. The poem is well grounded on the union of his mental vision and external reality. It bears the best testimony of Soyinka's glorification of anything that is African. Being endowed with a prophetic urge and visionary strength to aid his

African generation, Soyinka proclaims gospel that "Earth will share the rafter's envy the air will not deny you." He considers all the oppressions that were done under the sun to be vicious. He beholds the tears of such as were exploited and they had no comfort and there was power on the side of oppressor. He envisages that there is vanity and vexation of spirit in the world of Africans that can be dissipated by the illuminating master forces rising out of abundance in African soil.

> Yield man tides like the sea
> And ebbing leave a meaning on the fossilled sands.

The poet prophetically views the future of Africa. He has a firm faith in the order and benevolence of Mother Nature and land. He contemplates upon a kind of living on a higher plane to go to a higher platform.

> Child—your tongue arch
> To scorpion tail, spit straight return to danger threats
> Yet coo with the brown pigeon
> Tendril dew between your lips.....

The poet apprehends the cardinal facts and generate his visionary experience to the Mankind. He endeavours vigorously to refashion the human existence in conformity with the existing patterns, values and systems of African society. He has been a participant in the history of his own troubled generation as well as the recorder of the great African trial (*Three Nigerian Poets*).

> Earth's honeyed milk, wine of he only rib
> Now roll young tongues in honey
> Till your cheeks are swarming honeycombs
> Your world needs sweetening child.....

This part of the poem offers a contrast picture, and a positive view of life to necessarily inculcate well-stimulated zeal and zest in the future generation of Africa. The poet not only explores a sense of alienation between him and his environment but sustains the world with the element of hope that exists in the underlying principles of life. He treats of certain metaphysical concepts grounded in optimism and faith.

Be ageless as dark peat, but only that rains
Fingers may wash you not the feet of men tread upon you.....

He directs his thoughts towards African community, channelising to ease the masses encumbered with loads of care and distress.

Long on your lips, of salt that you may seek
None from tears. This rain water is the gift
Of Gods—drink of its purity bear fruits in season.

In counselling the forthcoming generation with a series of instructions, Soyinka attempts to observe the world around him. He had respect for the terrestrial world of common reality. He opens an intercourse with the natural world guided by boundless enthusiasm and didactic strain. He grapples with some of the actualities through communication of his feelings and the penetration into the natural world outside (*Poems by Wole Soyinka*).

The major contention of this poem 'Dedication' is to record the veracity that duty bound Soyinka takes the strength of his art to propagate the universal human ideals so as to promote solemn aspects in the life of man. 'Dedication' is a modern poem that makes an imagistic representation of the moral strategies needed to transform the present state of affairs in the African world. This poetic piece comes to the readers as a prime object of courage and inspiration promoting optimistic directives to encounter the future challenges. The poet says that like the vampires of imperialism, the Mother Nature will not partake in inflicting pains on the citizens of Africa. Though Africa experiences a seeming fall due to the heinous attitude of white, Africa clutches oars of progress zestfully and grasps the essentials of life. The liveliness and vitality in black masses compared to yam that is wholly earthed yet retains its warmth of water, convey the symbolic implication of unassailed, undaunted spirit of blacks after the intense scars of the racial prejudice wreaked by the imperialist. No diabolical force can uproot the African nation, which is ageless as the Mother Earth, which is not for trodden upon but to receive fertility from the showers of rain.

Lawrencian principle handed down to the younger generation draws much similarity to that of Soyinka. This poem as a beacon light ushers the masses of African to be as innocent as a brown pigeon and as vile as scorpion tail. Earth is the abode that shields people as the heart of kernel. The patriotic fervour of Soyinka runs though the poem 'Dedication' and undoubtedly instills in his people a hope of regeneration and renewal after the heavy odds and assaults inflicted by the colonizer. The poem achieves its objectives with an inkling of sermon to gospel the forthcoming generation to run a good race and complete the course of life. The poetic expression "haste to repay the debt of birth" requires many ways of interpretation. "Yieldman tides of sea ebbing" refers to the active and ambitious soul, for a great enterprise of Africa for splendour is the upbuilding of man.

The poem 'Dedication' unfolds a spacious venue for the articulation of thoughts of illumination on the mental health of the blacks and prospective future of Africa. The poet has a vision on particular future for Africa. He yearns for establishing a kind of relativity between the life of man and the life characterized by progressive features. He combines within himself the evolutionary instinct exemplified in this poem. He upholds that man should not have any fellowship with unfruitful works of darkness but reprove the frailties of man.

Soyinka was among the one who rose to the defence of the individual against the injustices and brutality of colonizers. He studied African life from a new angle. It is indeed a panorama of the new life in Africa, a disillusionment of the past and a new search for values of life. He is a nationalist like Tagore who said "Into that heaven of freedom let my country awake." He synthesizes with the feelings of varied human emotions and directives, evolved out of dreams, hopes, prophetic urge, sense of solidarity and progress. He impresses "Yield man tides of the sea ebbing." In his poems, there is an apparent leaning towards moral principles combined with the thirst for dispersing the seeds of such directives, hailing from great masters to confer benefits upon the entire human race. As a cultural critic of Africa, Soyinka points out the rising up of new mental enlightenment and emancipation, extolling African zest, analytic frame of mind, moral principles, unity and enriched experience scored out of bearing the cross adversity that leads to human wisdom. Thus as a literary master, he dreams of the formation of well-ordered sociopath; he wants the deliberate expansion in all spheres of society.

In the larger human context, the dreams and visions of the poet inescapably reflect the existential problems of his own nation, race and fellowmen. As a literary master, he envisions on the well-ordered socio path and the deliberate expansion in all spheres of society. It was chiefly the oppressive features that crippled Africa but the poet is in trance about sufficient increase in revival consciousness. The anxieties, idealism, aims, deep sympathy for the suffering masses, his abhorrence of social injustice, misuse of power all these have been the features explored and poetized.

Soyinka renders the subtle nuances of the life of Africans, uniquely in coloured vibrations instituted by images, symbols, impressions, satire, pathos and irony. His style though simple, very powerfully executes desirable objectives of the poem. It is the human world that he paints with true colour. The setting for the portrait of Africa has been sketched both historically and geographically with a fine sense of local colour and his characteristic image.

He uses the external world as a mirror to reflect his internal feelings, directness of speech and self-revelation. Earth, soil, wind, roots, squirrels, fruits sun, pigeon, honeycomb, rainwater. He enriches the texture of his verse by means of symbols. The multiple perspectives and symbolic dimensions add stateliness to his poetry. His symbolism opens a venue for the identification of the self with the nation, mankind, himself and with the universe. The symbols bring before the mental eye of the readers umpteen associations related to themes. The choice of words encourages the readers to form the images. The similes and metaphors used by Soyinka in his poems are so enthralling that can present a long catalogue of theme.

The poems of Soyinka encompass the forces that tormented the African masses in colonial period. African black and their affairs constitute the major part of his work. The impact of his works is wider as the promotion of healthy social life has been firmly recommended. His literary world gains prominence through depiction of facts that have direct bearing upon African phenomena. Twentieth century African world, its varied landscape of wilderness, historical features, modified social, political customs, transcending situations, colonial scenes, attitude of the white, aspirations, whims and fancies of the administrators all those aspects are subsumed into the poetry of Soyinka. Imbuing redemptive principles, Soyinka recommends some of the fundamental values of Africans for the serene state of existence on earth. As a leader of thoughts he has succeeded in interpreting aspirations and hopes and the attainments of African world for the formation of national character. He has directed his attention to the African themes the essential dignity of African men, wealth of African colonial experiences with all African tragic conditions, complexities and ambiguities. Thus colonial literary scene just as other transformed faces of the human world in all the spheres experiences a surging tide of progress characterized by the extended critical tastes and expanded impulses for the modified trends in literature.

Works Cited

African Literature Today, Haeinemann Educational Books, Annual, London.

Bier Ulli (ed.), *Introduction to African Literature,* Longman, London, 1967.

Dyson Michael. *The Plight of Men,* Z. Magazine, Feb, 1989.

Freire, Panto. *Pedagogy of the Oppressed,* New York, Seabury, 1970.

Harper World Poetry Database: *Poems by Wole Soyinka,* 2nd edition, Rex Collings, 1972.

Heywood Christopher (Ed.), *Perspectives on African Literature,* Haeinemann Education Books, London, 1971.

King, Bruce (Ed.) *Introduction to Nigerian Literature,* London, Evans, 1972.

Memmi, Albert. *Colonizer and Colonized,* New York: Orion Press, 1968.

Narasimhaiah, C.D. *An Anthology of Commonwealth Poetry.* Macmillan, Madras, 1990.

Research in African Literature, African and Afro-American Research Institute, University of Texas, Binannual.

Soyinka, Wole, (ed.), *Poems of Black Africa,* African Writers Series, Haeinemann Education Books, London, 1967.

____________, *Idanre and other Poems,* Eyre Methuen, London, 1974.

Tanure O Jaida, *Wole Soyinka Biography,* Fountain Publication, Lagos Malthonse Press, 1994.

Udoeyop, N.J., *Three Nigerian Poets (JP Clark, Christopher Okigbo, Wole Soyinka)* Ibadan University Press, Ibadan, 1973.

Walker, Alice. *Colour Purple,* Harcourt, New York, 1982.

Walsh, William. (Ed.) *Readings in Commonwealth Literature,* Oxford: Clarenden Press, 1973.

Watkins Gloria, *Yearning: Race, Gender and Culture,* South End Press, Boston, 1990.

William McPheron, *Curator for American and British Literature,* Stanford University Press, Stanford, 1998.

2 Black Consciousness in White: A Study of Nadine Gordimer's *A World of Strangers*

— Dr. M. Prabhakar & K. Ram Mohan

> The idea of Black Consciousness is not to institute black racism, or return some aspect of vengeance upon white society, but rather to enforce a sense of solidarity amongst blacks in South Africa...
>
> —Wiki

The history of the Black Consciousness Movement is traceable to 1960s in Africa. Steve Biko, a black medical student, and Barney Pityana, have led the movement. The Black Consciousness Movement is a grassroots anti-apartheid activist movement. It has emerged out of the imposition of ban on the African National Congress (ANC) in the mid1960s. The Black Consciousness has a great impact on the South African Society and its writers. Inspired by the Black Consciousness Movement and its ideals, the writers have launched an attack on the white monopoly in the form of their writings.

The Black Consciousness Movement is a source of great inspiration for Nadine Gordimer, one of "the guerrillas of the imagination" as well as the first South African to be awarded the Nobel Prize for Literature in 1991. Gordimer is an activist writer who questions and challenges the dialectic of apartheid in South Africa through her fiction. In spite of being a White, she has used her fictional house as a means of conscientizing blacks as well as radically altering the mental attitudes of whites. In other words, she is on a mission to educate the blacks and creates an awareness of the blacks tragedy among the whites. She has portrayed Toby, as a white protagonist in her novel *A World of Strangers,* who has confronted the apartheid regime. Thus, she shows, in her novel

A World of Strangers, how even some white people are conscious of the victimization of blacks.

A World of Strangers, Gordimer's second novel (1958), has been banned by the white apartheid regime for its anti-apartheid overtones. It is a social document on the condition of the blacks. It is about the tragedy of the Black South African society. The novel exposes "the battle of the races": between the blacks and the whites caused by the imposition of apartheid. The apartheid has divided Johannesburg and other cities of South Africa between the blacks and whites areas. *A World of Strangers* is the story of a white Toby, who virtually has the black consciousness committed to the human rights of the Blacks. Gordimer, the Geiger counter of Apartheid (Wastberg) as well as the humanitarian raises her voice against the unjust racial segregation of apartheid regime through the dramatization of the black consciousness in white in *A World of Strangers.*

The novel is set in Johannesburg, which is divided, like other towns, on racial grounds into two separate zones—the whites live in Johannesburg and the blacks in Sophia Town. Toby himself associates with a revolutionary white woman, Anna Louw, who builds her cottage on the borderlines of these two zones in order to challenge the racial discrimination of apartheid 'The High House' represents the fashionable white society, whereas 'The House of Fame' stands for the Black circle. The novel is thus structured around 'The High House,' and 'The House of Fame.'

A white Englishman, Toby, the protagonist of *A World of Strangers,* moves in and out of Johannesburg of the white people and Sophia Town of the black people. He is of the view that the white people have racial prejudice. They believe in white superiority and are determined to rule the black. But Toby soon leaves all that white community and associates himself with the warm-hearted blacks. In spite of being a white man, Toby is conscious of the victimization of the black people. He follows the ideology of Liberal Party and African National Congress. He becomes the spokesman of Gordimer's vision of black consciousness. The black consciousness in Gordimer's novel integrates the blacks, who are forcibly separated on racial grounds, into a single racially united South African nation.

Toby Hood has come from England to look after his publishing firm when South Africa is in turmoil due to apartheid. There is a battle between the blacks and the whites. Toby is determined to be apolitical and socially neutral, because he wants to enjoy life for himself without subscribing to any particular ideology or belief. He intends to establish a healthy and balanced relationship between the blacks and the whites. He does not want to judge human beings on the basis of race, colour or gender. He is humane and naturally believes human rights of the blacks. He says: "I want to see people who interest me and amuse me, black, white, or any colour. I want to take care of my own relationships with men and women who come into my life" (Gordimer 36).

Toby is able to be aware of how the rigid white race has brutally divided South Africa along racial lines. The whites, who are proud of their colour, exercise power over the blacks. The blacks who are seriously disadvantaged, are treated as second class citizens. They are looked down upon and humiliated at the slightest provocation. The white 'superiority' has caused severe discontentment among the blacks leading to conflicts. This is the situation Toby faces in South Africa. He is not like the other whites, but a humanitarian who transcends the boundaries of race and class. He, in fact, feels ashamed of the white race for being inhuman. He feels sorry that he belongs to a race, which has exploited and racially segregated the South African nation. He sums up his black consciousness thus:

> I felt that what I really wanted was to enjoy what was left of the privileged life to which I and my kind have no particular right, and which exists, even in its present reduced condition, much as it was gained, by discrimination and exploitation. I felt, with a kind of irritated relief that I really belonged to that bad old good life which my parents helped push down into a dishonoured grave (35).

Toby is aware of how he is introduced by his parents to the world of 'The High House' of fashionable society who "thought of courage in terms of gallantry, spirit in terms of gameness" (243). Toby, thus, witnesses their rich lifestyle and finds it to be in stark contrast with the poor living conditions of the black community.

Toby's encounter with Anna Louw, a South Afrikaaner woman born black, is an important event in his life. She is the woman who puts Toby in close contact with the black community and its political movements. Thus, he is aware of the new developments in South Africa. Anna is a revolutionary white Afrikaaner lawyer working for the Legal Aid Bureau. As a committed lawyer, she addresses the legal problems of people who cannot afford approaching courts of law on their own. She says: "Most of the people we help are Africans"."... Not only are they poor, they're also the most ignorant of their rights. Those that they have, we help them know and keep" (70-71). She makes Toby increase an awareness of the right of the black people.

Thus, Anna brings Toby to the world of blacks who is a stranger in Johannesburg. He is uncertain of his future. As he enjoys absolute freedom, he does not know what to do with it or for that matter where he is heading. Anna assures Toby: "You will have, soon." "... Anyway you must arrive with some idea, all ready" (79). Anna guides him along the right way, and helps him overcome his personal conflict. Toby's association with Anna is, thus, a remarkable event. It is through his association with Anna that Toby comes into contact with another world the world of the blacks. For Toby, Anna is the 'spiritual mother' who teaches him about the current situation and politics of South Africa.

During a get-together party organised by Anna, Toby has an interaction with the Black South Africans such as Steven Sitole, a coloured man of mixed parentage, Sam, a Black and Peter. In spite of being a White man, Toby moves closer to the Blacks in search of understanding and 'meaningful relationships.'

Toby's interaction with Steven Sitole is another important event in his life. Toby and Steven are drawn to each other in their very first meeting because of their ideological concerns and common talks. In course of time, their 'relationship' blossoms into a symbol of 'ideal friendship,' which transcends the racial segregation. Toby and Steven have set no particular ambition except meaningful relationship in their lives. Toby forms an 'inter-racial bond.' In the slums Toby seems "to have found a soul brother" (Obugbesan) Thus, Toby exemplifies Gordimer's black consciousness.

Toby also establishes a meaningful personal relationship with a white young woman called Cecil Rowe of 'The High House.' This relationship blossoms into a love affair and Toby is emotionally attached to Cecil for some time. His attachment with Cecil fades, as she hates the blacks.

Anna is anti-thesis to Cecil. She provides Toby an insight into her family background. Anna is born in an Afrikaaner family at Karroo village of Neksburg. Unfortunately, she is dark complexioned: "she was short, dark woman, young with the neat head of tidy bird" (70). She has her schooling in Bloemfontein. As a child, she has used to play in the yard of her house with the children of the coloured servants, in charge of looking after her. Her parents are prejudiced against the blacks. Anna's black colour makes a great difference to her parents. They have always discriminated against her although she is their own flesh and blood. Anna says:

> In a way, I understand my family's reluctance to own me, their own flesh and blood, reminding them of everything they're afraid of. And have you noticed how dark I am? I'm like a blooming Spaniard. Huguenot blood, they say (182).

Anna launches her revolution from home itself. After graduating in law, she has worked in Bloemfontein and then in Johannesburg taking part in active politics against the wish of her parents who have dreamt for her to have "smart clothes and dances and plenty of boy friends" (181). Contrary to their wish, she becomes an activist and a trade union leader. She also becomes a member of the Congress Party. She participates in the Defiance Campaign and the Passive Resistance Movements. Thus, she is committed to the upliftment of the blacks.

Anna leads a life of 'ideal'. She marries Hassim, an Indian Muslim, defying her parents, who are ashamed of her marriage with a 'coloured' man. Unfortunately her relationship with her husband breaks due to the apartheid laws, which do not allow mixed marriages. She proves her courage and commitment by associating herself with the black people. Her life is the symbol of struggle for human rights of the blacks. She deliberately builds her cottage between the two racially separated zones of the blacks and the whites of Johannesburg as a mark of her protest against the apartheid impositions: "Anna was a real frontiersman who had left the known world behind and set up her camp in the wilderness; the skirmishes of that new place were part of the condition of life, for her" (175). She renounces the world of privilege into which she is born in order to work with the blacks. She wages an uncompromising war against the evils of apartheid.

Inspired by the vision of Anna, Toby lives in a white suburb and frequently visits the black township where Steven and Sam live. He mingles with the members of the black community. It is his close association with Anna and his humanistic element, which urge him to go to the slums and meet the black people. It is very unusual for a white man to visit the black towns during the fifties. Thus, Gordimer tries to raise black consciousness in the white through Toby, in order to humanize race relations. Toby takes a special note of the 'economic differences', which have widened the gap between the rich whites and the poor blacks. He has a great concern over the backwardness, poverty and terrible living conditions of the blacks—"behind, and down below everything teemed, rotted and flourished" (161). Toby, who is humanistic to the sufferings of the blacks, is deeply moved by their plight. He questions himself, "Why it is that the life of poverty is regarded as 'more real' than any other life" (157) He feels disturbed when he compares the lives of these poor black people with that of the rich members of 'The High House.'

Toby is thus, aware of how life in the black township is more 'real' than the life of 'The High House'. The greatest reality of these people is that they face the financial crises, in their day-to-day affairs. Among 'The High House' white people Toby meets Cecil, and other frustrated whites who have given themselves up to golf and horse-racing and girls who have broken their love affairs in order to go to Europe. For this reason, Toby regards the life of 'The High House' circle as 'unreal.'

Tom also associates with Sam who has been brought up in the slums. He feels that he has a 'moral responsibility' to serve his fellow Black people. He is determined to improve their conditions. Toby appreciates Sam's commitment to the cause of the Blacks: "He had his inner eye fixed quietly and steadily on his and his people's destiny as decent bourgeois, his curse fell equally upon the roistering wretchedness of life in the townships" (161).

Toby is very sensitive to the suffering of the black people. He feels neither ashamed of nor insulted by living and mingling with them. Instead, he tries to understand their problems. He often sleeps in the house of Sam. Toby's friendship with Sam and Steven is 'deep-rooted' and raises his consciousness above the social barriers of race, colour and class. The black and the white men living together is an unimaginable thing for the black people living in the vicinity of Sam's house. When Toby steps out of Sam's house, after spending the night there, the black men and women look at him quizzically and pass sniggering comments: "a white man slept in the house of Africans was unheard of and under the greatest suspicion" (162). They think that he has come to the black township looking for sexual gratification. The members of the black community are unaware of "a world of strangers."

Toby not only visits black townships but also calls his black friends to his flat in the white suburb, which is unusual happening. He does not care for how other people respond to his actions and he mixes with the black people without any reservation. He thinks that Steven is also like himself, and the colour of his skin should not be greatly relevant. Toby loves the company of his black friends who, according to him, are honest, faithful and warm-hearted, whereas, the white people of 'The High House' are dishonest, unfaithful, and unduly prejudiced. A further reason for Toby's goodwill for the blacks is that the white community totally ignores them. The whites of 'The High House' are much concerned about their own politics, particularly about the struggle between the Afrikaaners and the English nationalists.

Toby is shocked to know that Steven has been killed in a police raid. He rushes to the 'mortuary' and asks for permission to see Steven's body. Steven is still alive in Toby's memories. He is very anxious to see him. Toby says:

> But I knew I must look at him because otherwise I would never be able to believe that he was gone. I would go away back to England one day and it would seem to me that he was merely left behind, he would begin to live again, forgotten by me. I wanted his death to come home to me, as his quickness had done. (251)

Toby is deeply moved by the tragic death of Steven. He is very much disturbed and finds it hard to cope with the reality of the situation. He has never had such experience of pain on the death of either an intimate friend or a relative. He says: "Despite the war, despite the death of my father, I had never proved the fact of death in my own experience; since I was a man, I had never lost anything that meant more to me than a pet" (251). He has never loved anyone more than he loved Steven. Steven's death is really heart-rending for him. It changes the future course of his life itself. It is the first time in his life that he undergoes a strange suffering over the loss of a friend. He has treated Steven as his own 'brother' and viewed himself as one with him: "He was me, and I was him" (252). Thus he has 'ideal friendship' and 'strong personal bond' with blacks.

Toby raises his voice against the white government's policy of racial segregation. He finds fault with the in human and prejudiced rule of the whites. He feels his moral responsibly to resist the apartheid. He feels guilty of being a member of the white race, which has caused the death of his beloved friend, Steven. He is sorry for his white race's dehumanization. He says: "What I believed should have been my own was destroyed before I was born heir to it" (252). Steven's death awakens in Toby those emotions that have always lurked in the irrational part of his psyche. He contemplates revenge against the white government, which has killed his dear friend. Commenting on black consciousness in Toby, Kolawole Ogungbesan says:

> ... Toby, full of confidence in his self-sufficiency and pride, returns from doing violence to birds to confront the violence of a divided society, moves towards his reconciliation with his fate, and accepts the price of the risk of human condition. The incidents of his life, which have 'predestined' him toward the proud denial of his own humanity, are echoed. (Ogunbesan 151)

The death of Steven brings home many truths to Toby. He realizes his responsibility to himself and to his fellowmen. Toby forms friendship bond with another black man, Sam, as a compensation at the loss of Steven. Steven's loss strengthens his 'personal relationship' with his black friend, Sam more than earlier. From now onwards Toby pays regular visits to Sam in his house. He admits: "I began to spend a lot of time with Sam and his quiet wife" (256).

Toby indicts the white people of 'The High House' who prefer to live in their illusion, and are jealous of their privileges. He decides to sever his relationship with them. He is convinced all over again that the black people have 'true love' and 'affection' for him. Therefore he would like to continue his association with them. Toby realizes how the aimlessness of his freedom, because it does not propel him towards a destination. He admits: "Like a neurotic struggling against cure, I hugged to my aimless freedom that had hung about my neck so long. Suppose when I went back to England, I should find that, for me, reality was left behind in Johannesburg" (258). Even as he is going through a psychological turmoil, Toby receives a letter from his uncle, Faunce, asking him if he would like to return to England. Toby does not give a reply as he is playing with the idea of staying on in Africa for a few more years. This suggests that he would like to work for the cause of his black friends following the footsteps of his 'political mother' Anna. He gets even closer to the black community in order to face the challenges of apartheid. He begins to participate in the political discussions, which take place in Sam's house, where he meets different people including the leaders of the Congress Party.

There is a mass political imprisonment of the Congress leaders during the fifties. One hundred and fiftysix Congress leaders have been arrested in December 1956 on the charge of High Treason. Anna is also arrested because of her connection with an organization for which she acts as an unofficial legal adviser. Anna and the other Congress leaders have made a great sacrifice for the nation. Reminding the immortal sacrifice of those leaders Toby says:

> I felt myself suddenly within the world of dispossession, where the prison record is a mark of honor, exile is home, and family a committee of protest—that world I had watched, from afar, a foreign country, since childhood. (265)

At the end of the novel, Toby leaves for Cape Town for a month to promote the sale of books. Sam comes in a hurry to the railway station to meet him as he waits for the train. He is pleased that Sam has come to see him off. The meeting between Toby, a white and Sam, a black, kindles the curiosity of the other white people at the railway station. The friendship between the blacks and the whites is unusual, unheard of and unprecedented in the racially divided South Africa.

Sam tells Toby that he would send a telegram when his child is born: "If it is a boy we're going to call it after Steven. I wish you could have been godfather" (264). Toby accepts with a smile to be the child's godfather and assures Sam that he will return before the child is born. Thus, Toby a white man, wishes to become the 'godfather' to a child of 'a black man.' Commenting on Toby's black consciousness, Stephen Clingman says: "Toby is able to transcend social barriers through a purely human interpersonal relationship. To this extent his triumph is a triumph of consciousness" (Clingman 47). Further, Clingman says, "The child represents the fertility of the future in a truly integrated society based on respect and human commitment, likewise a cultural synthesis" (Clingman 47). Thus, he forms a bond with the black community. Commenting on his brotherhood with blacks Toby says:

> ... he [Sam] was there before me, laughing and grasping, and we held each other by the arms, too short of breath to speak, and laughing too much to catch our breath, while a young policeman with his innocent face, on which suspicion was like the serious frown wrinkling the brow of a puppy, watched us. (266)

The symbolic arm-clasp of Toby and Sam represents Toby's commitment to the black consciousness. The novel ends with Toby's hoping to dedicate himself to the black men's struggle. He is determined to play his role in the South African politics revolting against the apartheid system.

Toby, a young Englishman, who has come to Johannesburg professing detachment and non-commitment to the South African politics, finds the racial disharmony among the people. He comes into contact with the world of the blacks by establishing 'inter-racial personal relationship' with Steven, Sam and Peter. He understands the parasitic nature of apartheid and decides to put an end to the deep-rooted syndrome. He is now determined to commit himself to the cause of the black people and end the racial differences imposed by apartheid. Toby thus becomes the symbol of Nadine Gordimer's vision of the black consciousness.

Through *A World of Strangers*, Gordimer drives home the message that the whites should realize that the blacks are also human and the whites are not superior to the blacks. She is of the view that both the races—the backs and the whites should live together in peace and harmony as brothers.

Works Cited

Clingman, Stephen. 'Multi-racialism, or A World of Strangers,' *Salmagundi* 62 (Winter 1984), pp. 21-47.

Gordimer, Nadine. *A World of Strangers.* London: Penguin Books, 1958. (Subsequent parenthetical page references are to this edition.)

Ogungbesan, Kolawole. 'Reality in Nadine Gordimer's *A World of Strangers,' English Studies* 61.1-6 (1980), pp. 140-151.

3 Wole Soyinka: A Known African Voice of the Unknown in *The Road*

— Dr. G.J. Sathyaseelan

Soyinka is an epoch making writer of modern African state. In his essay "the writer in a modern African state." He writes, "The writer has always functional in African society as the record of the mores and experience of his society and as the voice of a vision in his own time." It is even said, he is the most original and challenging literary voice in African literature today. As a historian he presents his peoples cultural past for present needs and aspirations. As a playwright he is simultaneously a traditionalist and a pathfinder. He plays many roles as a writer of the modern African state.

When Soyinka started writing plays in the late 1950's there was hardly any major play in Nigeria or for that matter in Englishspeaking West Africa. The ordinary man's notion of drama at that time was Shakespeare or something foreign or distant and probably unattainable for Africans. It is to Soyinka's credit to have placed drama about Africa and Africans on the world stage. He is not merely a force but an inspiring writer to other contemporary African dramatists. His main objective in drama is to bring out his native yoruban myths into contact with great African myths of other cultures.

Soyinka is intensely active, controversial productive and remarkable by any standards. There is an uncompromising commitment to his art and to his political and moral views, which has earned him the title ' Tiger on stage'. He is even compared to James Joyce for his excellent capacity to bridge two different cultures in his criticism with a dazzling power over the resources of language. Yoruban background is the one in which we find the roots that nourish his extraordinary energy and also the inspiration of his plays. Soyinka's *The Road* is a play which can be understood only in relation to the traditional background of Yoruban drama. In most of the African language's they don't even have an equivalent word for 'drama', though they do have terms for play, music and performance. African drama is a collective communal experience without any reference to the individual reaction of a participant. It is a ritual drama since it is deeply rooted in community festival. It is also a renactment of historical events in which actors and audience share equally. In traditional masques in Africa actors may lose their personality by impersonating others. The climax of an impersonation is possession by the spirit impersonated, this is not something which the audience can experience to the same extent.

Yoruban artists originally emerged from the two societies known as 'Gelede' and 'Egungun'. The Gelede was run by women, and its prime function is in appeasing witches by sacrifice, prayer, praise songs and ritual dancing. But the 'Egungun' society worshipped the dead ancestors, which seems to have become a regular feature of court entertainment by the seventeenth century. They cultivated special skills in dancing, miming, poetry and acrobatics. They even travelled form one place to another as professional entertainers. This kind of ritual drama slowly declined in the nineteenth century due to the invasions of Christian missionaries from Europe and other parts of the world. Originally it was performed by the members of the ruling class to the accompaniment of drumming, recital of elaborate praise songs and chorus usually by women. Their subjects are mythological, the creation of the world, of God, the lives of ancestors and their mutual relationship.

In *The Road* Soyinka has extended this state of possession by a god in the figure of Murano. It is the state of an indefinite suppression between life and death. It is this impersonated figure which appalls Kotonu when he puts on the masque of Ogun. This has been described by Ogunba 'A masked figure as a festival, whether he dances or speaks or does neither, has by mere appearance created a situation of potential dramatic value. Since, he is a visitor from the land of sprits; it is the atmosphere, which his sheer presence creates that generates the drama. The audience, help to create this atmosphere by their reception of him and in a highly charged and emotional situation, commonplace things tend to take on other worldly qualities. The costume of the actor becomes sanctified and the maker is totally depersonalized and assumes the role of his ancient forbears or the spirit of the tribe'. The person is identified with the spirit of God. God is made of flesh and the individual personality of the actor is of no importance whatsoever. The mask completely covers his head and body. The driver's festival, which frames the action in *The Road,* is the festival of Ogun. They are his worshippers and at one point the maskers enter with a sacrificial dog.

The road is full of ideas and traditional values. It is also a new form, which commands both the past and the future. In the play it is Ogun, the god, who lurks beside the road demanding to be fed by the ritual slaughter of people and dogs. The physical world is thus shadowed by the demands of the metaphysical world of gods. In yoruban world there are innumerable gods. Olodumare is the supreme god who gives the breath of life to his creatures. Obtala, moulds human beings from clay. 'Erinle' is a forest god. Song is the god of lightning. Yoruban faith centres upon 'orisha', all the three things a god, a force in nature and a figure in history. Therefore being one image or idea is being transformed and adopted into another. This is the key to Ogun's nature and to his complete manifestations is Soyinka's work.

Herber Ogunde was the first Nigerian artist of the contemporary theatre group. He has made his roots in the traditional festival of drama quite plain. He even tells "I was playing drums with the masqueraders in my home town when I was young and these Egungun people gave me the urge inside me to start a company of actors." They are drums, flues and balls, and a song is sung in yoruba by a solo actor and chorus. It's range of subjects is originally tribal myths, superstitions Biblical story, social and political satire and clowning. This complete and vibrant texture was originally performed without written texts and improved from a basic story. Among the Nigerian playwrights, the three last known dramatists are Soyinka, J.P. Clark and Ola Rotmi, the university teachers. University patronage in Nigerian has established drama departments at Ibadan, Ife and Zaria. This particular play *The Road* is different from the original yoruban play and other morden plays where they concentrate on the Christian concepts of heaven and hell by the yoruban idea of reincarnation; this kind of freedom to adopt, merge, borrow and create a new is a feature of yoruban culture and a strength of playwrights.

Ogun has a dual nature; he is both a destructive and creative force, a fearsome god known for his recklessness and an embodiment of the idea of indiscriminate waste. He is popularly known as a destroyer. Yet he is a protector of orphans, a roof over the homeless and a terrible guardian of the secret Oath. His worshippers are all those who work with iron. He has been called the national god of the yorubans. This terrifying deity and his presence hover to over every line of *The Road*. He is known for what Soyinka calls 'rigidly restorative justice' through sacrificeman and animals. Soyinka in his essay' *The Fourth Stage*' has described Ogun as the master craftsman and artist, farmer and warrior, essence of destruction and creativity, a recluse and a gregarious imbiber, a reluctant leader of men and deities. He is the lord of the road Ifa. He opens the way to the heart of Ifa's wisdom thus representing the knowledge seeking instinct, an attribute which sets him apart as the only deity who sought the way; it was he who led them, his was the first rite of passage. Thus, in yoruban mythology Ogun was the first god to cross the abyss, the first to dare to cross the traditional boundary between annihilation and existence, between death and life.

The Road is a piece of literature which can only be fully appreciated in its enactment on stage as a live presentation. In this play there is an universal dependence on movement, song, music of various types and ritual design. It is simply a play about a day in the life of a group of drivers at the side of a Nigerian road. Their aimless existence, waiting for jobs to turn up, dull routines of talking, drinking, sleeping and dreaming of an exciting, future is dominated by the obscure but powerful performance of a professor. He runs a store providing spare parts for vehicles and second-hand personal property, both mainly looted from road accidents. This occupation supports a personal quest for the meaning of death.

The action of the play takes place during an interrupted festival of Ogun. During the festival a masker who has been impersonating the god Ogun has been knocked down by Kutonu's lorry and almost killed at the moment when he possessed the spirit of god in him. He has been immediately removed to the accident store and concealed by professor who believes that

Murano holds within him the secret knowledge which he desperately searches. Even though Murano is mute he is expected to supply the answer to the professor's puzzling questions. But the Egungun masqueraders are searching for their lost mask bearer. The violence infects the drivers and the professor is even killed as an intruder into the Ogun rite. The professor has intervened with his own personal search for a revelation of the word with heavy Christian overtones challenging the climax of the Ogun masquerade. He even expects the spirit of god to be made flesh through Murano but he does not want a public manifestation of death's meaning. He engineers a road death by uprooting road signs and forged driving licences for inexperienced and unqualified drivers in pursuit of the experience of death. He wishes to experience death vicariously by directing others to the boundary of life and death while he himself remains uninvolved and ready to learn from their direct contact.

The Road depicts a state of transition between the certainties of established religion and confused uncertainty in which savage gods exhibit their powers over other beings. The central image of road is a symbol of progress of an actual road, marked by reckless driving and death. The professor's quest for the meaning of life through the essence of death is the pattern of everyman's quest for knowledge in a world of confused values, false prophets, wrong turnings. The professor is a symbol of restless quest for intellect; always questioning the world he lives in, ready to grasp the power of god and use it for own ambition but eventually destroyed by his pride and lust for damnation.

In the first part of the play Samson and Salubi exchange their customary insults. Samson's name is symbolic and ironic. The Biblical Samson is a strong man but this Samson is without either dignity or purpose. He is a proud man with a fixed loyalty to his driver Kotonu. The professor has been depicted in this contest as a fraud, a forger of driving licences. Salubi considers this man as insane but Samson provides more information, that he sleeps among the dead in the churchyard; he exercises his control over a group of unemployed former drivers. His idiom is always characterized by words such as miracles, secret, mystery, spirit, communion, that connote religious revelation. He often makes references to the 'word' that may evoke many possible interpretations but none is specifically indicated. The accident deaths are regarded not as chance happenings but as signposts in his search for the word, which is the essence of death itself. In the church near the accident store, through the open window the *Bible* is glimpsed resting on a bronze lectern in the shape of an eagle. This is the word of god but it is only glimpsed for a moment.

Kotonu even recites a liturgy of famous drivers killed on the roads as though mere heroes killed in the battle. The road is thus linked with the battlefield and travelling on the road becomes a metaphor for destiny itself. Say Tokyo kid feels very proud of carrying a good quality timber in his lorry. To people like Samson timber is a dead object but to Say Tokyo timber is full of life. He tells,"There is a hundred spirits in every of timber trying to do you down cause you've trapped them in, see'There is a spirit in hell for every guy of timber spirits, which protect him from the carnage on the roads. The third dirge is an incantation, a warning about denying the power of gods and functions as an omen for the future transgressions of Samson and the professor. It in accompanied by a violent war dance, song and shouting.

The fourth driver's dirge suggests the professors, association with obscurity, denial of life, with passivity, obsessive individualism, apathy, the depending centre of a declining world, which was once vibrant with vigour and action. He exploits his intimacy with their daily encounters with death on the road in his chance of discovering the secret of death. A lorry is *seen bringing* the road accident victims to the church. It is witnessed by Kotonu and Samson. He even remarks,"The road and the spider lie gloating than the fly buzzes along like a happy fool (178)." To the professor such a wholesale slaughter has obscured the individual mystery of death. He even remarks that the dead have been selected by a malevolent sate. The professor is even waiting for the church to break apart and to recall the word. Kotonu reveals the visual sign of his obsession, the mask of Ogun which Murano had been wearing during the drivers festival. He had been knocked down and almost killed by Kotonu's lorry and is thought to be carrying within him the secret knowledge of death which the professor so desperately seeks. Salubi's casual mention of suicide enrages the professor who regards this form of death as a cheating, evasion of its real essence. Salubi tells, "I must get a licence now, now. This job is first class. If I don't get I will commit suicide" (183). The professor's deepest obsessions are aroused by the casual remarks on death, as through his private system of taboos gives him authority over every usage. Even Muraro's entry coincides with the communion hour inside the church. He even talks of revenging his expulsion from the church by finding the hidden word and by extracting the secret of death from Murano, the "one person in whom the word reposes and whose big toe rests on the slumbering chrysalis of the word." He even replies to Samson, "where the ascent is broken and a winged secret plummets back to earth."

When Samson returns from the accident spot empty-handed the professor gets annoyed, neither spiritual nor material, he even tells, "that shop sustains over souls and feeds our bodies." When Kotonu narrates the accident it seems his near fatal approach to the broken bridge signifies a personal boundary between life and death, between his past life and his present nightmarish predicament, between the known and the unknown. Samson even warns kotonu that it is necessary to make a propitiatory sacrifice to the god of the road, by killing a dog, if he wishes to preserve his life. The professor is purely materialistic and depicts himself as the one who gleans the harvest. It is clear that his egocentric will to dominate implies disaster for everyone, around him and the imagery of harvest implies a collective death from which he will gain the secret knowledge he seeks. Others will be sacrificed to satisfy his lust for the ultimate mystery. He examines minutely the paper contained 'guruguru' as an unconscious medium, a channel through which the word is communicated to him. It suggests his inability to see the most ordinary things in a normal way, a kind of mental derangement. Samson supports this kind of viewing and interpretation of a football pool of one of his friends.

The professor even gives an account of his earlier life as a lay reader of the *Bible*. His earlier faith and reforming zeal had collapsed leaving the word 'hanging, in the coloured light of sainted windows, a mere empty symbol. He has fallen from grace and is now an exile from organized religion. But his reaction is not repentant. He sets himself as a church critic, and the whole edifice of dogma and spiritual leadership is distortion of the true word, which has been chosen to reveal.

The drivers festival takes a new turn, the mask followers are searching for the mask bearer (Murano). Kotonu comes under the terrible grip of fear as he has smeared the blood of Murano. He even gives an account of his part in the events of the driver's festival. The injured Murano had been brought to the accident store and had then disappeared leaving only the mask. The professor distorts the investigation of particular joe and his speech is as obscure as ever, he even adds, "Today was my day of error" (220). He allows his group to sing his favourite praise song about communication with the spirit world. In the song he is depicted as their protective patron and the link between the worlds of men and gods. He expresses his contempt for the drivers and point out that he is merely using them as means to an end. He tells, "Your lives whittle down the last obstacle to the hidden word" (221). The policeman again attempts to identify the missing man who was possessed at the festival of drivers, a palm wine taper by trade. At this point he enters, carrying a gourd full of palm wine. It is now professor's time for evening communion, a chance not to see god incarnate but the reverse, to see flesh dissolve. Finally, The professor makes it clear that Murano is merely a man but with the spirit of god in him, and he has been held captive by the professor as a means of cheating death by fore knowledge. He even hopes to experience death and therefore learns its secret mysteries through Murano, without dying himself.

A lengthy passage is interrupted by the emergence of the *egungun* mask from inside the mammy wagon. Salubi remarks, "No one is playing around with my sanity. I am not staying to witness this" (226). Professor has conjured up the spirits of the dead and is pushing his companions towards a terrifying revelation of death. Say Tokyo puts it, "You are fooling around where you ain't got no business." The *egungun* is building up to a state of procession and they reach a climax. Say Tokyo kid takes a violent action to stop it. He grabs the mask during the struggle,The professor tries to intervene but Say Tokyo kid plunges the knife in the professor's back. He even makes a gesture very vague with a hand 'like a benediction' and delivers the last words of the play. There is no hidden knowledge revealed, no revelation of the essence of death. It ends not on a note of harmony or resolution or clarification but with a confirmation of uncertainties, ambiguities and violent death.

The Road is about a search for hidden knowledge in a world of broken traditions and cultural confusion. It takes the form of an individual's quest for the essence of death. The established religion has failed to retain men in its hold nor able to answer his queries. In its place there is a spiritual vacuum and the person is left alone to seek his salvation. It is also an attempt that man will destroy man by his seedless search for progress by the domination of individual will by his pride and arrogance. It is symbolically conveyed through the myth of Ogun. The professor is trying to exercise his will over others. None of the drivers can understand his world but they all feel the power behind them. He is a crook, a forger, a thief; he engineers deaths and ruthlessly manipulates others towards the boundary of experience between life and death in a personal search for knowledge.

The remarkable feature of the play is its combination of the familiar with the unfamiliar, a fusion of Christian themes and yoruban ideas. The only target of the professor is the word and its effect. But unfortunately he dies without comprehending the ultimate significance as the key to the mystery of death's essence. In one sense the meaning can never be experienced, the essence of death is incommunicable to the living. No traveller has ever returned from death's kingdom except through the resurrection (Christ) or through possession (Murano) who can never convey his experience in words. The professor's intention is to push his men close to the experience of death on the road so that he himself can cheat death by foreknowledge.

In the church the professor had been given the task of reading passages from the *Bible* and also teaching its content to Sunday school children. He had been expelled from the church for two reasons: theft of the church funds and an attempt to take over the task of interpreting the scriptures from the priest. He even believes that he has fallen from the grace towards the end of play with resurrection. It is a fundamentally Christian conception. In the opening verses of the gospel according to St. John, "In the beginning was the word, and the word was with God and the word was God. The same was in the beginning with God." All things were made by Him and without Him was not anything made that was made. And the word was made flesh and dwelt among us full of grace and truth. According to the Christian concept of theology the word is the source of life and light, a creative and creating principle and the idea of the word becoming flesh through the figure of Christ. His elusive quest for, the word has arisen from the collapse of his conventional beliefs in the church. He assumes God-like powers of a priest, prophet, Judge, and executioner and believes that he has personal monopoly of the truth.

He looks for the word on the road among its travellers, drivers, passengers and among the victims who are brought to the graveyard; he sleeps in the churchyard hoping to pick up clues. He even thinks that his own version of the essence of death will be superior to the Christian concept. He looks for the clue in newspaper, road signs, football coupons and all verbal garbage posing deaf ears to spiritual dusting. It is not a theatrical research into the essence of death, but he commits two errors, causing road deaths and perpetuated by particulars Joe, and the interference of Ogun festival, which evokes powers of violence and destruction leading to death.

The professor closely resembles in his activities the leader of both a Christian and a traditional cult. His distribution of palm wine to his followers in the evening synchronizes with the Holy Communion inside the church. His final speech is uttered in the manner of a priest giving benediction at the end of a service. Soyinka has blended the tradition with a parallel cult. It features the traditional African temple (Accident store) and a priest whose duty is to keep the community in touch with its ancestors (maskers). He trains his apprentice Sergeant Burma, and Kotonu with his psychic ability to divine secret meanings and a skill with learned talk. Moreover, a priest and a cult leader should lead his respective community to knowledge and wisdom. But the professor is driving his followers to destruction. He works against his community and is even prepared to sacrifice, it for his personal possession. He even goads his drivers with a vivid threat, "play and burst your flooded threats before I draw the bowstring in the word and veiled shaft bores paths of faith across your cowering mind. Do I feed you wine for nothing? Play, you foulmouthed vermin of the road" (93). He even expresses a highly charged statement; 'before I poke them off. Do you think I would commerce? How dare you! It is true I have not found the word but tempt me and I shall unleash its elemental truths on your head" (63). To the professor there are signposts everywhere but Murano is the key. Murano has become his evensong, the professor is waiting for the god incarnate to reveal through

Murano the secrets of death's essence, until that he must substitute the evidence of lesser mortals, the drivers. He questions Kotonu in the beginning of part II, "what did you see friends? What did you see? Show me the smear of blood in your brain" (56). Though he is very close to the professor he cannot articulate the experience because of the shock induced by the road accident. To Samson death is a fact, a necessary price for using Ogun's road.

The word is always associated with wisdom and the divine pattern from which the material world is copied. To him Christ is the word. He experiments with the word, which is the dissolution of flesh, the secret knowledge of transition between life and death. It is the mask of Agemo hovers in the background throughout the play. Murano is trapped when he is experiencing the transition. He is not fully aware of the significance of the word himself, no one can know it but each feels its presence. He even states his belief that the church has in fact concealed the true meaning of death by its doctrines of comfort and consolation, since Christ's example has shown that death can be overcome. He doubts this doctrine and forces himself as close as possible to a *confrontation*. He even tells, "I don't permit shuttered windows in my household". They are the ones who bar up the windows. I have nothing to hide".

In English the best-known exponent of the masque is Ben Jonson. There is also a masque in Shakespeare's *Tempest* and Milton's *Comus*. Soyinka's *The Road* owes nothing to this specifically European background, but styles of expression. It belongs to a secret ritual, performed annually on certain festival occasions. It includes dance, music, mime, poetry and elaborate costume, all combined for a solemn celebration of the ancestors. The audience renews its contact through their performance with the ancestors. It is a constant reminder of the means whereby the living can enter the stage of transition between the past and the present over and above the professor's own search. The maskers actually erupt in violence while searching for the lost god apparent, and this injects great urgency into the professor's quest. The driver's festival is only an interruption of the twelve hour's play.

The driver's dirges provide a thematic chorus elaborating the central idea of death, disobedience, and sacrifice. They are all sung in Yoruba underlying the traditional validity and customary strength. The first song concerns the road to heaven. The second one is a sexual parody of the idea of ancestral spirits becoming the flesh; the third one is Say Tokyo's speech about death on road by invoking Eshu, the trickster god. Samson tells the story of Kokolori's death. The professor even attempts to restore his damaged self-confidence by listening to his favourite praise song. In addition to this there are three more devices which manipulate the concept of time: impersonation, flashback and renactment. He also gives Kotonu's parentage and the details of his father's death. The professor even renacts bridge. It in this event, which has so deeply shocked Kotonu and led to his abandonment of the driver's profession. Particular Joe narrates the depressing experience of ex-soldiers returning home to an indifferent society. Samson impersonates Burma and realizes the horror of death. In the play the yoruba concept of time is presented as a continuum of the past, present and future.

It is a common sight in Nigeria to see a mechanic advertising his services as 'Doctor of Volkswagen', a repairer of the office equipment as 'Doctor of Typewriter' To them an enterprise demands an impressive title; the professor is no exception to this kind of practice. His name connotes false credentials. He is an impostor dominated by words. He is as enigmatic as the word itself. It said he was a former Sunday school teacher. He has assumed the dignified appearance of a professor.

Murano embodies the incommunicable experience of the life to death. The professor even regards him as god on his doorstep. He has no mind sound enough to react. He neither speaks, hears, nor remembers, and one leg is shorter than the other. He is merely the vehicle of god's possession, an unconscious actor in Ogun's ritual. He is a palm wine tapper. Palm wine is Ogun's drink and it is he who brings the version of communion wine to the drivers. He is the only man who has been depicted with traditional occupation, all others are either crooked or unemployed or rooters.

Kotonu has been portrayed as a troubled character, psychologically affected after the road accident to look after the accident store. He is indifferent to everything except the possibility that he almost killed, the god incarnate Murano. He is almost stunned into apathy by the brutal violence and corrupt practices of the contemporary world. He even requests the professor to identify Murano as god apparent who is never answered. He is drifting aimlessly through life until he is roused by some form of resurrection and renewed purpose.

Samson reminds us of the biblical Samson once but now he is a limbo because the driver has abandoned the road. He even tries to rehabilitate Kotonu and questions the professor. He is now condemned like the biblical Samson in frustration and inactivity until a new purpose in life is revealed to him. Salubi is a driver trainee and a comic character.

Say Tokyo kid is a lorry driver and captain of thugs. He connects the spiritual world and ordinary world of violence and corruption. He believes in the protective timber spirits. He even warns the professor at the end.

> I reckon this has gone too far.... I am telling you, you are fooling around where you ain't got no business.... I am say to you kid. I don't give you one damn. Chief in town is another corrupt politician. His name is ironical particulars Joe, a corrupt policeman.

Sergeant Burma is a war hero, trained to kill dispassionately but not properly rewarded by his commencing officer. It is said he was not decorated properly because of his colour. He has been depicted as a man of no scruples. He robbed the dead, grown rich and died when his brakes failed going down a till. He preyed on road deaths like a vulture, until his turn came to be made a sacrificial victim.

Traditional beliefs are competing with the imported Christian themes. The professor's threatened 'resurrection' ends in his own death. The search for enlightenment ends in violence and darkness. His search for the elusive word never materializes. He even addresses the drivers from the brink of life, "Dip in the same basin....be even like the road itself (96). Those who wish to know the essence of death must collaborate with it and be its constant companion. Death cannot be cheated by foreknowledge because nobody dies by proxy. Knowledge of death is what the professor wants but actual death is what comes to him. The broad panorama of the road of life is completely overshadowed by the presence of death, the great destroyer. Like Satan himself the professor moves into death's kingdom urging his disciples to aid and abet the universal process of destruction.

Works Cited

Dhawan, R.K., *African Literature Today, Prestige Books,* New Delhi, 1994.

Jones, Eldred Durosimi, *The Writings of Wole Soyinka,* Heinemann, London, 1973.

Moore, Gerald, *Twelve African Writers,* Hutchinson University Library, London, 1980.

Ogunba, Oyin, *The Movement of Transition, A Study of the Plays of Wole Soyinka, Ibadan,* University Press, Ibadan, 1973.

Reddy, Venkata, *Critical Studies in Commonwealth Literature,* Prestige Books, New Delhi, 1976.

Soyinka. Wole, *Colleted Plays-1,* Oxford University Press, London, 1973.

______________, *Myth, Literature, and the African World,* Cambridge University Press, Cambridge, 1976.

4 Marginalization in the Select Plays of Wole Soyinka*

— K. Naveen Kumar

Marginalization is a very common term in Asian and African countries. There is a wrong notion about the term marginalization, that it refers to the downtrodden or dalits in India and blacks in Europe, America or African countries. But, in fact, marginalization prevails in each and every society. In our day-to-day life, we are marginalizing others, and at the same time we are also marginalized by others. According to *The Chambers 21st Century Dictionary* marginalize means"to push something or someone to the edges of anything (especially of society or one's consciousness), in order to reduce its or their effect, relevance, significance, etc."

Everyone has his / her own centre and it makes others to be in margin from their point of view, because one's centre will be and other's margin. G.J.V. Prasad gives an explanation regarding this as follows:

> If you write in English in India, aren't you immediately part of the metropolitan centre, your very language proof to the fact? But aren't you on the margins of the vast literary and cultural spaces of your own land? Don't you have to de-marginalize yourself into your layer contexts even as you de-centre yourself from the Anglophone hub? And what if you belong to a religious minority group as well—academic margins, margins of history, forgotten people, times and spaces. (1)

---

* Paper presented in the National Seminar on "Literature of Marginality: A Study of Dalit Writings in India and Afro-American Writings" organized by VHNSN College, Virudhunagar,(T.N) 30th & 31st March 2009.

To this point, marginalization is very common in all societies and it could not be removed. It is not a problem of some particular sect of people like blacks and dalits. Wherever there is suppression or pressure on an individual or a group, it is marginalization. It is a global problem. It is prevailing in every society and reflects in literature.

Literature reflects everything of the society. Especially it gives platform to expose social evil. Exposing such evils of a society to others is a right duty of a creator. When females were suppressed and oppressed, it gave way to rise of Feminism to support the females in all over the world, to express and share their problems and sufferings in the male chauvinistic society. It made revolutionary effects in past five decades in the women's society and in humanities, all over the world. Like that, marginalism or marginalization can be used as a literary device to state the suppressions and sufferings of marginals. It is like a literary theory to analyse a literary work from the point of view of marginalization. In this perspective, marginalization prevails in all literary works and it can be divided into three categories:

i) Marginalization of a society,

ii) Marginalization within a society or group, and

iii) Self-marginalization.

The Nobel Laureate Soyinka's plays, *Death and the King's Horseman, Kongi's Harvest* and *The Lion and the Jewel,* the three different kinds of plays, are analysed from the point of view of all the three types of marginalization.

Marginalization of a Society

People in a dominant group of a society marginalize another society, who belongs to a different caste / creed / race, etc. The dominant group humiliates and gives no respect to the other group in any aspect of life and also keeps them away from all important decisions and events of the society.

In *Death and the King's Horseman,* white officer, Pilkings, is marginalizing native Africans by hindering their rituals and the age-old traditional beliefs. Robert Gnanamony observes the play as, "The Colonizer's cool-headed and systematic attempts at cancelling and negating the cultural difference between the

Yoruba Native and visiting White is a historical factor that forms the core of the play" (253).

According to the customs of Yoruban society, when the king dies, his favourite horse, dog and his horseman should accompany him to the eternal world. It is the duty of the horseman to cross the realm of transition and reach his master to escort him with honour to the next world. Elesin Oba is the horseman in the play. His society assigned him the role of a saviour, who would safeguard the spiritual well-being of the people. He is in his last day of his life, that night he has to perform the ritual of sacrifice. Already his mind oscillates between life and death. At the time, he hesitatingly performs the ritual, the village officer, Pilkings, intrudes and ceases the ritual performance by arresting Elesin and puts him in jail.

The reason behind his arrest is not that he values the life of Elesin, but that he does not want any commotion at the time of British Prince's visit to his district. Through his actions, Pilkings marginalizes the native Africans. As a colonizer, he never worried about the age-old traditional beliefs and rituals of the natives. As Leela Gandhi states, "Colonialism, then to put it simply, marks the historical process whereby the West attempts systematically to cancel or negate the cultural difference and value of the non-West" (16).

In one scene, he and his wife, Jane, wear the sacred *egungun* dress for fancy dress competition. Actually, the dress is used by the native African Obas, while they perform the dead cult. Amusa, a native Muslim policeman, sees the *egungun* dress is not respected properly by them. He boldly points out their mistakes and he requests them to behave rightly as government authorities. But they dismiss the belief as nonsense, barbaric and horrible. In addition, Pilkings threatens Amusa for his words by making him eat pork.

Pilkings marginalizes and subdues the natives by attacking their religious beliefs and customs. But he sends Elesin's son Olunde to study medicine in England. By educating Olunde, Pilkings is executing Kipling's theory of 'the Whiteman's burden'. Here the intension of 'the Whiteman's burden' is to destroy the originality of the colonized land's tradition and culture from the minds of natives. That is the reason when Olunde returns from

England to his native place, for his father's ritual sacrifice; Pilkings and Jane expect that his character would be transformed into whites'. But he does not lose his individual quality of loyalty to his roots and people. When the Whites come to know about his strong mind in tradition, they are shocked and suspect the black people's nature of love to fellow humans and particularly the blood relations. The whites could not get into their philosophy of life and death.

At last, Olunde sacrifices his life to save the society and honour of his family. Instead of his father, he performs the rite and makes him to feel ashamed of that, and also he breaks the marginalization of whites. For the whites, they need the people to be under their collar. To keep them subdued, the whites marginalize every aspect of life and traditions of blacks. The whites' marginalization leads to the destruction of a custom in the society but Olunde defeats their marginalization by his actions.

Marginalization within a Society or Group

It is similar to marginalization of society but here the difference is that an individual or a group of people in a society / caste / creed / organization marginalizes an individual or a group of people in the same society. In the play, *Kongi's Harvest,* two different groups in politics, tradition and modern, fight for power in the state. The modern leader Kongi marginalizes the traditional leaders to usurp their powers and privileges in the society. Traditionalist, Oba Danlola is the religious and political leader of Ismaland. Kongi is the new modernist government head. As a champion of new values, he wants to marginalize the traditional systems of the land at the root itself. He has already marginalized Oba Danlola from the mainstream of politics by seizing his power and keeping him and his people in a preventive detention camp. He orders the traditional leader to surrender publicly and acknowledges his supremacy, and then the traditionalists can be released from the detention camp. But the traditionalists are not ready to give up their privileges, power, legitimacy and dignity for the sake of establishment of new government in the state. Kongi projects his image to public as a rationalist. He believes that he can improve the society through his modern ideas. But in fact, all his modern ideas are like, old wine in a new bottle. His new trendsetters, the Reformed Aweri Fraternity and the Carpenters' Brigade are his modern idea, but they already exist in the traditional political system.

Kongi marginalizes the traditional and religious leader in order to capture power in the state. He is a mere political leader and power-monger. He has no quality of spiritualism in him to enlighten others. But he ceases the rights of spiritualism in order to hold all titles and prestigious roles in the society and also to prove himself as an omnipotent leader. He looks at spiritualism as the power, which controls people. He is not ready to share his power; he wants to be the sole authority of the whole power of the nation. So he wants to be the spirit of the harvest and to get a public show of the Oba's surrender of power to him. In connection with this, Basavaraj Naikar states, "He, thus wants to humiliate Oba Danlola doubly and establish his position as the new ruler of the country" (91).

However, the old Oba Danlola does not want to be marginalized from his stature. To protest against the marginalization, he refuses to surrender himself by submitting the yam of the year to Kongi. At last, his heir apparent Daodu convinces him, to surrender his power to Kongi for the condemned men, who are in jail. But Oba wants to know whether Kongi will keep his promise of reprieve or not. When he comes to know the cancellation of the reprieve by Kongi, he calls it. "A Plain incitement to murder." Daodu persuades him to attend the festival, because he seeks to rejuvenate the tradition in the festival celebration by executing his plan of assassinating Kongi with the help of his ladylove, Segi.

In the festival, Oba Danlola surrenders the new yam to Kongi and he places his hands over it in benediction. At this moment, gunfire bursts out. The men in the detention camp, including Segi's father, are killed. It is partly a success to Kongi to his power of marginalization. Kongi begins his speech in the festival, after killing the condemned men.

> The Spirit of Harvest has smitten the enemies of Kongi. The justice of earth has prevailed over traitors and conspirators. The Spirit of resurgence is cleansed in the blood of the nations' enemies, my enemies, of our collective spirit, the spirit of planting, the spirit of Harvest, the spirit of Inevitable History and Victory, all of which I am (*Kongi's Harvest* 129-30).

These words state the suppression of the traditionalists. Those who are ready to accept the marginalization are allowed to live, while others are shot to death. In the festival, Daodu and Segi cannot act according to their plans. At the end of the festival, Segi places a copper salver in front of Kongi. In that, she keeps the head of her shot dead father, instead of the new yam of the year. When Kongi sees it, he remains speechless in terror and the festival ends in chaos.

In this play, a back (Kongi) suppresses and marginalizes his own people for his personal establishment in the society. The level of marginalization goes to the extreme point to eradicate tradition and religion from the society, to show the power of modernism and politics.

Self-Marginalization

Self-marginalization is the problem of individuals, who are restricting themselves from their society and in day-to-day life, because of the fear of their own conventional ideas or tradition or culture of the society. In fact, it is a psychological problem of the characters. They never know that they are marginalizing themselves in the midst of others of the society. Even if they know, they do not want to come out of the sufferings, because sometime freeing from suffering will be more sufferable than their present sufferings.

In the play, *The Lion and the Jewel*, Sidi is the best representation of the above-mentioned category. Outwardly, one can say that Sidi is marginalized by the village chief, Baroka, for his desire to marry her after seeing her beautiful pictures in a magazine and because of that, she faces all troubles. Actually, she marginalizes herself intentionally (mentally) by the tradition and culture of the society. Moreover, she never allows any rational idea into her mind, which is advised by Lakunle, her lover. She greatly supports and argues for her society and its tradition. She does not want to come out of the conventional ideologies. She does not know that she is marginalizing herself for the ideologies of the society. She accepts the slavery in the name of accepting the customs of the society. It is revealed from her dialogues with Lakunle. When he proposes his love and wishes to marry her, she insists on the traditional bride price as:

I have told you, and I say it again
I shall marry you today, next week
Or any day you name.
But my bride-price must first be paid.

According to the customs, a girl marrying without the bride price is a disgrace to her. She fears that and refuses his proposal as:

Will you make me
A laughing - stock? Well, do as you please.
But Sidi will not make herself
A cheap bowl for the village spit
They will say I was no virgin.(*The Lion and the jewel* 8)

When Lakunle tells her that he is not seeking a wife to fetch and carry, cook and scrub, and to bring forth children. But she does not agree with him and argues that child-bearing is a sacred part of married life. He assures her that he will treat his wife as an equal partner by giving full rights. After marriage, he and his wife will dine together from plates at a table, walk together in public, visit nightclubs in nearby cities to dance, etc. The rosy picture that he paints of their life does not impress her, because she believes that, it is not the duty of a woman to do such things in the African society. She does not want to differ from other women in the society. She subdues and marginalizes herself and does not want to be like modern women in other countries. That is the reason that when she sees her photographs in the Western-magazine, she claims more bride price. To her, bride price is more vital than her own progress in the society.

At the end, Baroka cunningly seduces her and she decides to marry him. Even though Lakunle offers him to marry her, she rejects and she is firm in her decision. Her decision shows that she wants to be under the control of manliness. Thus, the tradition has marginalized her psychically not to think rationally.

Conclusion

In all these three plays, Soyinka employes the various shades of marginalization in different aspects in the lives of the blacks. In *Death and the King's Horseman*, the whites marginalize the blacks by stopping and hindering their traditional beliefs and customs. It is not only a tragic end to Elesin and his family, but also to the tradition of age-old ritual sacrifice. In *Kongi's Harvest,* a black dominates his own society for his welfare and to show himself as, "a great and benevolent politician, magnanimous and supreme leader of power, eminent and esteemed speaker, versatile and ingenious writer and above all, Messiah of Ismaland" (Kumar 72). Here the marginalization of blacks by a black, leads to destruction of a group of people in the same society. In *The Lion and the Jewel,* Sidi, a typical African young girl, cannot break her bond of tradition. Her tradition prepares her mentally to face suppressions, but not to defend herself. Therefore, she marginalizes herself to survive in the society. She does not want to come out of the sufferings, because freeing from suffering will be more sufferable than her present sufferings.

Soyinka uses drama as a device to expose the lives of the blacks (the third world countries) to others. Through these marginalized characters, Soyinka brings out the agonies, sacrifices, losses, and miseries of native people into light. In addition, he brings out the different levels of marginalization of native people and their day-to-day life, manners, religions, customs, beliefs, etc, to the reader's attention and judgement.

Works Cited

Gandhi, Leela. *Postcolonial Theory: A Critical Introduction.* New Delhi: Oxford University Press, 2000.

Gnanamony, S. Robert. *Literary Dialectics: Notes and Chords from East and West.* Chennai: World Book Publication, 2006.

Kumar, Naveen. K. 'Social Problems and Conflicts in Kongi's Harvest.' *Dialogue,* IV. iii (Dec. 2008): 70-77.

Naikar, Basavaraj. S. *Perspectives on Commonwealth Literature.* Jaipur: Book Enclave, 2004.

Prasad, G.J.V. 'From the Editor's Desk.' *Journal of the School of Language, Literature and Culture Studies,* 4: Autumn 2005.

Soyinka, Wole. *Six Plays.* London: Methuen, 1984.

__________ *The Lion and the Jewel.* Chennai: Mohan Pathippagam, n.d.

__________ *Collected Plays* II. London: Oxford University Press, 1974.

5 Hurtle as Vivisector and Illuminator in Sir Patrick White's *The Vivisector*

— Dr. V. Sangeetha

The theme of quest is a recurring theme in the post-colonial fiction. The quest takes shape in various forms—quest for one's roots, quest for cultural identity, women in pursuit of ascertaining their separate role in society and religious quest identifying the "Divine Presence" (White, "Credo" 16) with the downtrodden, dispossessed and oppressed.

The quest theme is a pervasive element in Western literature. The heroes of great works are portrayed as pursuing their quest with vigour and sometimes with audacity. The protagonists of Virgil's *Aeneid*, Homer's *Odyssey*, Dante's *Divine Comedy*, Spenser's *Faerie Queene* and Bunyan's *Pilgrim's Progress* explore the uncharted realms to realise their own selves. The mythological quest motifs range "from the Argonauts' search for the Golden Fleece to Captain Ahab's pursuit of the Great White Whale" (Ziolkowski 137). Northrop Frye identifies "the central myth of literature in its narrative aspect, with the quest-myth" ("Archetypes" 431) In his *Anatomy* he refers to a number of stories in relation with the heroic quest-romance and the quest heroes—Don Quixote, Perseus, Theseus and Beowulf (180,189,190,191).

Jessie Weston's *From Ritual to Romance* deals with the legend of the Holy Grail, the cup used by Christ for his Last Supper in which the blood of the saviour was collected when he was crucified. It signifies the quest-myth for the knowledge of the self, and T.S. Eliot has drawn heavily on this myth in his work *The Waste Land*.

Man's desire to discover his self has been explored by many writers and thinkers. But Patrick White gives it a completely new, unique and individual dimension through his ability to bring diverse kinds of human beings together in search of a common goal.

Apart from the hero going in search of a concrete treasure and winning the hands of the bride there is also another type of quest where the writer himself is the quester and his work is either the product or the image of his quest. John B. Vickery claims a seminal role for Frazer in modern literature, when he views the total oeuvre of an author as a quest,

> for the thematic quests of Eliot for redemption, Joyce for a father, Lawrence for a Golden Age, Yeats for the buried treasure or hidden mystery, and Miss Sitwell for purification are all adumbrated in *The Golden Bough.* (130)

Similarly the oeuvre of White stands for humility and simplicity and faith.

The quest for vision has, in the twentieth century, a special relevance, because it holds out a ray of hope to many people who experience a feeling of alienation in the modern world. Many writers have explored this need or urge of man to establish an experimental contact with the divine. Writers like D.H.Lawrence, Ernest Hemingway, W.B. Yeats and T.S. Eliot have depicted, in one way or another, man's struggle to see himself in relation to the cosmos, his lonely self confronting nature and trying to establish his identity by moving back into himself and thus to the innermost core of reality. About not following any orthodox doctrine in religion which is the central concern of his novels, White himself has said:

> Religion—that's behind all my novels... the relationship between the blundering human being and God.... I belong to no church, but I have a religious faith. I have lifted bits from various religions in trying to come to a better understanding. (qtd. in Driesen, "Unprofessed Factor" 77)

White reveals his preoccupation with the theme of quest through his novels.He has an understanding of the interactions between the writer and society, the work of art and the reader.

Most of White's novels centre on the metaphor of the journey, quest or search which will lead man to a vision of reality and self-awareness. White seems to regard the quest as an integral part of the progress towards the redemptive vision. The search for truth and fulfilment gives direction and dignity to the lives of the individuals with emphasis to the fact that all quests ultimately turn out to be quests for self-knowledge.

The metaphor of journey which White introduced in the novel *The Living and the Dead* achieves prominence in subsequent novels. According to Barry Argyle,"...the journey, extended into a metaphor of the mind, is an exploration of the past in order that the present should be in a fit state to have a future...." (4).

The Vivisector (Vs) is about the gradual development of Hurtle Duffield as a painter whose spiritual quest is almost satisfied and reaches near perfection towards the end.

The fiction writers up to the early twentieth century emphasised on the conventional morality. Thereafter men began losing faith in tradition and religion. Materialism engulfed them. A sense of loneliness and loss of faith drove novelists like James Joyce, D.H.Lawrence, Somerset Maugham and Virginia Woolf to look into their struggling selves and project the vibrations of their own creative agony in their novels. They introduced the artist theme and pursued the quest-myth of self-identity where they explained the self of their artistic heroes. An important subgenre of novel Kunstlerroman "represents the growth of a novelist or other artist into the stage of maturity that signalizes the recognition of the protagonist's artistic destiny and mastery of an artistic craft" (Abrams 133). Novels such as *Sons and Lovers* (1913) by D.H.Lawrence and James Joyce's A *Portrait of the Artist as a Young Man* (1914) belong to this type. Both the novels portray the novelists' quest for self-identity.

This artist theme has influenced many Commonwealth writers. White sets *The Vivisector* against the Australian culture. As in his other novels he explains the hero's journey through the interior regions of his soul. It is concerned with the artist's quest for self-identity. As Robert S. Baker puts it:

> ...The theme of *The Vivisector* most exclusively stated, is the intellectual and psychological maturation of an artist evoked in terms of the dialectic between self and world, mind and nature, imagination and reality of dialectic, moreover energized by Duffield's decisive experience at Sunningdale and dramatized in a series of crisis. (215)

White views art in close relationship with religion and sensual pleasures. In his novels, Chellappan observes:

> The tragic triumph of the visionary is linked with the life-in-death of the artist, and if the human sufferer partakes of the passion of Christ, the artist-God is an image of the God-artist and in his journey towards his vision and redemption he is assisted by women with whom he is in apparent conflict. (Chellappan, "Self" 24)

In *The Vivisector* Hurtle tells Rhoda "... I'd like to tie the end of my life to the beginning. I think, in that way—rounded—it might be possible to convey what I have to" (Vs 450). Thus the three, namely, art, religion and sensual pleasure may be interconnected to form a continuous cycle.

Through art, Hurtle reaches the ultimate spiritual vision. The spiritual vision is made possible only after overcoming the physical passions. The medium to attain the spiritual synthesis for Hurtle is painting. The novel's first epigraph from Ben Nicholson, "As I see it, painting and religious experience are the same thing, and what we are all searching for is the understanding and realization of infinity" shows the relationship between painting and religion both aspiring to infinity.

The artist in Hurtle is always alive right from his younger days. In the school he draws "Death" symbolised by an elephant in a lion's skin. He is able to see only the negative in every object. While the teacher Miss Adams feels that the elephant is such a gentle creature, Hurtle considers the elephant as an animal which "can trample its keeper, without any warning, and rip with its tusks" (Vs 41). The art of vivisecting and highlighting the destructive aspect of any work of art is inherent in Hurtle. That is why he draws "poor black 'Jack' Shewcroft jumping off the roof... the blood running out of his cut throat, through his veins, and from his heart, which was like a little fountain squirting from his chest" (Vs 100). For Mrs Courtney, the drawing is a horrifying revelation of the destructive side of Hurtle.

Like most other novels of White, *The Vivisector* also centres round the spiritual quest of the hero "....The journey of White's protagonists is primarily inward into the depths of their own natures, there to discover undesirable qualities repellent to themselves, and there to seek a happier state" (Morley, Mystery 22).

Hurtle conceives his struggle towards omniscience as artist and as visionary in archetypal terms that excludes his share in common humanity. But his self-portrait stands as a testimony of:

> ... his failure to assert his absolute authority of his creativity. He is confronted by an image of his cruelty, his narcissism and his depravity. The painting accuses him of dishonesty in his self-conception and, accordingly, untruthfulness in his view of the world. He is forced to admit that he has 'created' what he found not only in Nance but in himself and in the physical world. (Williams 106)

Nance becomes the first prey to his vivisection in the name of painting. He uses "the architecture of the [Nance's] body" (Vs196) as a vehicle for the expression of that vision in which she is shown to be "vegetable in form and essence" (Vs 200). He regards her as little more than an animal, dissociating his creative self from "his own animal" that responds to her sexually (Vs 210).

Hurtle never loves her, never really takes part in her life, but only uses her for his art. Nance herself is very well aware of his inability to love her. But she is drawn towards him not just sexually but sees him as her spiritual complement. She feels that her own aborted spiritual aspirations and unfulfilled sexual desires centre on Hurtle as the dreamt-of young man who will teach her to "see things as they're supposed to be" (Vs 245).

Indeed Hurtle loves her form and not her soul which he transforms into art. That is what happens in his painting titled "Marriage of Light." Yet he needs her as she resuscitates him and his art "which probably never entered Nance's consciousness" (Vs 210).

Seeing the rock paintings, Nance accuses him, "You aren't a 'uman being. You're a kind of perv-perving on people- even on bloody rocks" (Vs 224). He has failed to express himself other than through paintings. His participation in Nance's life has been a kind of vivisection of her, Nance's grumble, "... you're obsessed—by what you like to think is the truth... use of yer in the name of the Holy Mother of Truth. He thinks. The truth" (247)! is appropriate with the epigraph from Saint Augustine. "They love truth when it reveals itself, and they hate it when it reveals themselves." He does understand that his painting accuses him of dishonesty in his self-conception and untruthfulness in his view of the world. Realising the truth of St. Augustine's words, he smears his self-portrait with his faeces and throws it away.

Nance's agonizing death leaves him to admit his cruelty and dishonesty to himself for the first time. Yet that does not change him. In his conversation with Cecil Cutbush, he says he believes in the Divine Vivisector while Cutbush believes in God. Hurtle views God as the Divine Vivisector and himself the instrument in executing His order through painting. Only when he is afflicted with a stroke does he realise that God as the Divine Vivisector is not a destroyer.

The next woman to be vivisected is Hero Pavloussi. Hero marries Cosmas, the millionaire for his money and his robust body but is disappointed with him. On the other hand, Cosmas is shocked at the fervour of his wife to get sexual gratification.

If Hurtle's relationship with Nance is to offer him experience of physical love, he thought Hero's will offer him an inspiration free of earthly contamination. As he explains it to himself:

> He was falling in love with her, not in the usual sense of wanting to sleep with her.... In his aesthetic desires and their consummation he believed himself to be honest; and in his desire to worship and be renewed by someone else's simplicity of spirit, he was not forsaking the pursuit of truth. So he was falling in love with Hero Pavloussi. (Vs 321-22)

But it is unfortunate that Hero never becomes the ideal soul. Neither does he help her in her search for sanctification nor sexual gratification.

Hero senses in herself a division between the innocent ideal both Hurtle and her husband Cosma (*sic*) want her to represent, and the highly sensual woman she knows she is. The blatant mind-body dissociation has made her virtually schizophrenic. (Steven 97)

Hurtle, the pervert and timeserver never fails to grab the opportunity to explore. Hero by vivisecting her body and deforming it in the name of art. Hero is not happy about the paintings because Hurtle is not helping her out of her debacles, instead reflects them in his paintings. His paintings only add to her plight. She frantically pleads to Hurtle:

> 'If you do love me, as I think you are perhaps too sensitive to admit,' she said, putting out an encouraging hand, 'why can't we make together, out of our love, something beautiful and lasting instead of morbid, drowned cats?' (Vs 359)

But Hurtle will not play the role of a lover in a play with the end like "they lived happily ever after." Hurtle recognises this love for its sentimentality and refuses to compromise himself with it. His uncompromising nature and lack of understanding are revealed by his showing Hero the painting which depicts her in a self-destructive pose, and which gives her the clue for her attempted suicide. "His repeated downfall was his longing to share truth with somebody specific who didn't want to receive it. Was it why he had failed so far in love" (360)?

"Why do painters have to deform everything they see" (315)? is a relevant question voiced by Hero. The fact that Hurtle does not sign his paintings shows that he himself is aware of his vivisecting attitude but does not want to acknowledge.

Here is one form of White's failure motif and also one aspect of the theme which underlies the emphasis on Dreck, the identification of inner human corruption with physical putrescence; 'nothing develops as conceived; the pure soul, for example; the innocent child, already deformed, or putrefying, in the womb'. (Morley, Mystery 220)

White brings into the novel the character of Boo Hollingrake alias Olivia Davenport so as to satirise the upper class shams and the philistine life led by them. Boo makes the best criticism of Hurtle's paintings. Although Hurtle spots in Boo "a core he desired to possess, and which she was apparently determined he shouldn't" (Vs 298) till the end the relationship reflects her refusal to share the personal core, either sexually or psychically.

In his later life, Rhoda's kinship is forced upon Hurtle's consciousness and conscience. Near the end of his life, says White, he can finally "recognize... himself in the glass she was holding up to him" (Vs 603). White makes the connection explicit, making Rhoda tell her brother, "Almost everybody carries a hump, not always visible, and not always of the same shape" (Vs 469).

Rhoda first refuses to stay with her brother when they meet after a very long gap because she feels, "I might be vivisected afresh, in the name of truth-or art" (Vs 445). She knows very well that she has already been vivisected by her deformity. That is why she remains unaffected by his drawings "Pythoness at Tripod" a series of paintings revealing her and her deformity in a cruel manner. She confronts him for his spuriousness of his pursuit of truth. In her nihilism and isolation, she also alerts him to the dangers of his solipsism. During a conversation Hurtle says, "I believe... in art....I have my painting" (Vs 518). Rhoda replies, 'your painting". And yourself. But those, too, are 'gods' which could fail you" (Vs 518).

Shortly before the stroke which ends his life, Hurtle acknowledges this crucial failure:

> To be honest: he had failed to love Rhoda. Pity is another matter: his 'Pythoness at Tripod' had expressed a brilliant, objective pity for an injured, cryptic soul and a body only malice could have created. But pity is half-hearted love. (Vs 614)

It is interesting to note that the art theme in the first part of *The Vivisector* is contrary to the norms of any of the archetypal patterns of painting art. Though art is beauty and beauty is truth, Hurtle sees only ugliness and cruelty in everything he comes across. He vivisects and projects in his paintings everything that is ugly, vulgar, and repulsive in a horrid and grotesque manner. In the words of Hero, "The painter is cruel. Why do painters have to deform everything they see" (Vs 315). On another occasion she calls his paintings as "pornography" (Vs 360). "Dreck" and cruelty and not beauty does he find. White who is the creator of this protagonist is himself of this mould.

In the biography *Patrick White: A Life,* David Marr says:

> White was not searching for beauty. Raw creative ideas excited him, and a blare of colour filled him with pleasure. He liked to see the pain and struggle of creation in a painting. Menace caught his eye. He was stimulated by the prospect of a long tussle to make a difficult work yield up its meaning. Here, too, a little suffering was important. Abstract art was White's first love, but he was excited by paintings with a sharp satiric edge....(466)

Hurtle's rebellious nature, his alienated self, his unconventional and peculiar way of thinking and observing his surroundings are noticed right from his childhood. He conceals his feelings as well as his paintings, and dislikes the idea of sharing these with others. The glamour of Mrs Courtney affects Hurtle, the precocious vivisector and forces him to join the army. The more she becomes fond of him, the more he becomes isolated. He finds the army an easy escape from her intrusions. This alienation leads to creative activity.

Like many other of White's characters, Hurtle is voluptuous and erotic and is shown as gaining strength through sex. This aspect also is the considered view of White himself. In the biography by Marr, White says:

> I expect a lot of people will be furious and disgusted, but it has to come out the way it is coming. I feel more and more that creative activity in the arts is very closely connected with sexual activity, and that an awful lot of the insights I have had have come from that source. It isn't necessary to 'sleep around' but to investigate the variety of regularity. (486)

Veronica Brady comments on Hurtle's near obsession with the basic instincts.

> Hurtle Duffield, the novel's protagonist is a provocative figure.... True, as an artist he does not accept conventional beliefs and values. But far from exalting imagination at the expense of physical facts Hurtle Duffleld's life insists on the primacy of facts. The goal of life for him is physical; he wants to know the truth, what he saw rather than thought. ...For the questions he wrestles with throughout his life are ones our culture tends to repress: death, pain and the intransigent otherness of the physical world. Against the grain of our illusions which centre upon the body beautiful and the happiness of all? White insists upon the tragic facts of the human condition, its subjection to death and physical necessity. ("Artist" 136-37)

With Kathy Volkov, Hurtle's art of vivisecting comes to a close. Kathy symbolises the spiritual purity of Hurtle's artistic endeavour. The union of Hurtle, the painter and Kathy, the concert pianist is far more than sex. Kathy gains knowledge, control, and self-esteem from Hurtle. In the letter she writes from Europe, Kathy acknowledges that her father-lover has helped her to understand herself better, "It was you who taught me how to see, to be, to know instinctively" (Vs 539). Her letter also mentions the things we haven't said" (Vs 539). The vast age difference of nearly forty years never bars them from becoming lovers, patron and protègè, and spiritual father and daughter. The progress made by the two artists during the short time they had known each other testifies to the vitality of their spiritual cross-fertilization. Kathy's ability to shatter his adult defences also redeems him. By becoming childlike, he allows himself to be led by a child.

Hurtle spreads all kinds of traps before Rhoda to force her to stay with him. The main reason as he himself expresses: "At least by his sister's presence Kathy Volkov would be protected from debauch and himself from destruction" (Vs 450).

Hurtle is an amoral creator as well as a destroyer. He thinks of himself as God and not as a humble instrument of a creator God. The stroke he suffers by falling at the feet of Cecil Cutbush, whom he very much despises makes him doubt for the first time whether he possesses a soul at all. It is the soul he must now seek. When he falls down, he undergoes a metamorphosis which enables him to understand and acknowledge God, and he seizes on the clue "to the last and first secret the indigo" (Vs 549). Subsequently he finds himself, to his amazement, "looking for a god-a God-in every heap of rusty tins amongst the worm-eaten furniture out the window in the dunny of brown blowies and unfinished inscriptions" (Vs 561). Thereby he seeks, the ultimate ordering principle, God in the world of "Dreck" (Vs 392) and uncertainty. He now employs art as the medium to serve God whom he has now understood. It is ironic to note that till then he used this very art to oppose God. Through his paintings he now seeks redemption.

Hurtle has always relied on his own will. But, when he starts painting what is called the "God paintings" he is forced to surrender his will. His surrender is similar to that of Alf Dubbo and Voss. "Stroked by God", he responds like a willing lover (Vs 613).

The final God paintings reveal Hurtle's acceptance of the stroke and his acknowledgement of God's supremacy. His first God painting remains as a testament. As White describes it, Hurtle must confess himself and be shriven. "Before he could contemplate his vision of indigo, he had to paint out the death which had stroked him" (Vs 565). In his second painting 'The Whole of Life" (Vs 607), he expresses the encompassing vision which he has been bestowed upon like the other Whitean illuminates. He tries to bring out all the experiences of life, some of which he never experienced. However he strives for a vision which "would convey the whole" (Vs 604). As Bliss remarks, This painting is a paean raised to life in all its fragmentation and to flesh in its ephemerality, both of which he now affirms" (129). Hurtle's last work is full of religious fervour. Hurtle dies in his studio while busy at his easel. The last scene shows him not only active but also acted upon. Faced with death, he acts instantly, intuitively, and freely. His moment of naked enlightenment resolves all differences. When he tries to acknowledge the Grace of God in his painting, he dies and his soul is sanctified. Hurtle is stroked by God in His twin aspects of Vivisector and Illuminator. By suffering, Hurtle is at last able to acknowledge God.

White identifies the filth which Hurtle portrays with man's inner spiritual state. The filth complicates the search for God. "Dreck" stands for glory as well as doom of man's bodily existence. Hurtle's search for God is through rot, putrescence and Dreck. One has the final vision only after coming to terms with the filth with the understanding that ugliness is equally important as beauty. That is how Hurtle attains wisdom in the end. His series of paintings—rather vivisections enable him to have the "indi-ggoddd" vision (Vs 617).

As life is both beauty and ugliness combined, White feels that an understanding of this is very essential for knowing God. The four women who play important role in Hurtle's life are composed of beauty as well as ugliness. Kathy stands for beauty while Rhoda for ugliness. By accepting Kathy as well as Rhoda for what they are, he reveals his reconciling beauty with ugliness. Rhoda's affliction becomes a metaphor for all the sufferings of mankind. Beauty and brilliance; ugliness and deformity seem to be the two equal sides of the balance for understanding God.

Hurtle views life and art as consisting of beauty and ugliness and God as the author of both. Peter Wolfe observes:

> The artist is no copyist. Rather than reproducing photographic replicas, he distorts in order to capture a reality beyond appearances. Sometimes an inner truth lies in the mangled and the deformed. Ugliness can convey truths beyond the ken of sanity, reason and politeness. (164)

Hurtle's rage for beauty knits with his urge to damage and destroy. In his dunny, itself both a shabby outhouse and a "shrine of light" (Vs 307), he scribbles an inscription he is unable to finish.

> God the Vivisector
> God the Artist
> God (Vs 307)

For Hurtle, God is both creator and destroyer, kind and cruel. He leaves the inscription unfinished because he cannot find the mediating term between these polarized extremes. White wants to justify Hurtle's approach to God through vivisection. Brady observes:

> It is true that Hurtle Duffield is also preoccupied with the question of God. But this preoccupation does not withdraw him from a concern with the human condition. For his god is not an abstract concept but a God like Blake's who 'only Acts and Is in existing Beings and Men.' In fact he is bound up with central human questions, the existence of evil, pain and death. Hence he figures as the vivisector of the title, and Hurtle's attempt to interrogate him or, rather, what he does to man, makes him a champion of human integrity. For where others either submit to or avoid confronting the God who is ultimately man's antagonist, Hurtle wrestles with him and, paradoxically, this struggle enables him to fulfil his ultimate possibilities of freedom and power. ("Artist" 137)

White wants to justify Hurtle's approach to God through vivisection. Hurtle has to come to terms in some way or other with the moral dimension of the world and he embodies it in Rhoda Courtney. In her mission to save the cats of Sydney's gutters, Rhoda becomes an archetype of moral compassion. Rhoda saves the cats which both Hurtle and Hero avoided. Thus it is through the ugly deformed Rhoda does Hurtle try to attain salvation. The stroke completes Hurtle's journey in quest of God as vivisector, God as Artist and God as he himself scribbles in his dunny. The stroke humbles him and finally his quest for the vision is fulfilled.

Works Cited

Abrams, M.H. *A Glossary of Literary Terms*. Bangalore: Prism, 1993.

Argyle, Barry. *Patrick White*. Edinburgh: Oliver and Boyd, 1967.

Baker, Robert S. 'Romantic Onanism in Patrick White's The Vivisector.' *Texas Studies in Literature and Language* 21 (1979): 203-25.

Bell, Michael, *Literature, Modernism and Myth: Belief and Responsibility in the Twentieth Century*. Cambridge: Cambridge UP, 1997.

Bergonzi, Bernard, ed. *T.S. Eliot: Four Quartets. A selection of Critical Essays*. London: Macmillan, 1969.

Bliss, Carolyn, *Patrick White's Fiction: The Paradox of Fortunate Failure*. London: Macmillan, 1986.

Bradbrook, M.C. *Literature in Action: Studies in Continental and Commonwealth Society*. London: Chatto and Windus, 1972.

Brady, Veronica. *A Crucible of Prophets*. Sydney: Theological Explorations, 1981.

______________ .The Artist and the savage God. Patrick White's *The Vivisector'*. *Meanjin* 33.2 (1974): 136-45.

______________ . 'Patrick White and the Difficult God.' *Crucible of Prophets*. Vernice Brady. Sydney: Theological Explorations 1981. 69-89.

Chellappan, K. 'Self. Space and Art in a Few Novels of Patrick White.' *Literary Half-Yearly* 24.1 (1983): 24-34.

Driesen, Cynthia Vanden. 'Patrick White and the 'Unprofessed Factor': The challenge before the Contemporary Religious Novelist.' *Patrick White: A Critical Symposium*. Eds. R. Shepherd and K.Singh. Adelaide: Centre for Research in the New Literature in English, 1978. 77-86.

Frye, Northrop. *Anatomy of Criticism*. Princeton: Princeton UP, 1973.

______________ . 'The Archetypes of Literature.' *20th Century Literary Criticism*. Ed. David Lodge. London: Longman, 1972. 422-33.

Goodwin, Ken. *A History of Australian Literature*. London: Macmillan, 1986.

Joyce, James. *A Portrait of the Artist as a Young Man*. London: Flamingo, 1994.

Lawrence, D.H. *Sons and Lovers*

Lawson, Alan, ed. *Patrick White*. St. Lucia: University of Queensland P, 1994.

Marr, David. *Patrick White: A Life*. London: Vintage, 1992.

McLaren, John, ed. *Prophet from the Desert*. Melbourne: Red Hill P, 1995.

Morley, Patricia A. *The Mystery of Unity: Theme and Technique in the Novels of Patrick White*. Montreal: McGill- Quenn's University Press, 1972.

Nandan, Satendra. 'Beyond Colonialism: The Artist as Healer.' *South Pacific Images*. Ed. Chris Tiffin. St. Lucia: U of Queensland P, 1978. 11-25.

Steven, Laurence. *Dissociation and Wholeness in Patrick White's Fiction*. Canada: Wilfrid Laurier UP, 1989.

Vickery, John B. *The Literary Impact of The Golden Bough*. Princeton: Princeton UP, 1976.

Walsh, William. *Commonwealth Literature*, London: Oxford UP, 1973.

______________ .*Patrick White's Fiction*. Sydney: George Allen and Unwin, 1978.

White, Patrick. *The Vivisector*. 1970. London: Vintage, 1994. Page reference are to this edition.

______________ .'Credo.' *Overland* 3.6 (1988): 16.

______________ .'The Prodigal Son.' *Patrick White Speaks*. Eds. Paul Brennan and Christine Flynn. Sydney: Primavera Press, 1989. 13-17.

Wilding, Michael. *Studies in Classic Australian Fiction*. Sydney: Shoestring P, 1997.

Williams, Mark. *Patrick White*. London: Macmillan, 1993.

Wolfe, Peter. *Laden Choirs*. Kentucky: University Press of Kentucky, 1983.

Ziolkowski, Theodore. *Hesse: A Collection of Critical Essays*. Englewood cliffs: Prentice, 1973.

6 Aestheticizing Aboriginality in Jack Davis's *No Sugar*

— Dr. S. Robert Gnanamony

> There is a happy land,
> Far, far away.
> No *sugar* in our tea,
> Bread and butter we never see.
> That's why we're gradually Fading away.
>
> (*No sugar*. Act IV: s.v)

This paper is an attempt to bring out the various struggles and oppressions of the Australian aboriginal community had to face and their indigenality in the depression years. Through Jack Davis's aboriginal play *No Sugar* one learns how the natives of Australia were conquered, then colonised and then turned into the Other. The play not only documents how the natives were made to think that their culture was not enough for humans to live in, and their languages were not enough for humans to speak by, but also the white colonisers' biased attitude to the natives that they should always be illiterates, so that the white could exploit them for ever and for ever. The indigenous people were so alienated in Australia that they became strangers in their own land. They even seemed to have lost their will power to survive due to the white's invasion, occupation and dispossession of the natives. The play talks about the various pressures that the governmental agencies exerted on the indigenous people to conform to the state laws. Their predicament is such that those who conform and also those who do not conform are on the point of decay; this may perhaps be due to the historical process. Jack Davis does not romanticize the poverty of the aborigines of the Moore River Native Settlement in his play.

No Sugar tells the story of Joe Mullimurra and his girl friend Mary Dargurru's fight for survival at the time of the depression (1930's) and the ways in which they were humiliated in the hands of a couple of white officers like Neville and Neal. The indigenous people in the play suffer "a rape of the soul" (Wangka 4) due to their existential condition. The play also brings to light the human warmth, the spontaneity, the chivalry, the inner strength and humour of the native people even when they pass through a difficult phase of their life. Of late the indigenous people's predicament has become the focus of both the white and black writers of Australia. This has resulted in the emergence of a strong literature, which is ever growing in Australia. With out doubt, indigenous literature has increasingly become the basis for the construction of aboriginal history. As Milli Milli Wangka has observed, "life stories (often in collaboration), novels, short stories and poems are devoting their words to the indigenous existential being in what is now said to be a 'multicultural' Australia [...]" (3).

The natives of Australia lived as extended family groups very close to each other, squabbled, fought, intermarried and came together in peace in certain village squares where they held joint ceremonies. See how the native writer Mudrooroo shares his experience with one in his book *Us Mob*, "At the joint family gatherings, we managed to settle our differences, for we knew that families must cooperate for survival and well-being" (1). In *No Sugar*, when the native Jimmy Munday sees some three lorries of black aborigines transported from one reserve to the other, he says in exasperation, "You fellas, you know why them wetjalas marchin' down the street, eh? I'll youse why. 'Cause them bastards took our country and them blackfellas dancin' for 'em. Bastards!" (16). Wetjalas means white persons, a corruption of the English 'white fellow'. There is no hint in the play that the uprooted aborigines violently reacted against the move of the white master; this may be one of their survival tactics.

There was a widespread segregation practised against the black aborigines in Australia in the depression years and thereafter. Even though there was a special officer called Chief Protector of Aborigines, the white officials do not take any interest in protecting the aborigines. In *No Sugar* Auber Octavius Neville is the Chief Protector of Aborigines. In his office in the

Government Well Aboriginal Reserve, there are separate entrances for the white and black respectively. The privileges that the white enjoy are not extended to the aborigines. The white can carry liquor and consume as much as they want; but as Sergeant Carrol says in the play, "[...] it is an offence to supply liquor to an Aboriginal native under the Aboriginal Act." The native Frank Brown who tries to sell some liquor to some natives clandestinely is strictly warned by Carrol. Frank does it as a profession, because as he says, "I got a wife and two kids staying with her parents in Leederville. I can't even raise a trainfare to Perth to go and see them" (18). There is discrimination even in weekly rations and doles given to the white and the black/ aborigines. The native is entitled to get two shillings and four pence per week whereas the white would get seven shillings per week. No meat is given to the native in his ration and soap is also discontinued. Sergeant Carrol wants the natives to understand that they have to work and earn money to buy luxury items like soap.

The white coloniser does not really want the aborigines to be educated, because the former thinks that education is a weapon and it should not be handed over to the aborigines. The whites want the aborigines "to be educated into his ways of seeing things, of thinking things", of doing things (Mudrooroo 3). But the natives want to be educated in their own ways, think their own thoughts, and see with their own eyes. If the natives were educated, the white would never get the services of the native girls at a cheap rate. In the play *No Sugar*, some eighty girls went out from their reserve in the domestic service and "thirty returned to the settlement in pregnant condition" (21). Neal, the Superintendent of the Moore River Settlement instructs Sister Eileen not to lend books—it includes novels too—to natives. Astonished the sister asks him, 'That you don't encourage the natives to read" (95). Neal's answer confirms his earlier stand: "That's right" (95).

The natives have to keep themselves in their reserves; they are not supposed to go out into the town/city. In *No Sugar*, Jimmy ruefully brings out this when he tells Frank Brown, the unemployed youth: "None of us are; you know we're not allowed in town, not allowed to go down the soak, not allowed to march [...]" (28). If they are found in the town, they will be handcuffed and sent to prison.

The aborigines do not want to surrender their spirit and body, their land and their possessions to the coloniser, come what may. They do not fail to register their protest whenever they meet a shabby treatment from the white master. Jimmy, the native, is never tired of calling the white constable "you white bastard" (33). When they get paid lowly to their work, they say it to their bosses. Listen to the conversation between a couple of aborigines and Sergeant Carrol:

> *Milly:* Look, last week my Joe cut a hundred posts for old Skinny Martin and you know what he got? A pair of second-hand boots and a piece of stag ram so tough even the dawgs couldn't eat; skinnier than old Martin 'himself.
>
> *Gran:* And we couldn't eat the boots.
>
> *Milly:* You wait till brother Jimmy hears about this no soap business. He'll make you fellas jump.
>
> *Sergeant:* Yeah, and you tell that bush lawyer brother of yours, if he comes here arguing I'll make him jump; straight inside (23).

The white coloniser has a natural predilection to consume nature mindlessly; but the native has a tremendous concern for nature; his wants are limited; he wants "all trees remain and continue their natural growth around that great Grandfather Tree which is Australia, to respect Australia and its ceaseless and unending variety"(Mudrooroo 4). The aborigines of Australia do not unduly worry about modern notions of culture and civilisation. If no soap is found in the list of rations, well, they have an alternative which is nature-given. See what Granny says in *No Sugar* when Milly says that the Sergeant will not give soap any more: "Don't worry, we can use tjeerung bush. I know where some growin" (26). 'Tjeerung' is an expression in Nyoongah language of the aborigines which means medicinal leaves.

The indigenous people of Australia know pretty well that Australia is not Europe; any attempt to europeanise Australia, according to them may not bear fruit. In *No Sugar* plenty of efforts are taken to 'civilise' and 'australianise' the natives, but of no avail. The Chief Protector of Aborigines, Neville is of the opinion that if each native child is issued with a handkerchief, then "you are half way to civilising him" (24). Since there is every chance of losing the handkerchief, Neville suggests to "attaching them (handkerchiefs) to their sleeves by way of a tape" (24).

The Australian white, themselves a settler community, do not recognise the Other as their equal. They are prepared to accept the natives as artists, writers and musicians but not as politicians sharing of power. The white think that they have a moral sanction to 'civilise' the Other. That's why the JP tells Frank: "[...] but it's my duty to protect natives and half-castes from alcohol" (35). So saying he sentences Frank six weeks in imprisonment with hard labour for supplying liquor to another native, Jimmy.

The play *No Sugar* makes it clear that though the natives are deprived of all their privileges, they are not at all chicken-hearted. They stand firm even in the face of great adversity. An intimate conversation that goes on between two natives—Mary Dargurru and her boyfriend Joe Millimurra makes it clear to us:

> *Mary:* I don't want to go up there to marry an old man.
>
> *Joe:* You're meant to be gettin' married to me.
>
> *Mary:* Mr. Neal not gonna let us get married.
>
> *Joe:* [exploding] Jesus! [Indicating running]
>
> We're doin' this tonight, right this fuckin'minute.
>
> *Mary:* Joe, you'll get in big trouble!
>
> *Joe:* I'll get in bigger trouble if I have to chip that walrus-faced bastard. I'll kill him (69).

The white master grabbed the land of the natives without any compunction. In *No Sugar,* Frank Brown had once his own farm at Lake Yealering; due to his bad time, the crops failed and the loan he took from the bank consumed everything that he had; finally he had to surrender his land to the creditors. Frank is separated from his kids and it is six months since he last saw his kids. He hasn't even sent them any money. He thanks profusely when the Millimurras share their food with him: "And thanks for the really nice meal" (30).

The natives in Australia do not exist in isolation; no matter how remote the reserves are, they keep in touch with each other; they have never existed as an isolated culture in Australia. Like any other group of people, they quarrel but then they become friends once again forgetting their enmity. In *No Sugar,* Jimmy and

Sam are locked together cursing each other over a silly issue. Joe even bleeds on his nose. See what happens:

> *Gran:* Don't you hit, Sam.
>
> *Sam:* I will if he bites me.
>
> *Gran:* I'll stop you two fellas (30).

Gran Munday (Jimmy's mother) then charges at them and tries to separate them by grabbing them both by their hair and pulling them viciously. She then takes her walking stick and gives them both a solid poke in the ribs. They separate and get up. But shortly Jimmy lands in jail for possessing liquor. The prison cell echoes the song of Jimmy:

> Hail, Queen of Heaven [...]
> Save us from peril and from woe (32).

Though Jimmy gets prison sentence for six months, he says, "Six months! I can do that on me fuckin' head" (33). Plenty of restrictions are imposed upon the native community. Even entry into a native reserve and exit from there is forbidden. As Mudrooroo observes:

> For better or worse, everyone is bound up in a system of personal, social and political relationship, and these cannot be avoided, if they ever could. Even when reserves were set aside for the Native and entry restricted, the outside still penetrated, and even when Australia was Indigenous Australia, there is enough evidence in our traditions to suggest that our land was never the isolated continent as established in the Master texts (6).

Australian aborigines are also referred to as 'blackfella'; however there are some groups who dispute any term signifying blackness. The aborigine women are sadly nobodies in Master texts; As Mudrooroo says, the native woman is "doubly opaque, almost a material object" (8). Native women are mediated through maleness. If the black male was inferior to the white master, then the black female was doubly so.

In the Australian social structure, the white positions himself as the subject and considers the aborigine as the object. As

Mudrooroo writes, "His is the all-powerful gaze and consciousness" (8). In such a hierarchical superior attitude, the native image is obliterated. The white politicians are portrayed mindless in *No Sugar*. They don't show much difference between the dogs and natives. The natives are not supposed to keep any dog in their reserves. If any dog is found there, as Jimmy says in the play, "They can shoot our dawgs, anytime they want to. Bastards. They shot Streak [...]. Kill and show dawg, used to catch meat for every blackfella in Northam and they shot him" (29).

One of the saddest things is that the natives have to see their past through the Master text; this is because the oral tradition is not recognised and the native language/dialect has no validity. It is the white master who studies the past of the aborigine community and brings out the prehistory before the arrival of the Europeans. The Master text carries the phantoms of the past as seen by the master. It is through the Master text, the natives have to reconstruct their past. But the Other is only an insignificant trace in the Master text that has other concerns than to present a true picture of the aborigines.

The aborigines are not comfortable with the names given by the white. To name is not only to define but to own, and so 'counter-names' are being used by aborigines, such as Koori, Goori, Boori, Yolngu, Yamadji, Nyungar, Anangu, Munday, Millimurra, Dargurru and Murri, which signify a regional indigenality. The masters came, saw and named the aborigines. They continue to do so, and there is even a map of tribal areas and boundaries created by the master. As Mudrooroo observes, "We know that the masters invented tribes as they perhaps invented language groups as a way of ordering their world" (11).

The indigenous people have a 'feeling for the land'. They feel very upset when they see their original reserve, the Government Well Aboriginal Reserve at Northam, burned down in their forced absence. Joe says that his mother will be very much sad when she sees the place. Mary, Joe's girl friend comforts him saying, "Never mind, it's all over now" (79). But Joe says, "It'll never be over!" (79). When Joe questions Sergeant Carrol why the reserve was burned down, the Sergeant replies, "We're simply following orders" (80). The natives have a closer kinship with the big animals of their reserve forest. The biggest animal that they kill is the rabbit; most of the days they survive only on it. They call it"underground mutton" (*No Sugar* 28). They used to live on them whenever they are on the farm.

Joe Millimurra invites Mary Dargurru to his birthplace: "I'm gunna show you my country. Got a big river, swans, beautiful white swans" (70). They have a fund of stories to tell and a host of folk songs to sing. The natives Jimmy and Bluey get themselves painted with *wilgi* (a specially prepared paint for ceremonies) and both dance; Jimmy sings an old song; he calls it his "grandfather song" (65). They dance with increasing speed and energy, stamping their feet, whirling in front of the fire, their bodies appearing and disappearing as the paint catches the firelight. The dance becomes faster and more frantic until finally Sam lets out a yell and they collapse, dropping back to their positions around the fire. Billy congratulates Jimmy saying, "You song man, you fella dance men. This still your country" (66).

Going to the jail is not at all a shameful thing to the aborigines. Many native leaders are imprisoned for flimsy reasons. As Mudrooroo has pointed out:

> "For many adult males, a gaol sentence may be accepted as an indicator of Indigenality [...] and it is in the prisons of Australia that many of Us Mob develop a consciousness of nationwide Indegenality which is overtly political" (15).

In *No Sugar* when Gran Munday advises her son Jimmy Munday not to contradict the white Sergeant, lest, he should put Jimmy in gaol for six months, Jimmy says, "I can do that standing on my head" (26) Turning to his sister Milly Millimurra, he says, "You know how many times I been in gaol? [Holding up four fingers] That many times" (27). The charges framed against him are drinking, fighting and snowdropping. After undergoing the gaol term, Jimmy has to wait for a whole day in the Chief Protector of Aborigines Mr. Neville's office for train fare to go back to his reserve camp. To Jimmy the jail is "a wetjala thing" (71), which means a white man's burden.

The indigenous community of Australia has to undergo all sorts of hardships to eke out a living. When Jimmy's sister Milly wants the sergeant to supply her a blanket for her sick girl in the hospital down with pneumonia and pleurisy, the sergeant says,

"Sorry, blankets not here yet, Milly" (43). When Milly goes to the vicar of St. John for help, the vicar closes his eyes and says, "The Lord will help you" (43).

Sexual harassment is something common in the native camps; invariably, it is the white master who pesters the native women. In *No Sugar,* the young girl Mary Dargurru has to undergo a lot of hardships in the hands of the Superintendent of the Moore River Settlement Mr. Neal. She doesn't like the way he looks at her; she tells Joe, her boy-friend: "He's always hangin' around where the girls are workin'; in the cookhouse, in the sewin' room. And he's always carryin' that cat-o'-nine tails and he'll use it, too" (62). Joe and Mary come closer and even decide to get married at the earliest. Mary has all sorts of stories to tell her friend Joe. She shares the ordeal undergone by her intimate friend in the hands of her white boss:

> "My friend went last Christmas and then she came back boodjarri (pregnant). She reckons the boss's sons used to belt her up and, you know force her. Then they kicked her out. And when she had that baby them trackers choked it dead and buried it in the pine plantation" (62).

The reaction from Joe is, "The bastards. The fuckin' bastards" (62). That Mr. Neal is a womaniser is known even to the fellow white; it includes his wife too. He will not allow Mary to marry Joe. And that's why Joe and Mary elope with the knowledge of Joe's parents and friends. Since Mary does not toe the line of Mr. Neal, the latter lashes her with cat-o-nine-tails even though she is pregnant.

The white authorities shuttle-cock the natives as and when they please, sometimes with an ulterior motive of grabbing their land. This happens in *No Sugar* too. Mr. Neville with the help of Dr. Aberdeen examines the natives of some 89 people from the Government Well Aboriginal Reserve, Northam, who are reported to be "rotten with scabies" (47) and got them transferred to the Moore River Settlement. In reality, only one or two has got scabies. Even their dogs are free from scabies. But still they are taken on foot to a quarantine camp at Long Pool much against the wishes of the natives. But the quarantine camp is not a happy place to stay in; to Jimmy it is "a load of bullshit" (63). They have to be in the new reserve "until the scabies are cleared and a new reserve is gazetted" (48). Before they are transferred, the authorities arrest them and then shift them with police protection. The natives however, see through the white's game plan. Jimmy, the native knows it better:"You reckon blackfellas are bloody mugs. Whole town knows why we're goin'. 'Coz wetjalas (the white) in this town don't want us 'ere, don't want our kids at the school, with their kids, and old Jimmy Mitchell's tight 'coz they reckon Bert 'Awke's gonna give him a hidin' in the election" (50).

In conclusion, the play *No Sugar* throws more light on the early struggles of the aboriginals in the hands of the white settler. Nearly a century ago, Australia treated her unfortunate indigenous people in the cruellest manner possible. In Tasmania region alone, the play shows, "some six thousand natives disappeared and only one was left alive" (87). In the same region, from 1829 to 1901, some thirteen thousand natives were reduced to just 1,419. The cruelty inflicted on the black natives of Australia could be compared to King Herod's butchering every first-born baby boy under two years old at the time of Jesus' birth. The play also has a reference to it. To escape the cruelty of King Herod, Mary and Joseph (the parents of baby Jesus) had to flee to Egypt. The native people of Australia had to undergo a similar trauma whenever violence was unleashed upon them by the white administrators. It is natural that when an under privileged people are confronted by a privileged race armed with technology and power—political and economic with the accompanying strange and terrifying things, then everything is lost to the underprivileged people and those unfortunate people unable to adapt themselves become extinct. The title *No Sugar* is suggestive of the aridness of the native reserves. One by one, all those items in the ration-list have been taken away and at one stage, the natives do not even have such basic items like sugar, bread and butter. From the play it is clear that the white Australians do not see eye-to-eye with the black natives. There is a terrible distrust between them. Mary does not want to be admitted in the settler's hospital even for childbirth, and when the child is born, she tells Gran Munday, "Don't let Matron see Baby. Granny, go and hide him. Please, please, don't let Matron take him away" (103). She is afraid that once the baby is taken to the hospital, "The trackers will get him and kill him" (103).

From *No Sugar* one can understand that the Australian indigenous people are proud of their descent, they love their country and they have a deep attachment to their community. Whatever happens to one person in the community is considered happened to all the others in the community and they jointly devise ways and means to tackle it. The play teaches us that the natives unlike the other so-called cultured white are not at all lonely people; it is impossible for them to exist in isolation. It is time that they were recognised as the royal citizens of Australia and their culture was recognised as Australian culture.

Notes

Indigenality is a word that has become so common over the past couple of decades to denote the Australian aborigine community. The adjective of indegenality is indigenous. Mudrooroo, the native writer, however prefers the term Us Mob to Indigenality. The Native, the Indigenous person and the Aborigine are used as synonyms in this paper.

Works Cited

Davis, Jack. *No Sugar.* Sydney: Currency Press, 2000 (1986).

Mudrooroo. *Us Mob. History, Culture, Struggle: An Introduction to Indigenous Australia.* Sydney: Angus & Robertson, 2001 (1995).

Wangka, Milli Milli. *Mudrooroo. Indigenous Literature of Australia.* Victoria: Hyland House, 1997.

7 "The Will to Live": A Study of Survivors in the Novels of Mordecai Richler

— Dr. S. Ganesan

Many of Mordecai Richler's leading characters exhibit great survival ability. In fact Margaret Atwood's concept of survival is relevant not only to life in Canada but also to worldwide human predicament. The term 'survival' carries many connotations. To quote Atwood:

> The central symbol for Canada... is undoubtedly survival, *la survivance*... for early explorers and settlers, it meant bare survival in the face of hostile elements and/or natives: carving out a place and a way of keeping alive. But the word can also suggest survival of a crisis or disaster, like a hurricane or a wreck... for French Canada after the English took over, it became cultural survival, hanging on as a people, retaining a religion and a language under an alien government... But the main idea is the first one: hanging on, staying alive. (32-33).

Richler's characters often battle for survival against all odds. Many of them have faced the brunt of anti-Semitism and McCarthyism. Their experiences have made them tough, cunning and ruthless. In the words of David Sheps,

> ... much of their energy is consumed by the strategies of survival in a competitive and hostile world. The Richler characters often have the wary, suspicious, necessarily egoistic psychology of the survivor. They move through life like tacticians, are survivors of concentration camps; various forms of persecution, war, or poverty; or simply painfully traumatic personal experiences and shattered dreams and ideals. They are frequently the floating debris of the wreckage of the modern period and this mental set

> conditions them to ruthlessness [to me, Chaim is an exception], emotional detachment and scepticism (xv).

Richler's protagonists are mainly Jews though there is a sprinkling of Gentiles too among them. Richler is concerned with the survival of the Jews in Canada and elsewhere. His novels celebrate the survival ability of the Jews. They achieve not merely physical survival, but material prosperity too. There are some Jews marked by an endless hunger for success; others reveal their wisdom and strong common sense which help them in trying situations.

In *The Acrobats*, Chaim, an East-European Jew, flees from the Holocaust for his safety to America. There he falls in love with and later loses his lover to disease. After the pogroms and Holocaust, even after his own sufferings, he does not lose hope in life. He is able to transcend his unpleasant past to help the needy. He regroups himself and after many years, returns to post-war Poland which is in shambles. He encounters the remaining Polish Jews who still mourn their murdered sons and daughters. He meets a young man with a number-tattooed hand and readily offers his passport; to enable the young man to move to the safety of America to join his lover. There onwards, he has to remain without a passport moving from place to place.

Chaim is ready to help Andre, a disillusioned, sensitive young man to start family life with Toni, a young club-girl in Paris leaving the squalid post-war Spain. He remains a friend, philosopher and guide to Andre. Andre is plagued by self-inflicted guilty feelings over the death of Ida, his lover during abortion. He still reels under the resultant trauma. To complicate things, in his self-imposed exile to Spain, he encounters Krausthe-Nazi. He realizes his being stalked by Kraus both physically and psychically. He remains obsessed with these two nagging feelings which make him unable to paint; unable to respond to the genuin love of Toni who is ready to marry him.

Chaim has a thorough understanding of Andre's predicament. To him, it seems that Andre, instead of thinking of the future, needlessly tortures himself with the traumatic memories of the past. He feels that it is better for Andre to move to Paris with Toni to start a new life. While Andre is hell-bent on confronting the Nazi, Chaim is practical. To him, one has to accept the reality and has to act accordingly. Hence, he admonishes

Andre: "There are times to fight and times to run. Knowing that is the difference between being a foolish hero or a useful man" (TA 140).

Chaim believes that the self-centeredness of human beings makes them magnify their own problems. This results in suffering, ennui and suicidal tendencies. According to Chaim, Andre is in no way responsible for Ida's death. Still he keeps brooding over his imaginary guilt. His Hamlet-like-situation is of his own-making. Since the past cannot be altered, there is no use in lamenting over it. Also, it is futile to clamour for revenge against the evil forces.

In his essay, "What I Believe", E.M.Forster, while advocating a pragmatic kind of living, invokes the Scandinavian legend of Niebelung's ring. According to the legend, Fifnir, the dragon which is capable of destroying the world is in deep slumber. In the meantime, productive and intelligent life goes on in the world as symbolized by the *valkyries* (61). It is foolhardy to taunt and beard the sleeping danger and invite trouble. In the novel, Chaim is a vulkyrie and Andre is a foolish hero who courts death. What matters is, living life as decently and as meaningfully one can.

In the final scene of the novel, having been betrayed by Kraus, the Nazi, Chaim has to leave the place for safety. But he is reconciled to his lot. He tells the worried Toni: "You decide to live in a certain way and you know what it's going to cost you. It's worth it. I like it" (TA 209). Though facing constant threat, Chaim nurtures a passion for marriage, children and settling in Israel. The survivor never gives up hope. He grapples with all trying situations and overcomes them. "This longing to beat the odds, to conquer our own weakness, has carried humanity through its long history. It is the cry of the heroic" (Whitman 42). This is what one sees in Chaim.

What is the secret of Chaim's survival? Amidst all his ruins, he stands tall, thanks to the Judaic wisdom he had received. For him, human life is a chance to serve others. He believes that one should transcend self-centredness. No individual is the centre of his own universe. For, it is in living for the welfare of others, one can find meaning in life and can achieve salvation. Having an indefatigable faith in the worthiness of living, he utters the last words of the novel: "There is always hope. Always. There has to be" (TA 209).

In *Joshua, Then and Now,* Joshua comes to know of Carlos the Marrano, in his Spanish days. The Marranos in reality, are Jews who embraced Catholicism to save themselves from the Spanish Inquisition in the fifteenth century. They suffered a lot during the inquisition. Carlos's ancestors were expelled from Toledo to Majorca. The word 'Marrano' itself was a denigrating epithet, meaning pig.

Though outwardly converted to Christianity, the Marranos could not forget the religion of their birth. For centuries, they secretly kept practising Judaism at great risk to their lives. Their "surviving as Jews consisted in resorting to crafty stratagems and carefully thought-out ruses in order to preserve certain symbols of the Jewish tradition.... At the risk of death, they kept the custom of unleavened bread and of commemorating the parting of the Red Sea on Passover" (Brenner 129).

After facing religious persecution and massacres, they still retain their Jewish roots and their affinity with Israel, the historical homeland of the Jews. In the novel, Carlos is deeply conscious of his Jewish identity. He regularly prays "Shema Israel", affirming his bonds with Judaism; studies Hebrew and Jewish history, showing his desire to reintegrate into Jewish culture.

While Joshua regards his Jewishness as a sign of weakness and a burden, the Marranos do not think so. They feel proud of being Jews and at great peril to their lives, keep their Jewishness alive. While Joshua eschews his Jewishness seeking values elsewhere, Carlos, the Marrano resolutely clings to his Jewish roots. "He... chooses to redress the injustice inflicted on him by the Gentile world by an active re-establishment of the severed bonds with his heritage and his people" (Brenner 129). Thus, in Carlos, the Marrano, one can see the embodiment of tenacity, the hallmark of meaningful survival.

While anti-Semitism is rampant in Canada, the elder generation Jews are obsessed with their sole aim of making it big in the material game. In Richler's autobiographical short story collection, *The Street,* the parents try their best to instil material values in their children at the expense of Jewish pride and traditional values. To quote from the book:

> No sooner had they [our grandparents and parents] unpacked their bundles and cardboard suitcases than they were planning a better, brighter life for us, the Canadian born children. The Main, good enough for them, was not to be for us, and that they told us again and again what the struggle was for. The Main was for "bummers", drinkers, and [heaven forbid] failures. (55)

In *St.Urbain's Horseman*, elders like Uncle Abe remain politically meek. They feel it is enough to bribe, placate, act in a conciliatory way toward the Gentiles in order to survive in a hostile world. In the novel, the anti-Semites harass the Jews. While the younger generation Jews represented by Joey scream for militant retaliation, the elders led by Uncle Abe prefer appeasement. He and other clan leaders contribute to the election fund of the political authorities to ward off evil.

> Abe is aware of the humiliations heaped on Jews by the anti-Semites in Canada. But the Canadian situation is nothing compared to the harrowing Jewish predicament in Hitler's Europe. Actually the Jews flourish in Canada while their brethren were sent to extermination camps in Europe. In *The Street,* Richler describes the ironic situation:

> It was when we read of the uprising in the Warsaw Ghetto and saw, in Montreal, the changeover from poky little "shuls" to big synagogue-cum-parochial school with stained glass windows and mosaics outside. During the war some of us lost brothers and cousins but in Canada we had never had it so good.... (59-60)

Uncle Abe, the prototype of the elder generation Jews believes that appeasement and lying low will achieve security for the Jewish community so that they could channelize their energies in fresh ventures on becoming materially successful. In a sense, Abe proves to be on the right side in choosing the road of Jewish destiny in Canada as when Jake Hersh visits his clan for his father's funeral, there is more of a festive than a mournful atmosphere. He is pleasantly shocked to see the flourishing clan and the fruitful transformation of the once meek community into a vibrant one, celebrating every moment of life.

Commenting on Richler's fiction, Mark Shechner has pointed out how Richler's fictional concerns differ from that of the traditional Jewish fiction. To quote Shechner:

> Jewish fiction has repeatedly thrown up figures of wisdom and endurance, observance and rectitude-Richler, by contrast, adheres to a tradition of dissent that runs from Issac Babel's Odessa Stories, Daniel Fuch's Williamsburg triology and Budd Schulberg's *What Makes Sammy Run*? Which finds more color, more life and more fidelity to the facts of Jewish existence in the demimonde of hustlers, heavies, strong-arm types, and men on the make than in the heroes of menshlichkeit. This counter myth is not Jewish 'self-hatred' or embarrassment, for it is a self-regard of a different sort, in which vigor and tenacity are celebrated instead of saintliness. Richler's affection for these quarrelsome, grasping jews is genuine... (31-32)

It is this sympathy that enlivens Richler's portrait of young men like Duddy. In *The Apprenticeship of Duddy Kravitz,* Duddy displays an indomitable will and an ability to survive amidst a hostile environment. The motherless Duddy has to survive - his indifferent family, shadow-figures like Jerry Dingleman and Friar, a near- bankruptcy, cunning anti-Semites like Irwin Schubert, the self-defeating idealism of good but impractical uncle Benjy, to make a mark in the world.

Even as a school boy, Duddy the tough hustler is juxtaposed with 'tender-natured' boys like Milton. He knows things far ahead of his age like sex and the creation of children which makes mothers warn their children not to mix with him. In the novel:

> Duddy is compared to the 'spiky' grass growing by the railroad tracks in the slums... Richler's image suggests both a phallic potency that symbolizes a mature manhood and also a tough vitality which thrives upon adversity. Therefore, the spiky grass epitomizes Duddy's adoloscent struggle to prove himself by overcoming the psychic trammels of his family and the ghetto and by succeeding as his own man in a tougher but larger world (Ower 424).

Duddy's role models keep changing. Initially, the survival story of Dingleman, a 'Jewish hero' from Duddy's own St.Urbain's milieu, impresses him. Dingleman, the poor Jewish youngster wins a card game amidst anti-Semites; disappears from the Canadian scene only to return from the United States as a tycoon. To Duddy, If Dingleman could survive, then why not he? Later, Cohen, the Jewish business man's cut-throat business ethics too appeal to him.

In the novel, Duddy is advised by many. Simcha, his zeyda advises him on the need of an identity for the Jews; his father Max advises on practical survival; Cohen sermonizes on the ruthless ways of doing business; uncle Benjy advises him to become a gentleman. As David Carpenter remarks in his afterword, "His [Duddy's] apprenticeship, rather his survival story", has been a process of choosing whose advice to follow in a world that offers a plenitude of advice..."(ADK 323). In the ultimate analysis, Benjy wanted Duddy to become a mensh; but Duddy emerges, an Ubermensh, one beyond good and evil.

Duddy's climb to top seems to have a social function. To Margaret Atwood, a heroic character, "[...] must struggle against obstacles, as heroes traditionally do; the struggle must be meaningful, it must have significance for people other than the hero himself, he must be fighting on behalf of his own group or nation (*Survival* 165)." In Duddy's case, his relentless drive to acquire the land is not only to carve a niche for himself as he himself claims: "I did it all for us... I'm going to create jobs... I'm a public benefactor" (ADK 317).

Uncle Benjy brands Duddy as an aggressive, money-minded Jew. This is again a simplistic judgment. Duddy has few choices before him. He sees his studious brother Lennie tormented by the Gentile circle. He receives further baptism from Cohen, the Jewish-tycoon: "[...] A plague on all the goyim... they're all Nazis. You scrape down deep enough and you'll see" (267-68). In such a situation, Duddy finds liberalism anachronistic and he feels that the situation warrants aggressive action and cunning. Frank Birbal Singh rightly observes that "[Duddy's] behavior is conditioned less by personal motives than by social pressures. His nastiness is his response to an existing social phenomenon, the antipathy between Jew and goy. Duddy is what he is because goys are what they are" (104).

It is this same survival instinct that marks Ephraim and *Solomon* Gurskys, Richler's heroic/trickster figures. Solomon

Gursky was Here deals with the eternal human dream of survival and social recognition. The novel depicts the ambitious quest of the Jews for Canadian credentials. The novel is the saga of the rise of the Gurskys to prominence. Ephraim Gursky, the clan's patriarch is noted for his Houdini-like survival abilities. John Leonard sums up, the Protean ability of Ephraim:

> Ephraim was always mythic: the son of a Minsk cantor, a pickpocket and a pimp in Dickensian London, a penal colonist in Tasmania, part of Franklin's Crew in 1845, peddler in St.Petersburg, gun runner during the American Civil War, a player of pianos in Klondike Saloons, a buddy of Geronimo, a shaman and a con man who converted Eskimos to Judaism. (227)

In other words, Ephraim is a Protean figure, ready for all seasons and could survive adverse circumstances. He survives the Russian pogroms, the notorious London prisons and is the sole-survivor of the doomed Franklin's expedition to find the Northwest passage and reaches the Canadian North having the menacing raven as his totem. There he indulges in gun running, making his own brand of country-liquor and fathering children. He teaches the survival skills to his chosen grandson Solomon Gursky by taking him to the Arctic North. Ephraim never returns to his clan, preferring to spend his last days in the North. Having survived gloriously, he has his spiritual quest remaining. He desires to see Yahweh, face to face like Moses.

Ephraim sees himself as a Messianic figure like Moses. Like Moses who released and led the Israelites to the Promised Land, Ephraim too has led his family from the burning Europe to the Promised Land of Canada. Again like the Biblical Moses, who did not reach the Promised Land, Ephraim too prefers the wilderness of the North to the materialistic mainland.

Ephraim's survival is significant in two ways: first as the escape of the Jew from the horrifying European-situation; secondly his surviving a hostile Nature. Moreover, throughout his life, he has overcome crisis after crisis gloriousiy. He also has fathered and nurtured his clan well. All these make him a typical heroic figure in Canadian Literature which gives paramount importance to 'survival'.

Solomon too is a Protean figure with an endless appetite like Ephraim, his *zeyda*. He learns from Ephraim, the fine art of fighting against odds, and later he becomes a past master of survival strategies. Thanks to his winning the poker game, the Gurskys buy a hotel and soon develop a liquor empire, making use of every legal loop-hole available. Solomon knows when to duck and when to jab. To escape court cases, he engineers his plane crash. He is supposed to be dead. But he surfaces again as Sir Hyman Kaplansky, a Jewish Knight in Socialite London. Now he has been knighted being the biggest donor for the Conservative Party. He takes revenge on the anti-Semites by throwing a party and making them to taste ritual blood. When his identity is found out by Moses Berger, the self-styled biographer of the Gurskys, Solomon eludes him yet again. Later, he ensures the future of the Gursky Empire, lying in safe hands.

Solomon is not merely adventurous. He is concerned with the Jewish sufferings in Europe. He tries his best to save as many Jews as possible. As Leon Rooke points out:

> The bootlegger has certain integrity, and loyalty to his people-while Bernard and Harvey Schwartz were adding new labels to McTavish booze, Solomon had a cot in his office and his ear to the short wave. As Hitler strode over Europe, Solomon was petitioning Ottawa on behalf of the Jews and buying land in the Laurentians where the refugees might settle (13).
>
> Throughout life, he involves himself in world events of Jewish interest like the plot to kill Hitler, the Israeli war of Independence and the Israeli raid on Entebbe. When he is eighty, he organizes the Entebbe Raid. "Solomon is that updated myth, the Wandering Jew as frequent flyer; part guardian angel, part avenging angel settling scores with Mr.Richler's sharp sense of humour" (Prose 222). He is like the mythical raven, with an unquenchable itch to meddle and provoke things, to play an endless game with the creatures of the world.

To survive the hostile geographical climate, the Richler characters are forced to throw all human norms to winds. *Solomon Gursky was Here* contains cannibalistic incidents. Sir.John Franklin's search for the North-west passage ends in cannibalism and

Ephraim has to turn a cannibal to survive. Later in the novel, "Solomon's son, Harry, the Hassidic Howard Hughes, dies in the frozen Northwest Territories, and his son Isaac actually eats him, like a drumstick" (Leonard 227). Of course, this is an extreme strategy to survive. But as Knud Rasmussen says in his *Across Arctic America*: "Many people have eaten human flesh. But never from any desire for it, only to save their lives and that after so much suffering that in many cases they were not fully sensible of what they did..." (Quoted in Cultures in Canada 17).

Apart from the survival of heroic protagonists, there are quite a few shadow-figures who too survive, rather disturbingly. At the end of *The Acrobats*, Kraus-the-Nazi flees to safety after killing Andre. In the words of Graeme Gibson, "... he's a very vulnerable man [morally], but he has survived,...."Similarly, in *A Choice of Enemies*, being tormented by Carp (the once-victim becoming a victimizer here), Norman Price bursts out: "The Best ones were killed, Carp; only the conniving evil ones like you survived"(Quoted by Gibson 286). In the same novel, Ernst, himself a victim of post-War political situation in Germany murders Nickie and still survives. Above all, in *Cocksure, the Star Maker* (who symbolizes the ruthless pursuit of success at any cost) survives at the cost of innocent human lives whose healthy organs are periodically fitted to his body to prolong his longevity artificially. Though Cocksure is a satire and the Star Maker is a caricature, as Graeme Gibson points out, there is a progression of the survival of shadow-figures in Richler's novels (287).

Thus in Richler's novels, both the heroes and villains survive. In the words of David Sheps, "One of the most interesting facts about these novels is that the ostensible heroes and the ostensible villains share many qualities" (xv). Some of the heroes save their lives, tradition and humane values by lying low against the hostile forces and by making intelligent compromises. Chaim, Uncle Abe and Carlos, the Marrano belong to this type. Some others use aggressive strategies, trickery and cunning. They are symbolized by Protean-figures like Duddy, Ephraim and Solomon. They are at times unscrupulous. But their over-all stature remains heroic. On the other hand, villains too survive marking "the destruction of innocence and the death of beauty" (Gibson 285).

Works Cited

Atwood, Margaret. *Survival: A Thematic Guide to Canadian Literature.* Toronto: Anansi, 1972.

Bavington,Jack. Et al. eds. *Cultures in Canada.* Toronto. Jack MacLean-Hunter- Learning Materials Company,1976.

Brenner, Rachel Feldhay. *Assimilation and Assertion: The Response to the Holocaust in Mordecai Richler"s Writing.* New York:Peter Lang,1989.

Forster, E.M. What I Believe: *Selections From E.M.Forster* ed. R. Krishnamurti. Madras: Macmillan India Ltd., 1984.

Gibson, Graeme. *Eleven Canadian Novelists.* Toronto: Anansi, 1973.

Leonard,John. "Sermon on the Mountie." Contemporary Literary Criticism. Vol. 70, Year Book 1991. Ed. Roger Matuz. Detroit:Gale Research Inc., 1991.

Ower, John. "Sociology, Psychology, and Satire in The Apprenticeship of Duddy Kravitz: *Modern Fiction Studies.* Purdue Research Foundation, Indiana, Autumn.1976, pp. 413-28.

Prose, Francine. "Hopping Mad in Montreal." *The New York Times Book Review,* April 8, 1990, p.7.

Richler, Mordecai. *Joshua Then and Now.* Toronto: McClelland and Stewart Limited,1989.

______________ . *Solomon Gursky was Here.* Markham: Penguin Books,1990.

______________ .*St.Urbain"s Horseman.* Toronto:McClelland and Stewart Limited,1989.

______________ .*The Acrobats.* Toronto:McClelland and Stewart Limited,2002.

______________ .*The Apprenticeship* of Duddy Kravitz. Toronto: McClelland and Stewart Ltd.,1989.

______________ .*The Street.* Toronto:McClelland and Stewart Ltd.,2002.

Rooke, Leon. "Tales from the Caboose." *Rev. of Solomon Gursky was Here by Mordecai Richler.* Ed: Doris Cowan. Books in Canada. Vol.18, No.8, Toronto, Nov. 89, pp.11-13

Shechner, Mark. "Books and the Arts: "Joshua Then and Now"." *The New Republic.* Vol.182, No.24, June14, 1980, pp.30-32.

Sheps, David. ed. *Mordecai Richler.* Toronto: McGraw-Hill Company of Canada Ltd., 1971. pp.ix-xxvi.

Singh, Birbal F.M. "The Early Fiction of Mordecai Richler: Novels and the Nation" *Essays in Canadian Literature.* Toronto: TSAR, 1995 pp.100-107. Whitman, Ardis. "Here"s What Survivors Are Made Of." *The Reader"s Digest: 75 years.* Mumbai:RDI Print and Publishing PVT.Ltd.,1997.

8 Mapping the North as a Female Space in Aritha Van Herk's Geografictione—*Places Far From Ellesmere*

— Dr. Raj Kumar Sharma & Asra Sultana Mouda

Places Far From Ellesmere has been brought forth in an innovative garb by Aritha Van Herk which she calls a Geografictione, a new genre which has emerged out of the fusion of geography and fiction in the literary panorama. Aritha Van Herk has brilliantly interwoven a logical pattern from some unconventional constituents unexplored so far, in this remarkable Geografictione. A well-orchestrated plot of this artistic creation immensely suits her explicit objective through which she successfully explores an exclusive domain for women bereft of male chauvinist interventions. By resorting to inter-textuality, Van Herk has endeavoured to subvert and reinterpret the views of Tolstoy in presenting Anna Karenina and ensured for her a secure place where she may establish her independent identity without being bruised by the male counterparts. In order to counter the male dominated West, Van Herk has justifiably projected the concept of North that may be identified by an attribute of female discourse.

The geografictione comprising one hundred and forty-three pages is an exploration for a different space for women distinct from that of male which is symbolically depicted in the exploration of landscape. It is divided into four parts comprising four exploration sites: Edberg, coppice of desire and return; Edmonton, long division; Calgary, this growing graveyard; and Ellesmere, woman as island.

The narrator in the process of her descriptive narrative describes the search for a place, her 'Home' from Edberg through Edmonton and Calgary which ends in Ellesmere. The text begins thus,

> Home: what you visit and abandon: too much forgotten/ too much remembered. asylum for your origins, your launchings and departures, the derivations of your dream geographies. Where you invented destinations. Always and unrelentingly (home) even after it is too late to be or to revert to (home), even after it pre/occupies the past tense (Ellesmere, 13-14).

The text begins with the word "home" that symbolizes the seat anchor, the point of origin wherefrom the mapping begins in life. Conventionally, Van Herk's exploration starts from home that marks the organic development of her plan that takes several twists and turns in the due course leading down to fruition in Ellesmere which is the final destination. This exploration vividly paints the feministic concerns of Van Herk which she takes up as her mission and lastly carves out a niche for women where they may breathe independently without experiencing the domineering attitudes of males.

Van Herk's feministic orientation is evident in her delineation of the female protagonists in which she sets them free from the clutches of enslaving patriarchal society imposing its rules and regulations. They are highly individualistic, struggling to raze the boundaries of male conventions and aspiring to attain what is unattainable. Thus they leave an indelible mark and lasting impression on the minds of the readers. Her protagonists drawn from varied walks of life and different sections of society, with their biblical and mythological tinge display extraordinary courage in their fight with the adversities of life.

Like her heroines breaking the boundaries of conventional norms, Van Herk experiments unconventional norms stretching the parameters of genre suitable for the profound insight of her complex characters. As a feminist writer, Van Herk appropriates the myth of the West and deconstructs the male discourse in her attempt to give a suitable and unbiased representation of women. She subverts the original myth in order to explore new horizon for women. Van Herk states, "Women can write kitchen-sink realism about the limitations of their lives forever. But realism can become its own prison, its own enclosure. Fiction's mandate is to explore the possibilities of the imagination, the possibilities of the world beyond its closure" (Jones 7).

Portraying the North as a space for woman's writing, Van Herk subverts the ideal male topography. From the male perspective, the North is considered as something challenging where men can reveal their valour. To her, North is not just a direction, but a geographical space which discloses the geography of the mind. She describes in her essay, "The Ethnic Gasp/ the Disenchanted Eye Unstoried." "North is not an ethnic designation in Canada; the notion of north is tossed about as casually as if it were nothing more than a direction, rather than a destination or even—quite possibly—an act of the imagination integral to Canada's collective ethnicity" (76).

Sherrill Grace in *Canada and the Idea of the North—Introducing the North writes*:

> Canada is not over. Indeed at the beginnings of the 21st century, the country is facing some splendid new beginnings, as well as some persistent changes. But it seems to me that now, more than ever before, it is important for the Canadians, to look north and in looking north to celebrate the creation of Nunavut, to appreciate the dependence of South on Canada's Northern resources, to recognize a crucial role we must play in safeguarding an Arctic environment, and in articulating politics for a circumpolar world..... North is an idea as much as physical region that can be mapped and measured for nordicity (Geogle books).

The subtitle "a geografictione", an amalgamation of map-making and fiction writing, "dismantles the conventions of the masculine north and deconstructs the hierarchy of an objective science (cartography) and subjective fiction (Mott 105)." Further, Van Herk, in her geografictione, draws a parallel between Anna and Ellesmere and transforms the landscape into an image of Anna's body. Anna, "a woman on the verge of flesh, with a full, solid figure is equated to Ellesmere which 'is a fat island, the tenth largest in the world, fat with the flesh of heated snow" (pp.96-97).

Marlene Goldman comments in *"Earth-quaking the Kingdom of the Male Virgin: A Deleuzian Analysis of Aritha Van Herk's No Fixed Address and Places Far From Ellesmere"*, 'In keeping with the tendency to view the landscape as a metaphor, the text identifies features of the Arctic...., with the character in Tolstoy's novel and the process of unreading (38).

As an intellectual and committed reader, Van Herk is interested in Tolstoy's *Anna Karenina,* the story and the heroine well introduced in the geografictione. Anna is introduced in the first section of the text 'Edberg, coppice of desire and return.' Van Herk's women driven by determination rebel against the patriarchal society, forge ahead in an undaunted mood of will power, and strive for independence. They negate the idea of blank submission.

Although the title of the last section *'Ellesmere:* Woman as Island' explicitly states the metaphor of woman as island, obviously she has used the same metaphor and envisioned the place as woman, giving female attribute to the landscape. "Everywhere is here... Edberg is an Ellesmere, an island shrouded in the wet snow of summer, with muskoxen waiting for their coats to grow. A movie un/made, with the auctioneer and pie makers as heroes... Anna Karenina will get off to pace the platform for a few moments" (p.36).

Van Herk has slowly introduced Tolstoy's heroine preparing our minds to accept her in a new situation. "(... Anna)... just long enough to see Tolstoy's coachman and to remember that illegitimacy lurks everywhere", she has only to read the story differently her own story waiting to be un/read by the light of places: "all places with acts of reading as their histories, and all of them your homes" (p.37). The meticulous care with which Van Herk has described the place Edberg is marvellous. According to Mott, it is "semi-fictive autobiography", as the protagonist describes her life through the description of landscape where she lived (Mott, 104).

Asta Mott, in the essay "Aritha Van Herk's *Places Far From Ellesmere: The Wild and Adventurous North*?" says thus: "The approach to autobiography in *Places Far From Ellesmere* is also unusual. The book is narrated through the description of places; thus the focus is not only on the individual but also on the landscape. If male northerns tend to emphasize that the male subject is in control of the menacing landscape, Van Herk's text offers a different relationship between a human subject and a landscape" (104).

The narrator's experiences, reading into her past, by reading-unreading of the text slowly lead us on to Ellesmere. The topography is in minute description which is analogous to woman's body. She hints also at woman's unyielding and unbending temperament. "In the basement of the person rests the village of Edberg, refusing to be dislodged, a continuous grounding" (p.37). Van Herk strongly feels that women must shake themselves from the stringent conventional beliefs that they can only be mothers, or sisters or home makers. In the light of this context she writes in the article, "A Gentle Circumcision," referring to the writing of Canada as a masculine kingdom of adventure.

> Try being female and living in the kingdom of the male virgin: try being female and writing in the kingdom of the male virgin. Women must come to a place in this kingdom themselves but until now it has been dominated by a romantic fiction that is disintegrating like paper cowboy put into water. The kingdom boasts adventure and chivalry; it proudly displays all the characteristics of romanticism: innovation, spontaneity, sensuous nuance, limitless aspiration. This is big sky country; both the fiction and its criticism have relied on endless landscape as a metaphor. But it is also a kingdom which practises a kind of perverse courtly love: don't touch the lady. She'll sully your purity (259).

The second section with the title Edmonton, the long division, begins with the following lines that symbolically signify division of the soul in an islanded sublimation. It also shows how Edmonton weans the traveller from Edberg. Each section begins with the subtitle Exploration site. The writer begins with the description of the North Saskatchewan. The place name blooms with the love later on, love of woman.

> The North Saskatchewan curving the town in half: north/ south;...Long division: what you were never good at, had to concentrate for practice. What choices are there? You set up the equation, begin with a thick stemmed land lady who rustles through your closets when you are in classes, who insists you are amoral because you resist falling in love: not yet, not just yet (pp.43-44).

The section "Calgary" presents the theme of death. She has chosen Calgary as a place of growing graveyard. She begins by saying,

"From within the grave you can only leave into light, burst through dark soil, arrival the admission of belonging: here/there/ within. Or coming from...." (p.57). She gives a definition of graves. "Graves are for their visitors.... Well yes, it is death that makes a place of its own" (p.59). Van Herk vents her thought on death and grave in an interview, "A grave is a fine and private place but none I think do there embrace. My fixation on graves and coffins is really strange. I guess, I think of death as a real act of freedom. That may sound quite macabre to you, but I do not think of death as such a negative slate. Not that I believe in heaven...." (Tamara Piano).

> For Van Herk death is a kind of escape, ... a very freeing space where you were not having to listen, pay attention, breathe and think, eat and sleep....we only have the coffin for the people who put the body away. The body does not need the coffin to be contained. We put them inside this thing to say they are really dead and so I guess I have this notion that coffins or genres of books or even lives can be escaped or even transformed. I am constantly trying to escape (ibid).

In the last section entitled Ellesmere, woman as island, multiple themes such as Ellesmere as woman, as envisioned by the writer, Ellesmere—the place as a state of mind, as a place to escape for woman, the northern influence, predominantly emphasized North as a utopian space for women. Finally Tolstoy's Anna as re/read by the author and literary critics, surfaces. Anna's consummate escape to Ellesmere from the clutches of Tolstoy or Vronsky and Karenin has been created by Van Herk with the intention of creating a space of freedom for women on one hand and for readers on the other. "Anna Karenina should have escaped to Ellesmere" (p.77).

> If Tolstoy had suffered her, if she hadn't been a woman created and governed by a blind and obstinate man. This is a remedy you want to propose to her, Ellesmere, as if it were a nectar she could swallow or inhale. A consummate escape from Vronsky and Karenin, Ellesmere, the most northerly of extreme Arctic islands, probably un/named when Tolstoy invented her, probably unheard of, like Anna herself. A lost heroine. Lost in Russia, lost in love, lost in the nineteenth century. The special lostness of an invented character whose inventor revenged himself on her through the failings he invented for her (p.77).

Regarding "her Island, tabula rasa" (77), in an interview with Nicole Dargent, on being asked if Ellesmere is a state of mind, Van Herk affirms, "Absolutely! And once if you actually go to the place called Ellesmere the only thing you will discover is that place is a state of mind. You won't find out that—I mean, you will find about Ellesmere but it is still very much a created space, it is an invention, it is an act of the imagination." (Tamara P'ano).

Men underestimating the capacity of women, and women writer's potential, she bluntly has a dig at men's inflated pride. She is equally persistent in asserting her female position, "War and peace exactly what you wish to leave behind in lower Canada. But you take *Anna Karenina*" (p.81). In Ellesmere, Anna reads her own experiences, her own reading/unreading. "You want to read yourself (in a mirror) and Anna, a fictional mirror of a male reading of women. Perhaps you can un/read her, set her free. There on that desert island, between the harebells and the blue dreaming of glaciers" (p.82).

In a conventional, patriarchal, male-dominated society, women are left with no options but to submit themselves to the mundane realities of life with the options of marriage, love, harassment, dejection and death. Van Herk boldly projects Anna as a symbol for all women characters caught in the web of male prejudice, relieving them from the entrapment of conventional plot, reading and interpretation. She states:

> You know at least a hundred Annas, stranded in fictional love affairs written by men who do not know that Ellesmere exists. Come to that, women are all Annas, caught or not, Annas sweating their way from one day to the next. They know their wars within their orbits, between their children and huband and lovers, need and desire and the desperate necessities of symmetry, how they will be always and forever, culpable, exiled for their visceras, eviscerated for their exiles (p.82).

As we journey along with the narrator, we understand that Van Herk constantly makes reference to North. We are given to understand that "Ellesmere is Anna, Anna's story, articulated in the geography of place. But you are Ellesmere, this mystery of polar desert, remote of all Canada's island flock. As far as it is possible to get away; and you will fly still farther north, not even close to Hazen yet, its eurhythmic allure" (p.89).

Van Herk admits women to Arctic space, the so-called male territory creating a space for women, exploring the unexplored mysterious female self, hence the complex reading becomes the exploration of the self through the exploration of the land. This discourse articulates feminist approach and post-modernist aspect in that it shows the relationship between the text and the reader and views reading as a creative act like writing itself, besides projecting a female image delineated through female gaze in conflation with the geography of the land. "Here on Ellesmere, you see, now how reading is an alien act, such a strange activity,... Only the north can teach what reading means, and you are a woman in the north, reading a woman written by a man to whom women were a mystery... A northern: unread Anna" (pp.132-133).

The choice of north as a female space is presented as a kind of counterpart to the male defined west, which Van Herk voices forth in the interview.

> I think males have tried to control the frontier always. That's their territory, and that's where they go, when they want to run away from women. So for them west was always a frontier to run away to. And when you run out of west, I mean on a certain stage you hit the west end of Canada, and can't go any further except into the ocean. And then actually by the time you get to Japan and to China, you are in the East again. And so they get really upset, because they have no more west left so they sort of did a turn and started going up north. But I think north is a more seminal space that does not permit itself to be colonized by the masculine interrogation and so I like the notion of north but also you noticed in *Places Far From Ellesmere* I am actually going over to Russia. If you keep going north you actually start going south. I think of the north as this wonderful kind of open space that does not already have a discourse attributed to it and that discourse you can alter or usurp or enter. So it is not so limited as the West (Nicole Dargent).

Van Herk seems to be inspired by the incredible north. She asserts that she likes "the notion of being Northern. Being enigmatic, being unable to read...." (*ibid*) "Go, north, Anna, go north. If there are westerns, why can there not be northerns?" (p.85).

Van Herk is heaping all her admonition and anger in a very satirical vein on Tolstoy's narrow views of women. Her intention in weaving inter-textuality of *Anna Karenina* is to analyze the difference between a man's writing and a woman's writing of the female character. She intends to read the voluminous novel of eight hundred and fifty pages "as a lesson, to solve a problem in how to think about love; to solve a problem in the (grave) differences between men's writing and women's writing; to solve problem in sexual judgment. To investigate viscera and mirrors; passions and polemics. Even though you know you'll be stuck with Tolstoy, that the order and the rules are male, that he writes Anna no choices" (p.82).

Van Herk becomes too sentimental. "Anna. All Annas are women written by men, now re/read by women. The reader un/ reading the Anna.

Vengeance is mine, and I will repay" (p.85).

As Van Herk weaves her childhood recollections about Edberg, Edmonton, and Calgary-"as a well-groomed cemetery', she sees Ellesmere as a 'languid body." "Ellesmere will appear like a languid body below you, the island only waiting finally to float into a geografictione, like Anna waiting so long backstage on the yet to arrive, the interminably delayed train" (p.87).

Leona Gom in her review of *Places Far From Ellesmere* eulogizes the way in which Van Herk has razed the male topography by her profound insight of male atrocities and her efforts to free 'Annas' from male clutches.

The setting of the text, a travel memoir, is spread over four places, cartographically starting from Edberg, moving through Edmonton and Calgary to Ellesmere towards North as exploration sites. Each site signifies the metaphorical meaning, beginning with yearning of the narrator leading to the long division symbolic of duality of body/ mind, truth/ fiction, victor/ victim, illusion/ reality, life/ death, and self/ other. Calgary—the growing graveyard symbolizing death which is actually an act of freedom--- from torture and injustice leads to Ellesmere, "a place for women to disappear to" North. It is a dream place, an inevitable presence, writing space and mythical identity. North is a prime point of significance in Canadian national identity too. 'North' in the fiction symbolizes an essential source of myth, a convenient place to escape to. For the narrator, the north represents creativity, charm, invention, space and adventure. She says referring to Tolstoy's *Anna Karenina*. "But whose invention is she? Tolstoy's? The nineteenth century's? Russia's? The novel's? Yours? She is the north's invention" (p.113).

This manifests the creativity of a northerner, the creator of Anna who provided an opportunity to Van Herk to go for a discourse, to show to the world the ways of males delineating the females. Through this she has tried to justify the imaginative potential of north wallowing in resourcefulness which women can tap and overshadow the west. The narrator visualizes north as all that is charming, loving and mysterious. Here, Ellesmere, Anna and north are all intertwined. Ellesmere becomes a state of meaningful existence for all the female victims who have suffered at the hands of male chauvinists. North is the place where this existence will bear the true meaning, where all the Annas can shape their future.

Hulan says in *Northern Experience and the Myths of Canadian Culture*:

> An analysis of gender is a useful method to address issues of political power and difference. Representatives of imaginary north have frequently depended on concepts that are defined by a masculine-feminine opposition. As a geographical location, the north provides writers with the setting for quest narratives, and heroic tales of survival. Such stories require their characters to attain qualities traditionally thought, exclusively associated with masculine identity, including self reliance, autonomy, and physical endurance. By having these qualities, the individual embraces and embodies the northern, "spirit" of character" (p.245).

The concept of north is thus multifaceted, all assimilating and powerful. It is equally associated with Canadian identity and Van Herk seems to be very much mindful of it. Even the cover of the book is symbolic of myth of place, culture and gender, making an entry of female self in an imagined place, defying the masculine writing, and subverting and infiltrating the masculine Northern. Referring to the cover of the book, Mott says, "The cover reminds us that while the explorations to map the Canadian North were driven by scientific, economic and political motives they also drew on the mythologies of place, culture and gender of the day" (Mott 106).

Thus, Aritha Van Herk's *Places Far From Ellesmere* is a typical post-modern novel analyzing the post-modern aspects and feminist concerns in a different ambience in which female self is explored in the exploration of space, fiction of self is determined through the geography of the land. Ellesmere, the place, hence, becomes an island in the world, which stands as a metaphor for escape, for fulfilment. Van Herk frees Anna from the pages of Tolstoy and presents her distinctly, different from the fictional mirror of male reading a woman. Anna takes refuge in potent North which is endowed with all the attributes needed for the women to explore the possibilities in life without any intervention from male counterparts. The notion of North is really all encompassing, multi-dimensional that is really the bedrock for the fulfillment of all the aspirations of women folk.

Works Cited

Beer, Ann. 'Thinking Too Precisely on Some Events.' Review of *Places Far From Ellesmere. Border Crossings* 10, iii July 1991. pp. 35-36.

Dargent, Nicole. 'Interview with Aritha Van Herk.' *Trier,* Germany. 15 May, 1994.

Gom, Leona. 'Places Far From Home.' Review of *Places Far From Ellesmere. Event* 20, ii Summer 1991, pp. 125-27.

Grace, Sherrill. *Canada and the Idea of the North. Introducing the North.* (Google books)

Hulan, Renée. *Northern Experience and the Myths of Canadian Culture.* McGill-Queen's University Press, 2002, p. 245.

Jones, Dorothy. 'Interview with Aritha Van Herk.' SPAN: *Journal of the South Pacific Association for Commonwealth Literature and Language Studies,* 25 October 1987, p. 7.

Mott, Asta. 'Aritha Van Herk's Places Far From Ellesmere: The Wild and Adventurous North?' *Canadian Literature 157,* Summer 1998, p. 101.

Van Herk, Aritha. Places Far From Ellesmere. A Geografictione: Explorations on Site. Red Deer, AB: Red Deer College Press, 1990.

______________ . 'The Ethnic Gasp/the Disenchanted Eye Unstoried.' *Journal of Canadian Studies.* 31.3 Fall 1996, p.76

______________ . 'A Gentle Circumcision,' in *Trace: Prairie Writers on Writing.* Ed. Birk Sproxton. Winnipeg: Turnstone Press, 1986, p. 257. <www.ucalgary.ca/lib-old/SpecColl/vanherkbioc.htm - 112k

Verduyn, Christl. 'The Grace of Living and Writing: An Interview with Aritha Van Herk'. *Aritha Van Herk: Essays on her Works.* Ed. Christl Verduyn. Toronto: Guernica, 2001.pp. 23-24.

9 The Transcendental Power of Love: A Study of Garcia Marquez's *Love in the Time of Cholera*

— Dr. Pradip Kumar Patra

Love in the Time of Cholera of Garcia Marquez is a novel in which the novelist shows the contours of love so clearly without any pretension and reservation. The context of the novel is so wide and the tone not serious. What is significant is the passion for love and its exploration till the protagonist is old. Old age may take away the physical charm, but definitely not the emotion of love. Marquez is like Shakespeare who delineates love with all the finishing, but nowhere does the reader feel that the author is present. The wider context that the author provides works as a broader background for the process of signification where love sparkles.

As its title implies, Gabriel Garcia Marquez's *Love in the Time of Cholera* is a creative amalgam of two starkly contrasting elements: the sacredness of love, and love's embodiment in everyday experience. Ultimately, the transcendental power of love emerges as the beautifully rendered theme of this evocative and paradoxical masterwork.

The historical setting of *Love in the Time of Cholera* is an "in between" time: from the end of the nineteenth-to the first decades of the twentieth century. The location is an unnamed Caribbean seaport: one resembling Cartagena. Florentino Ariza—who, with his long frock coat and melancholy air, resembles a "rabbi in disgrace"—is overwhelmed by love for Fermina Daza, a comely girl whose "doe's gait" makes her "seem immune to gravity."

Florentino's antiquated frock and excessive sentimentality symbolize the romanticism of the last century, which is parodied and caricatured here and extended, like the frock, beyond manageable proportions. Indeed, Florentino cannot even compose a business letter without incorporating lyrical flourishes. Love is his *raison d'être*, yet he reeks of it rather than shines, following always in its shadow, never seeming to grasp its essential light.

Florentino is placed in a precarious position when Fermina suddenly rejects him (after returning from an exile imposed by her father, who disapproves of Florentino for reasons of class). Her years of travel have so broadened her vision of the world that one quick glance at Florentino is enough to blot out every trace of her former passion and dreamy-eyed innocence. She simply tells him to "forget it", demands that he return her letters and gifts, and promptly decides to forget he ever existed.

Fermina embarks upon "a marriage of convenience" to the esteemed Dr. Juvenal Urbino, who in many ways serves as a counterpoint to Florentino's overblown romanticism. After completing a "course of specialized studies in France", Urbino becomes "known in his county for the drastic new methods he used to ward off the last cholera epidemic suffered by the province." He founds the Medical Society and organizes the construction of the first aqueduct and the first sewer system. He serves as president of two academies and is conferred with honorary titles from various organizations. In one of the most powerful passages in the book, he and Fermina fly in the carriage of an "aerostatic balloon that on its inaugural flight carried a letter to San Juan de la Cienaga, long before anyone had thought of airmail as a rational possibility." Thus, he clearly personifies such "rational possibilities." Therefore, it comes as no surprise that, when they marry, they do so in the absence of love. Even when they consummate their marriage, Urbino is "aware that he did not love her", yet he's "sure there would be no obstacle to their inventing true love", much like any other rational possibility.

There are three main characters: Dr. Juvenal Urbino, a very famous physician in Caribbean, Fermina Daza his wife and Florentino Ariza, Daza's "eternal true lover". The story is set into Caribbean and against the backdrop of Caribbean culture, Marquez weaves a superb funny, witty story of old age, love, wait, death, sex and sensuality. The story titillates one, tickles one, makes one think and some time frightens one (when one starts thinking of one's own old age and its repercussions).

Florentino Ariza, product of "an occasional alliance" between Transito Ariza (his mother) and well-known ship owner and one of the founders of a ship company Don Pius Loayaza, the occasional alliance failed to materialize into marriage and Florentino Ariza was brought up by his unwed mother (helped my secret helps from his physical father and after his death his uncle.) Ariza, a victim of chronic constipation, meets Daza, a school going girl, living with her father and aunt, when he goes to deliver the telegrams to Daza's father and for Ariza it was love at first sight with Daza. Ariza whose only talent at that time (or for that matter his profession apart from telegram office worker) was to write love letters and he used his talent to the fullest, writing love letters to Daza without a break, and soon she also started responding to the poetic love letters of Ariza, which were product of Ariza's talent and cheap poem books sold on the roads and memorized by Ariza. So far so good, but at one point of time Daza realizes that her attraction for Ariza is not love of teenage illusion and she leaves Ariza and in due course of time marries Dr. Urbino as per her father's wish. And here starts the wait of Ariza for Daza. He keeps on waiting for his first love. He waits for the death of Dr.Urbino, so that he can marry Daza, and his waiting does not last for years or decades; it goes on for half a century. Marquez's narrative is fantastic, his eye for details is beyond comparison and it never crosses the threshold limit of the reader. His depiction of a loveless marriage marred by old age and haughtiness of Daza will make one chuckle. The story is full of sensuality and Marquez's narrative and story telling gives one a "high" with description of numerous "physical loves" of Ariza, during his half century long wait for his first "spiritual love".

The story makes one familiar with numerous kinds of love, relationship and characters. To allay the pain of not getting Daza and to soothe the waiting heart, Ariza searches for love everywhere in whorehouses, in extramarital affairs with women twice her age, in beds of widows... everywhere. His affairs start with carnal desires and end in love, and some time vice versa.

Marquez has covered a plethora of human emotions in such a brilliant manner that one will not be able keep the book down.

Like many great novels, Gabriel García Márquez's *Love in the Time of Cholera* portrays the tension between illusions and material reality, especially in the context of love. In the novel's final pages, when Florentino Ariza and Fermina Daza are finally together in their old age, we are told that love "was more solid the closer it came to death" (p.345). This statement exemplifies the novel's method—instead of saying what love is, and in this way judging the strength of its characters' grasp of reality, it articulates the relationship between love and something else, giving different perspectives but no definitions. This circling around love gives *Love in the Time of Cholera* the quality of capturing the ineffable.

Different ways of understanding, experiencing, and representing love are embodied by the novel's three central characters: Florentino Ariza, Fermina Daza, and Dr. Juvenal Urbino. For Florentino, love has the properties of a dream; its fullest expression occurs in art (especially in writing), and it stands in opposition to everyday reality, entirely resistant to rational understanding. Like Emma in *Madame Bovary*, Florentino is filled with notions of love derived from popular literature; he also becomes a comic figure when reality unexpectedly intrudes into the world of his imagination. The bird droppings that fall on Fermina's embroidery when they meet as teenagers in the park and the intestinal disruption that betrays him when they meet following Dr. Urbino's death both testify to the unavoidable fact of the material world. But Florentino's fate suggests neither acquiescence to reality nor the continuation of his belief in a wholly illusory kind of love.

As the relationship between Florentino and Fermina unfolds following Dr. Urbino's death, it seems enabled by Florentino's emergence from the imaginary world in which he has lived for so long—the very existence of his imaginary world is made possible by Fermina's absence from it. The letters Florentino writes to her after Dr. Urbino's death possess, in Fermina's words, "a foundation in reality" (p.330), as opposed to the letters of his youth, inspired by "half-baked endearments taken whole from the Spanish romantics" (p.75). But other aspects of the novel's conclusion complicate this interpretation. Before making love, Florentino tells Fermina, "I've remained a virgin for you." In light of his many trysts and affairs, in what sense could this be true other than an imaginary one? When asked how long their ship will sail, keeping up its deception by flying the yellow cholera flag, Florentino answers, "Forever" (p.348), as if to specifically deny the reality of death.

Because of his belief in the power of the rational mind, Dr. Urbino often appears more grounded in reality than Florentino. He considers marriage "an absurd invention" (p.209), and his marriage to Fermina represents a lifelong effort to defeat the absurd and replace it with something that can withstand logical analysis. After his death, Fermina recalls his belief that "the most important thing in a good marriage is not happiness, but stability" (p.300). On the night they consummate their marriage, Dr. Urbino readily admits to himself that he does not love Fermina, but "he was sure there would be no obstacle to their inventing true love" (p.159). He thinks of love not as an unruly passion, but as if it can be brought into existence merely by an act of will. But his determination to avoid the chaos of emotion can make Dr. Urbino seem just as divorced from reality as Florentino. In his dissertation, Dr. Urbino asserts that, given the human organism's "many useless or duplicated functions it could be more simple and by the same token less vulnerable" (pp.158-159). Is this idea any less illusory than the most extravagant of Florentino's ecstatic proclamations of his love for Fermina?

Between the extremes of Florentino and Dr. Urbino is Fermina. When Dr. Urbino first tells her about the importance of stability, she hears in it a "miserable threat", but when she remembers his words after he dies, she thinks of them as "the lodestone that had given them both so many happy hours" (p. 300). She ends her first affair with Florentino by telling him in a letter that "what is between us is nothing more than an illusion" (p. 102). As coldly precise as this declaration is, Fermina is nevertheless open to the emotional upheavals that attend her marriage to Dr. Urbino. When he confirms her suspicion of his adulterous affair with Barbara Lynch, she wishes he had denied it, preferring the illusion of his fidelity to the feeling that "her rage would never end" (p.251). Sharing memories of Dr. Urbino with Florentino, Fermina could not conceive of a husband better than hers had been, and yet when she recalled their life she found more difficulties than pleasures, "admitting to Florentino that she does not really know if it was love or not" (p.329).

It is tempting to see Fermina as encompassing both the illusory and the real, but such symmetry would reduce her to a thematic device, as opposed to a fully alive character, capable of expecting nothing more from life after her husband dies and then falling in love with Florentino. The fact that neither she nor the novel ever arrive at a fixed definition of love suggests that its elusiveness is part of its very nature.

Love in the Time of Cholera is an "anatomy" of love. One of its most ingenious portrayals (in an anatomical and a visionary sense) is the growth of love out of the profane environs of "convenience." All the meaningless details of everyday life shared by two people bound together (all the unpleasant smells, degrading tasks, and dulling routines; all the unspoken bitterness and rancour; all the sullenness and gloom engendered by unlived possibilities) are unmercifully catalogued. Love's power to grow in such dark interstices—and to transcend life's profanity and to remain unscathed—is one of the most skillfully rendered themes of this work.

Just as love may have the power to transcend the limits of hyperrationalism, so, too, may it transcend sensual passion. Florentino's nostalgia of love is eventually transformed into an awareness of the reality of love as it must be lived in the present. While Dr. Urbino's studies in France include his tutelage under the "most outstanding epidemiologist of his time", one "Professor Adrien Proust, father of the famous novelist", Florentino is fated to live in the haze of a Proustian nightmare: one that evokes a bloated nostalgia for Fermina at his every turn. While much of his time is spent travelling from one to the other of his 622 erotic assignations, through it all he still considers himself a virgin untouched by anything other than his unrequited love for Fermina.

After waiting half a century for Urbino to die, Florentino ends his self-imposed emotional exile (of fifty-one years, nine months, and four days) of unrequited love. He declares his "vow of eternal fidelity and everlasting love" to Fermina, while she's attending to her husband's funeral. Outraged by his poor timing, Fermina forbids him to return. Yet, through a series of letters that are meditative and philosophic rather than flowery and romantic, he persists. And then, the final courtship of *Love in the Time of Cholera* commences.

Culminating in a steamboat voyage up the Magdalena River, the various themes of the novel coalesce in a symbolically complex and emotionally compelling adventure. Throughout the final chapter, Marquez deftly evokes higher aspects of love, while simultaneously maintaining a dark, earthly humour.

At one point during their riverboat journey, Florentine considers a quote: "Love becomes greater and nobler in calamity." Later on, as they paddle along and pass the sorrowful stretches of denuded forests, the "nauseating stench of corpses floating down the river", the "bogs of ashes", and the "vast silence of a ravaged land", the quote calls into question the survival of higher values in the midst of such decay.

Florentino's meditations mark the inception of a new era: one that's as stripped of natural beauty as it is profaned in matters of the soul. Just as mankind was ravaged by the cholera plague, now the first signs of a humanly induced ecological devastation appear. Thus, the voyage upriver bears witness to certain historical developments. Along with the personal signs of decay that reflect the aging process, one simultaneously witnesses the aging of Latin America and of the world-at-large. The passengers are unnerved by such horrific images and are sadly haunted by all that is forever lost:

> The imagery of finality is counterpointed by the human drama of "love eternal": comprising the fanciful flight of uncaring youth and the irrevocable conclusion of death.

Love in the Time of Cholera (El amor en los tiempos del colera in the original Spanish), published in 1985, was the first novel by Gabriel Garcia Marquez to be published since he was awarded the Nobel Prize for Literature in 1982. As abundant publicity surrounding the book's appearance in December 1985 revealed, the author was already working on a sequel to his novel *Chronicle of a Death Foretold* when the Nobel committee's decision was announced. With the award there came numerous public commitments obliging Garcia Marquez to interrupt the progress of his project until January 1984, when he resumed work on the existing material. *Love in the Time of Cholera* was eventually completed in August 1985 and published three months ahead of schedule.

Initial critical response took the form of summary notices and reviews, the most enthusiastic of which asserted that *Love in the Time of Cholera* was one of the great living classics of the Spanish language. It has been called a masterpiece of sensuous prose, because of its ability to summon up the textures, sensual pleasures, tastes, and smells associated with living in a particular place at a particular time. Because of this, it has been compared to other contemporary texts such as Toni Morrison's vibrant account of Harlem life Jazz. Overblown yet controlled, Garcia Marquez's story of life, love, and lust in a convention-bound provincial city on the Caribbean coast of Colombia displays great imaginative and narrative freedom. In addition, it has an almost novella-like discipline in its structuring of recurrent ideas.

Love in theTime of Cholera offers the same dreamlike quality of these other works, but for the first three quarters of the book, one feels trapped in a beautiful yet never-ending slumber. The protagonist of the novel, Florentino Ariza, barely enters the first fifty pages. Instead, one can learn to know and appreciate the compassionate, devoted Dr. Juvenal Urbino, Florentino's victorious rival for the affections of Fermina Daza for more than half a decade.

The prose is extraordinarily fluid and luxurious. Upon realizing his proclamation of his love for Fermina Daza was ill-timed on "her first night as a widow," Florentino reunites with one of his hundreds of mistresses. In the morning he

> walked out into a different city, one that was perfumed by the last dahlias of June, and onto a street out of his youth, where the shadowy widows from five o'clock Mass were filing by.... He could no longer hold back, not his midnight tears, as he thought, but other tears: the ones he had been swallowing for fifty-one years, nine months and four days.

The first three quarters of the novel recounts the youthful exuberance shared by Florentino and Fermina, through several years of love letters and a separation imposed by her father. The reader feels his pain when they are finally reunited and "instead of the commotion of love, she felt the abyss of disenchantment." The narration turns to five decades of her passionate marriage to Dr. Urbino and extensively details Florentino's attempts to forget her in the process of filling 25 notebooks labelled. "Women" with 622 entries significant enough to deserve a mention.

All of this proceeds in lush language at a sloth's pace under the specter of potential cholera epidemics. Corpses float along the river and litter fearful villages with contamination. Death is imminent even as the three main characters advance beyond their 70s, an age at which Urbino and Fermina Daza's children find "whispers and fleeting lover's quarrels repulsive."

Love in the Time of Cholera is a novel of patience, devotion, promiscuity, love and death—not necessarily in that order. The flowery and melodious images of dreaming yield to a surprisingly rewarding ending. But this is not a book for those who cherish an actively developed plot. It is meant to be savoured.

That Garcia Marquez portrays not just love, but also the love as experienced by human being, is the central motif of the novel. The entire novel in spirit remains high above the cultural denominations. Ethics and morality, for the time being, seem to be deactivated by the author. The novel begins with the love of the protagonist, Florentino Ariza, to a girl named, Fermina Daza, climaxes with her marriage to a doctor. The resultant frustration of Florentino Ariza is something worth-observing. The novelist puts the hero in a trial and shows how he fares. The tone of the novelist is balanced. Nowhere the reader feels that the novel is sentimentalized. The protagonist is never a puppet in the hand of the novelist. It appears he attains a life of his own in the novelist's hand. The phase of frustration for Florentino Ariza is never tumultuous, rather very peaceful. Garcia Marquez brings out the human as well as the godly qualities of the protagonists during this phase of his life. He rather reacts coolly to such an experience. Heaven doesn't fall upon him with such kind of unexpected separation.

It is not just love that finds expression, it is rather love with all its kindred that come to surface: love is not all about loving the other, it is also all about loving the other at one's own cost. That is why sacrifice is the other name of love.

Florentino Ariza visits the prostitutes in the absence of his love. He tries to live a normal life even without Fermina Daza. It was the emotion of Fermina Daza that the prostitutes were lacking. But he fails. But the failure doesn't matter. It is the exploration that matters. The novel seems to be reminding that. In life everything cannot be judged in terms of ethics. It is the undercurrent of aesthetics that works in the novel and takes the form of an archipelago in the end.

Hence, the novel works as a support for the silent seekers of the truth. It seems to be saying that nothing in life is meaningless. What seems to be meaningless today wears a meaning tomorrow. That human being will go on trying to accomplish something is the ultimate aim of human life, even though the consequences might be annoying. Garcia Marquez believed in this inner strength of human being. A civilization may be destroyed or erased from the earth, but the human spirit can not be. It is this idea of Garcia Marquez that shaped the character of Florentino Ariza. Never does one see that Florentino Ariza has ever lost his spirit.

The title of the novel suggests that love is eternal which is equivalent to the undying human spirit. Cholera is rather ephemeral. Love transcends the barriers of cholera ultimately. By juxtaposing love side by side with cholera the novelist prepares a broader area of signification in a process of contiguity where love sparkles.

The novel has an epic dimension for its thematic grandeur. It is the love of a human being that the novelist speaks about irrespective of caste, creed and religion. The novelist tries to give a recognition to it by putting it forth before the readers. In no other novel does Marquez celebrate love like that of *Love in the Time of Cholera*. It is the novel where life, art and aesthetics join and human emotion flows with dignity and spontaneity.

One significant aspect of love is its trans-moral appeal. It is not just the much hyped mainstream love which abounds in spirituality that matters, it is also about the love which human being always hankers with head down. It is the physical love which has never been portrayed with detest. The novel has been a steady progress through the so called 'perversion'. And true love takes a shape out of it.

The strength of the novel lies in the novelist's portrayal of the moments of love, awkward situations and more importantly the experience of physical love at the time of frustration. Marquez shows Florentino Ariza's exploration in an endless accelerated process when he comes to know that his beloved, Fermina Daza who is married to Dr. Urbino is out in Europe for honeymoon. In stead of going mad or hysterical for his unfulfilled love, he rather tries to find an alternative means of self-expression.

> On the morning of his return from his inconclusive journey, he learned that Fermina Daza was spending her honeymoon

> in Europe, and his agitated heart took it for granted that she would live there, if not forever then for many years to come. This certainly filled him with is first hope of forgetting. He thought of Rosalba, whose memory burned brighter as the other's dimmed. It was during this time that he grew the mustache with the waxed tips that he would keep for the rest of his life and that changed his entire being, and the idea of substituting one love for another carried him along surprising paths. Little by little the fragrance of Fermina Daza became less frequent and less intense, and at last it remained only in white gardenias. (148)

Love is not just portrayed with a conservative attitude, but with all dynamism. The protagonists has learned to change in keeping with time. Had Garcia Marquez stick to one woman, the novel probably would have taken a different turn. It would have put on a tragic robe. It is, however, evident that there are two selves within Florentino Ariza struggling to come up to bottom. One self is not able to forget Fermina Daza and the other tries its best to move forward with all its newness.

The novel is not just about the love between Florentino Ariza and Fermina Daza, it is also about the love between Florentino and a host of other women. One gets a glimpse into the sexual life of other women too. The novel thereby neither looks down upon the primordial instinct of these women nor highlights the vulnerability of the man (protagonist) and women. It rather shows that the underlying sexual urge is what makes a human being. Life's fullness rather depends upon it.

The novel also shows that the social and cultural construct imposed upon the women by men gives no scope for the former's self-expression. Beneath this repressive surface one finds an individual with all her natural urge.

She took off the taffeta blouse with the beaded embroidery and threw it across the room onto the easy chair in the corner, she tossed her bodice over her shoulder to the other side of the bed, with one pull she removed her long ruffled skirt, her satin garter belt and funeral stockings, and she threw everything on the floor until the room was carpeted with the last remnants of her mourning. She did it with so much joy, and with such well-measured pauses, that each of her gestures seemed to be saluted by the cannon of the attacking troops, which shook the city down to its foundations.Florentino Ariza tried to help her unfasten her stays, but she anticipated him with a deft manoeuvre, for in five years of matrimonial devotion she learned to depend on herself in all phases of love, even the preliminary stages, with no help from anyone. Then she removed her lace panties, sliding them down her legs with the rapid movement of a swimmer, and at last she was naked. (149)

The novel reaches an ecstatic point when Florentino Ariza is reunited with Fermina Daza after her husband's death. The novel begins with their love, takes a different turn with Fermina Daza's marriage with the doctor. She recovers from the sorrow of her husband's death and attains the spontaneity of her life with the celebration of their love in the sea where there is no impact of culture made by the humans. The same spontaneity reaches a crescendo when their ship on way back to the shore doesn't get the signal for anchoring because of the outbreak of Cholera. In the nature and culture conflict. Marquez shows that it is the nature which wins. Marquez doesn't show the ethics of love. Rather he shows that human being is capable of love. It is an eternal fountain which never dries up.

Work Cited

Marquez, Gabriel Garcia. *Love in the Time of Cholera.* London: Penguin, 1985.

10 Confessionalism in the Poetry of Kamala Das

— Lakshmi Pramod

M.L. Rosenthal first applied the term 'confession' to Robert Lowell's work. The first poem that was called confessional was Snodgras's 'Hearts Needle', which was a model of truthfulness. A notable critic, Irving Howe says, "a confessional poem would seem to be one in which the writer speaks to the reader, telling him, without the mediating presence of imagined event or persona, something about his life."

An integral part of the Indo-Anglican trinity, Kamala Das (the other two being A.K. Ramanujan and Ezekiel), has been labelled as a confessional poet. K.R.Srinivas Iyengar writes:

> Kamala Das is a new phenomenon in Indo-Anglian poetry, a far poetic cry indeed from Toru Dutt or even Sarojini Naidu. Kamala Das' is a fiercely feminine sensibility that dares without inhibitions to articulate the hurts it has received in an insensitive man-made world...

Kamala Das's poetry is confessional because it is largely autobiographical. She has revealed to the readers the secrets of her thought and feelings, thus taking the readers into her confidence. She has added a new dimension to the poetry of love and sex written by Indians in the English language. She is the only Indo-Anglian poet to have defined the complexity of the man-woman relationship and its physical aspects. Her experiences of love do not revolve round the traditional ideal of the Indian woman. Instead, they revolve round the extra-marital sexual relationship, which remains chaotic. Her themes range from the subject of marriage, to the dominance of males, to feminine sensibility, to unfulfilment in marriage, to the endless sexual relationships she sought for fulfilment and even to the Krishna devotee. She reveals herself without any sense of guilt or shame. Daringly she exhibits her frailties and virtues as a woman, her superior self as a mother and her inevitable exploitation as a wife, her weakness as a docile wife. Often her poetry verges on the brink of the unconventional and the taboo. But sharing and confessing is second nature to her. As she writes:

> "I must let my mind striptease I must extrude *Autobiography*"

Kamala Das's poetic output is rather slender. Contained in four volumes of poems, which include *Summer in Calcutta* (1965), *The Descendants* (1967), *The Old Playhouse and Other Poems* (1973), and *Stranger Time* (1977). Yet each collection has the same ring of true emotions experienced by one who dared to bare her. As S.D.Sharma writes:

> Her poetic collections, *Summer in Calcutta, The Descendants* and *The Old Playhouse and Other Poems,* contain a wide range of themes, yet they are largely confessional in tone and tenor...

Her poetry is a recordation of her own experiences and observations; her own unfulfilled love and her own sexual exploitation, frustration and disillusionment she suffered in a male-dominated society. The first published anthology of her poems, *Summer in Calcutta,* contains fifty poems and the dominant theme in most of them is love or failure in love. The only exceptions to this theme are the poems, 'The Flag' and 'Sepia'. The Flag is about the deprived, the Indian poor and Sepia is about the Indian lacking in originality and the vigorousness of her work. A draught landscape forms the backdrop in this volume. It is here that the poet manifests her inner feeling of dirt and sexual disgust. Her images are harsh, which are about sunburnt, a tropical world with the smell of decay and death. Even men have limbs like 'carnivorous plants', the trees dusty and lifeless. Only the sturdy bougainvillae and marigold survive. She executes the role of unhappy woman, unhappy wife, mistress to young men, hesitant nymphomaniac, mother, and as one pining for her lost childhood and innocence. Mina Surjit Singh finds in Kamala Das's poetry "confession of private humiliations of varying pathological degrees and kinds proliferating images of failure in short, by a literal self exposure."

The opening poem of this volume *'The Dance of the Eunuchs'* sets the tone of the whole volume, as well as the other two volumes. Eunuchs are a familiar sight in India. They are incapable of performing the sexual act and cannot produce offspring. Thus they are symbolic of barrenness. Kamala Das creates a world, which is emotionally sterile and unproductive, a world where outward ecstasy conceals inner vacuity. It is a world of dancing eunuchs who symbolize the suppressed desires within. In them the poetess finds an objective correlative for her own unfulfilled longings. Their adorned body and dance is elaborately described. The dance of the eunuchs symbolizes the dance of the sterile and therefore the unfulfilled and insatiable love of the woman in the poet. As she writes:

> Their voices
> Were harsh, their songs melancholy; they sang of
> Lovers dying and of children left unborn....
> Some beat their drums; others beat their sorry breasts
> And wailed and writhed in vacant ecstasy
>
> *(The Dance of the Eunuchs)*

Some touching images are portrayed here as she says their faces were harsh, their songs melancholic. Some beat their drums, and others beat their "sorry breasts", and they "writhed in vacant ecstasy", which brings to mind the barrenness of Kamala Das' own life. She wrote this poem to get even with a man who had hurt her when she was fourteen years old. She went through a number of relationships where her sexual needs were satisfied but the element of love was missing. Her efforts at love were futile. The futility of love has been projected in the last lines.

> The sky crackled then, thunder came, and lightning, And
> rain, a meagre rain that smelt of dust in Attics and the urine
> of lizards and mice.

The best-known poem in this volume is *'An Introduction'*. This poem is wholly autobiographical and lists all those experiences, which affected her till she wrote this poem. She writes about the physical changes her body underwent in the process of growing up like the sprouting of hair in one or two parts of her body, the swelling of limbs, etc. Then she writes the various kinds of advice handed over to her by people.

> .... Dress in sarees, be girl,
> Be wife, they said. Be embroiderer, be cook,
> Be a quareller with servants. Fit in. Oh,
> Belong, cried the categorizers

She was asked to play the traditional role of a wife, mainly to dress well, to order the servants to 'fit in' and 'belong'. She refuses to choose a name and a role but she defends her identity. She replies:

> ....I am sinner
> I am saint. I am the beloved and the
> Betrayed. I have no joys which are not yours, no
> Aches which are not yours. I too call myself I.....

The sense of alienation she experienced in her own house is brought out in this poem. She has boldly described her body parts and the rough treatment her husband meted out to her. She writes:

> He did not beat me
> But my sad woman-body felt so beaten.
> The weight of my breasts and womb crushed me. I shrank
> Pitifully. Then........

She was married at the young age of fifteen so the sexual act must have been torturous due to the lack of gentleness shown by her experienced husband. Her uninhibited manner of writing has brought a lot of flak on her works. But what she writes can be identified in many households across India where the wife is expected to satisfy the sexual urge of her husband meekly. E.V. Ramakrishnan rightly stresses that, in her poetry Kamala Das

> has always dealt with private humiliations and sufferings which are the stock themes of confessional poetry. The crucial factor in all confessional poetry is a matter of tone. The free verse of Kamala Das, by carefully avoiding all clichés of expression, has perfected a way of treating the

> most intimate experience without ever being sentimental or having any trace of pathos. Indian critics have found in her poems the voice of the new liberated Indian woman without realizing that she never speaks on behalf of anybody but herself, let alone any class or section of Indian society. Her frank admissions and bold treatment of private life have nothing exceptional about them and are perfectly in keeping with the nature and themes of confessional poetry.

Another notable poem here is *'In Love'* where she refers to the sexual act as a 'skin-communicated thing'. It is about a sexual experience, which she experienced and which created a dilemma in her mind. Though he made love with fervor, she wondered if it was sheer lust, which motivated his actions.She also admits being lustful and having no love in her heart for him. The failure to discover this meaningful relationship between the sexes invests her poetry with a deep sense of pathos bordering on tragedy. Yet another poem in this anthology is *'The Freaks'* where she presents a glaring contrast between woman whose mind is willed "to race towards love" where mind of man only trips "idly over puddles of desire", i.e, the sexual desire and act. He always satiates "skin's lazy hungers". In such a callous and loveless atmosphere Kamala Das's heart like every woman's is:

> An empty cistern, waiting
> Through long hours, fills itself
> With coiling snakes of silence...
> I'm a freak. It's only
> To save my face, I flaunt at
> Times a grand, flamboyant lust

Another fact of love that Kamala Das expresses in her love poetry is dual relationship, i.e., a strong sense of belonging to one and uniting with another. In her pursuit of realizing love, a woman, even though married, runs from one man to the other. This feeling is strongly communicated in *'The Testing of Sirens'*:

> I am happy, just being with you. But you...
> You love another.

Here the poetess describes her loveless sexual experiences with two men, quite different from each other. However in both the cases, she is disappointed, as the fulfilment she craves is not met with. Another poem in this collection expresses a mood of gloom bordering on despair is *'My Grandmother's House'*. Having spent most of her childhood at her grandmother's house, she has very fond memories of her grandmother. In fact, her grandmother played an important role in influencing her poetical output. She spent most of her happiest days with her and when she fails to find love in its true sense, she is dismayed when her grandmother also dies leaving her alone in this whole world. As she poignantly writes:

> I who have lost
> My way and beg now at strangers' doors to
> Receive love, at least in small change

Commenting on the first anthology of her poems A.N. Dwivedi writes:

> Despite the fact that the majority of poems in this volume are dominated by a tone of betrayal and present the poet as a prisoner of her own loneliness and complex moods, the poem *'The Wild Bougainvillea'* satisfies a peculiarly personal need as a necessary distraction from her mood of sadness and loneliness. The poem *'An Introduction'*, as mentioned earlier, is a candid and witty piece of self-revelation, and is a beautiful statement of her poetic credo and her attitude to language and experience. 'Fit in,' said they. 'Belong' cried the categorizers! But the burden of the poem, as indeed of Mrs.Das' entire work, is to have the freedom to be herself. Here she transforms her alienation from critics, friends, visiting cousins who say: 'Don't write in English' into a larger and more than universal alienation:
>
> I met a man, loved him. Call
> Him not by any name, he is every man
> Who wants a woman, just as I am every
> Woman who seeks love.

It is, however, clear from a large number of poems in *Summer in Calcutta* that Kamala Das's impersonal note or sense of universality is simply self-imposed and not natural for her.

The second anthology of her poems, The *Descendants*, comprises twenty-three poems. Apart from her usual theme of sexual love, Death figures prominently in this collection. She thus adopts a pessimistic attitude, which negates the essence of life. She exhibits a suicidal tendency in most of her poems for example in 'The Invitation', which is actually a dialogue between the poetess and the sea. The sea says to her:

> .... come in,
> Come in, what do you lose by dying, and
> Besides, your losses are my gains.

She experiences a pull from the sea which is as if coaxing her to commit suicide. So she has a lover on one hand whom she cannot disobey and the sea on the other which is suggesting suicide. The lover also, through his loveless sex makes her taste a metaphorical death. She feels as if she is:

> lying on a funeral pyre With a burning head."

Even after he has gone she recollects the intensity of their sexual experience. Another poem where the image of the sea is dominant is '*Composition*'. Here she narrates "ordinary events of an ordinary life." She begins with the fact that women are deprived of freedom before and after marriage. She says her husband ironically offered her freedom, as much as she wanted, after marriage. She further argues for equality among sexes, which was a long cherished dream of hers. Anisur Rehman writes:

> the poem finds an extension of meaning, acquiring new dimensions of thought and feeling. Kamala Das transcends her own mutilated self and transmutes her personal and private experience into something rich and universal. The poem has a therapeutic effect, the significance of which cannot be minimized.

In the same anthology, we also find her depicting one of her sexual encounters as a deeply sensuous experience. In 'Convicts' we have

> That was the only kind of love, This hacking each other's parts Like convicts hacking, breaking clods At noon. We were earth under hot Sun. There was a burning in our Veins and the cool mountain nights did Nothing to lessen heat. When he And I were one, we were neither Male nor female.

The imagery is blatant. Physical labour and heat are used to depict physical love. Again in the poem *'Substitute'* she mocks the hypocritical society and its artificial conventions. Though the tone is ironical one cannot but sympathize with her:

> It will be all right if I join clubs And flirt a little over telephone. It will be all right, it will be all right I am the type that endures.

Though she keeps repeating it will be all right yet the lines suggest something contrary to what is being said. David McCutchion writes:

> Her primary concern is to convey to her readers the intensity of her feelings, her frustrations and her disillusionments, and this concern determines her use of language, as well as frequent repetitions of words, and her frequent ellipses (use of dots), which have attracted a good deal of criticism.

Generally the conventions did not allow much freedom to a female writer, but Kamala Das not only defied the conventions but also shocked all by her brazenness and candour. She used words, which were unspoken in public, described the private parts of the human body, and described the action of urinating too in the poem *'The Looking Glass'*.

> Notice the perfection
> Of his limbs, his eyes reddening under
> Shower, the shy walk across the bathroom floor,
> Dropping towels, and the jerky way he
> Urinates. All the fond details that make
> Him male and your only man. Gift him all,
> Gift him what makes you woman, the scent of
> Long hair, the musk of sweat between the breasts,
> The warm shock of menstrual blood, and all your
> Endless female hungers.

So, *'The Looking Glass'* is a mirror, which faithfully images man's ego, and the exploited class of women in a male dominated world. She advises females to gratify her mate's lust. She must give herself to him completely, for that is what he expects. She should make him realize she has 'endless female hungers' and that by making love to her he is being kind to her. Such an action would feed his ego and male vanity. The anatomical images found in the poem seem to have their source in her intrinsic dislike of the body, which seems to limit the horizon of the self. Kamala Das may or may not be serious about women's emancipation from male domination, but as a poet she is creatively concerned with her own identity as a woman. Thus we have evidence of her awareness and liking of the human body and intimate details in this poem.

Another notable feature appearing in the poems of this anthology is her feminine sensibility. She deviates from the usual theme of sex, death, decay and disgust and beautifully narrates her experience of childbirth. Her first son is named Jaisurya and in a poem by the same name she writes about the actual feelings she experienced just before and after the delivery. From the time she conceived, the foetus grew bigger and bigger in her womb till the onset of labour-pains all have been realistically described. When her son is born she feels he has been separated from the darkness of her womb to enter the sun-kissed world:

> Out of the mire of a moonless night was
> He born, Jaisurya, my son...

The whole setting of the poem suits her temperament. It is raining continuously as if the rain was 'wailing, and roaring' to keep Kamala Das company who was groaning with labour pains. Another image deployed in the poem is that of lust being forsaken at the end of each sexual experience just like a snake sheds off its withered skin. She describes her son's coming into this world 'like a streak of light thrust into the faded light'.

Her husband subjected her to fierce domination. She represents the voice of many oppressed females in India. For men, often their wives may be mere means of sexual gratification. They may not even provide them with love or affection, which is expected of him. Thus she often adopts a resentful tone in her poetry, urging critics to label her poetry as the poetry of protest. She protests against the conventions of society and the restrictions which husbands or society impose upon women. Thus she advocates women to enjoy such freedom. She is referred to as a feminist, who tries to liberate women from becoming slaves to men. She remains iconoclastic in her approach to marriage. She finds it a cruelty on the part of the husbands. Her ego is hurt and surfaces when she ruefully depicts her loss of liberty through marriage. In the poem entitled 'Of Calcutta' she exposes the inner torment she experiences at the hands of her husband. She feels reduced to the status of a trained circus dog, and says her husband treats her as a 'walkie-talkie' to keep him warm at night. She asks:

> Where is my soul,
> My spirit, where the muted tongue of my desire?

She wishes whole-heartedly to abolish the male dominance and superiority, which she finds, renders women helpless. They are never allowed to express their feelings, or desires. It is promiscuous in society. She wants the women to be liberated in their thought and asks them to defy the hypocrisy of this male-dominated world. Even though her husband satisfies her sexual appetite, yet she longs to be free to acquire love and not merely sex in return. She asks if happiness is 'lying buried beneath a man?', she prods women on to explore the world, which exists beyond 'his six-foot frame'. Kamala Das even accuses her husband of not preventing her from involving in extra-marital affairs. She says he let his wife 'seek ecstasy in others' arms.'

The third collection of her poems is *The Old Playhouse* And *Other Poems* in which only thirteen new poems are included, the rest are borrowings from the previous two volumes. In the poem entitled 'The Old Playhouse' the poets mind is reflected as having different sensations but characters acting their parts seem to do so in the dark. The role she is assumed to play has been beautifully described in the lines:

> You called me wife,
> I was taught to break saccharine into your tea and
> To offer at the right moment the vitamins. Cowering
> Beneath your monstrous ego, I
> Became a dwarf, I lost my will and reason, to all your
> Questions I mumbled incoherent replies.

Thus her voice suggests how much she abhorred the exploitation of the females and their subsequent oppression by the males. She poignantly relates to how she lost her identity after marriage. She felt 'dwarfed' by her husband's 'monstrous ego'. She accuses her husband of being self-centred like a 'captor' who wanted to tame her. She likens herself to a 'swallow' in this poem. She says here her husband reveled in the bodily responses she made to his lovemaking but she finds it superficial because she never experienced a feeling of oneness with him. Her husband often treated her roughly while making love. She boldly describes how he forced himself onto her and yet instead of love it was her lust, which was satiated. As she writes:

> You were pleased
> With my body's response, its weather, its usual shallow
> Convulsions. You dribbled spittle into my mouth, you poured
> Yourself into every nook and cranny, you embalmed
> My poor lust with your bitter-sweet juices.

'The Prisoner' is another poem in this anthology, where she compares herself, to a convict who studies his person's physical attributes with hope bordering on distrust. Here too the poetess has manifested the feeling of being unable to free oneself of physical trappings. She knows this is not her ultimate destination in the realm of love but at the same time she lingers because of the satiation of her lust. As she writes in the lines:

> As the convict studies
> His prison's geography
> I study the trappings
> Of your body, dear love,
> For I must some day find
> An escape from its snare

The notable poem apart from the title one in this anthology is '*The Stone Age*', which describes her husband as an "old fat spider" who spins "webs of bewilderment" around the woman and encloses her in passivity and domesticity. She in turn has her freedom and revenge for when her husband leaves she climbs forty noisy steps to knock at another's door. Again the language used here in this poem has often been described as crass. She uses terms, which no one else dared to write about. Especially she being a woman, it was entirely unexpected.

> .... Ask me, everybody, ask me
> What he sees in me, ask me why he is called a lion?

A libertine, ask me the flavour of his
Mouth, ask me why his hand sways like a hooded snake
Before it clasps my pubis. Ask me why like
A great tree, felled, he stumps against my breasts
And sleeps. Ask me why life is bliss and love is
Shorter still, ask me what is bliss and what its price...

The poem, which best depicts the suffering and humiliation meted out to women is 'Nani'. The theme of the poem is a pregnant maid hanging herself unable to bear the shame resulting from the moral conventions of society. Ironically the real culprit, the society and its moral codes, go free whereas she as a 'puppet' in the 'hands of fate' is left all alone to hang from a rope as though performing a 'cosmic dance':

Nani, the pregnant maid, hanged herself
In the privy one day. For three long hours
Until the police came, she was hanging there
A clumsy puppet, and when the wind blew
Turning her gently on the rope;

Kamala Das's constant efforts to seek love in her husband's arms forms the core of most of her poetry. Were she satisfied with her marriage she never would have indulged in all affairs, which brought forth most of her poems. At times you can detect a certain pride she feels in her ability to make men love her. Bruce King rightly evaluates the tenor underlying in her poetry thus:

> In her poetry love and hate are often neighbours, just as an assertion of sexual freedom sits near feelings of self-disgust expressed through depression. The theatre of Das' poetry includes the revelations, the confessions, the various contradictory bits and pieces.

The fourth anthology of her poems is not very well known. Titled *Stranger Time*, it mainly has repetitive poems but the new theme recurrent here is one that is exclusive to Indians, that of the Krishna devotee. She seeks to find the equivalence of her quest for love in the mythological framework of the Radhakrishna myths. Thus we have the poem '*Vrindavan*' where she writes:

> Vrindavan lives on in every woman's mind and the flute
> luring her from home and her husband who later asks her
> of the long scratch on the brown aureola of her breast.

She is often described as the first Hindu woman to write honestly about sexual feelings and love. Through all the vicissitudes of her love with different persons in different places, it is the lure of the Blue god, which is constant, and the unconscious urges of her heart are providentially directed towards her ultimate decision, the union with her divine mate. Whatever roles she plays are mere reflections of the Jiva's yearning for the final union and merger with the divine:

> Krishna, I am melting
> Melting, melting
> Nothing remains
> But You

She says, "I always had a pink pillow with me when I slept. It has been my one companion, my husband which I would embrace and call out 'Krishna'." Thus the use of an objective correlative in the Radha-Krishna and Mirabai legends provide a mythical framework to extramarital sex in Kamala Das's poetry. Thus she even ventures into the celestial world in her search for the ideal love, lover and herself. When she fails to achieve this she isolates herself in poetry.

Thus Kamala Das frankly and frequently confesses in her poetry. Her confessions are tall, far-reaching and meaningful. She confesses a number of things exclusively related to her own self. The tone is pressing because of the pressure on her mind to give vent to her ire, not only against her husband but also against her other sexual partners and also against the male domination over women in India. Her poetry acquired wider dimensions and a wider range because she felt that she was speaking as much on behalf of the Indian women in general as on her own behalf. Thus her poetry, though subjective in inspiration, became objective because she realized that most women in this country were being held in a state of subjection to men and were serving their husbands merely as a means of sexual gratification. She realized that women, while not receiving the affection and the love they expected and which was the nature of all women to expect, were being treated as drudges, cowering under their husbands authoritative stare as they put saccharine tablets into their morning cups of tea. Thus the urgency in her tone was never contrived. It was the result of the intensity of the feelings in her heart, which led to her poetry acquiring an urgency of tone.

This urgency by no means reduces the artistic value of her poetry but rather adds to its artistic stature. One can find reflections of sincerity, honesty, realism, and spontaneity in her poetry. She has never written poetry for a cause, but what she experienced or felt strongly about, she wrote. She wanted to share her innermost secrets as they tormented her often. It's only a coincidence that feminist sensibility forms a major part of it. Her sensitivity of mind is manifested in her poems. She has written poems where men look repulsive, cruel, and merciless and women appear as mere puppets. She could not adjust herself to this situation, and thus what resulted is her poetry. In fact the result is confessional poetry obsessively mulling over love, sex and the 'body's wisdom'. Several faces of Eve are exhibited here—woman as sweetheart, flirt, wife, woman of the world, mother, etc. Love also appears in several roles such as a 'skin-communicating thing', an overpowering force, an escape, a longing, and a hunger resulting in satiety. Kamala Das's generally sex-dominated poetry has unfortunately obscured her few but sensitive poems, which evoke childhood memories of the ancestral home in Kerala.

> The first impression I got when I first read her poetry was one of embarrassment. I was unwilling to discuss her or her poetry. But then I came across her autobiography *My Story*. It helped me get a better insight into her poems. Now reading her poems gives a clearer picture of the image she tries to convey. She is no nymphomaniac but rather a love-starved housewife. Ever since her childhood she spent most of her time at her ancestral house in Malabar. The lure of life in the urban city enticed her to marriage. Little was she to know that she would feel entirely out of place there. Added to that her husband introducing her to the sex-act rather brutally, treating intercourse as a mechanical act was too much for her to bear. She admits giving into her sexual yearnings, with encouragement from her husband, who often asked her to bare her breasts, reminiscent of the devadasi tradition. She

> thus fell in and out of love with different partners hoping that one of them would love her in return. She always felt insecure and found only lust satisfied in these relations. Thus love became a 'swivel-door' for her, when one left another came in.

She is very much a poet of the body, which brings to mind the style of Ezekiel. But the similarity ends there. The language she uses is manipulated to show the various shades of feelings such as her 'joys', 'hopes', and 'longings'. She has never received formal education, yet she understands the potential of a language very well. She is selective with words and uses those, which express her feelings in the best possible manner. Interestingly words come to her effortlessly. She uses them effectively to express her emotions. As Srinivasa Iyengar puts it:

> It is no mean achievement that while giving the impression of writing in haste she reveals a mastery of phrase and control over rhythm- the words often pointed, envenomed, and the rhythms nervously almost feverishly alive...

Her diction is noted for its simplicity and clarity. Her style is simple and easily associated with. Her imagery too is familiar and commonplace. Her images are symbolic and thus they increase the expressive range of her language. All in all, her poetry is the quest of her woman persona to seek emotional fulfillment within or outside marriage. That is all there is to it and that is all, which should be perceived. Changing anything in her poems would be rendering it as someone else's style, one that is no more Kamala Das's. One should never read her poetry with a biased mind. Charges of obscenity and pornography are associated with her work, but only someone familiar with her predicament can understand what she lived and she wrote.

Works Cited

Das, Kamala. *My Story*, Sterling Publishers, New Delhi, 1976, p. 161.

Iyengar, K.R. Srinivasa. *Indian Writing in English*. Sterling Publisher, New Delhi, 1983.

King. Bruce. 'Women's Voice,' *Modern Indian Poetry*, Oxford University Press, New Delhi, 1987, p. 151.

Kohli. Devinder. *Kamala Das,* Arnold-Heinemann, New Delhi, 1975, p. 91.

Mina Surjit Singh, 'The Confessional Voice Of Kamala Das,' Iqbal Kaur (ed.), *Perspectives on Kamala Das' Poetry,* Intellectual Publishing House, New Delhi, 1995, p. 91.

Rahman, Anisur. *Expressive Form in the Poetry of Kamala Das,* Abhinav Publications, New Delhi, 1981, p. 52.

11 The Element of Mysticism in the Select Poems of Sri Aurobindo

— S. Kavitha

Sri Aurobindo is one of the most outstanding poets in Indian Literature in English whose contributions are many sided and magnificent. He is in the long line of the Indian seer poets whose poetry is a unique blend of the orient and the occident in theme and technique, philosophy and vision. Among other things mysticism is an aspect of his poetry, the attention of a good number of critics. This article is an attempt to study the element of mysticism in his minor poems.

India has been known for her mystics from the age of the *Vedas* and the *Upanishads*. Even in this age of science and technology, mystics are not uncommon and the interest in the study of mystical literature has not diminished. In India, mysticism and religion generally go together. A glance at the religious writings of the great writers of the past will undoubtedly prove that they were all "God-intoxicated."

Though all mystics agree that the Absolute is one, the expression of their experience differs according to the intensity of their experience and the religious environment in which they grow. A study of the inner, psychic as well as the external life of a mystic is a means to interpret the recorded experience in his poetry.

N.K. Gupta has rightly pointed out:

> There is a difference between spiritual poetry and mystic poetry. When the spirit speaks its own language in its own name, we have spiritual poetry. If, however, the spirit speaks out of choice or necessity—an alien language in a strange manner, e.g., that of a profane consciousness, or of the

> consciousness of another domain idealistic or philosophical or even occult, we have what we propose to call mystic poetry. (20-21)

According to V.K. Gokak, "Mystic poetry"- poetry in which a deep and intense inner experience is expressed through images and symbols that flash upon the inward eye of the poet" (74). For Sri Aurobindo, poetry proceeds forth from the Absolute and ends in the Absolute. Poetry aims at creating a life beyond, and the reader. In *The Future Poetry,* he asserts:

> The poetic vision of life is not a critical or intellectual or philosophic view of it, but a soul view, a seizing by the inner sense; and the Mantra is not in its substance or for poetic enunciation of a philosophic truth, but the rhythmic revelation or intuition arising out of soul's sight of God and Nature and the world and the inner truth. (Vol.1:34)

Indeed, mysticism "is the crown and the roof of all religious life" (Iyengar, *Adventures of Criticism* 168) and Sri Aurobindo's mystic vision has been transformed into literature.

Any insight or intuition that cannot be explained logically and which creates a mixed feeling of awe and reverence may be called mysticism. It is something mysterious, obscure and ambiguous for human comprehension. Mysticism is something indefinable, a hidden force that meets us everywhere, reminding of the existence of that which is beyond all human control. It defies reasoning. Yet, one may define mysticism, in the spiritual context, as a union with the Divine, a reunion of the finite with the infinite, an evolution of the soul. Thus, it is the unity of man and God.

Mysticism is also "the belief that knowledge of God and of real truth can be found through prayer and meditation rather than through reason and the senses" (Hornby 842). *The New Encyclopaedia Britannica* defines "Mysticism, in general, a spiritual quest for hidden truth or wisdom, the goal of which is union with the divine or sacred (the transcendent realm)" (470).

Otherwise, mysticism refers to a direct and immediate experience of the sacred or the knowledge derived from such an experience. Meditations, prayer and ascetic discipline usually accompany mysticism. It may also be accompanied by unusual experiences of ecstasy, visions, and power to read human hearts, to heal, and to perform unusual acts.

Mysticism occurs in most, if not all, the religions of the world, although its importance within each varies greatly. The criterion and conditions for mystical experience vary depending on the tradition, but three attributes are found almost universally. First, the experience is immediate and overwhelming, divorced from the common experience of reality. Second, the experience or the knowledge imparted by it felt to be self-authenticating, without the need of further evidence or justification. Finally, it is held to be ineffable, its essence incapable of being expressed or understood outside the experience itself.

Mysticism or mystical experience differs not only from an individual to another, but also widely from country to country. So, the world has Indian Mysticism, Chinese Mysticism, Persian Mysticism, Greek Mysticism, Primitive Mysticism, German Mysticism, the Mysticism of the Greek church, Sufism, the Mysticism of the Roman Church, New Testament Christian Mysticism and so on.

But "mystical" is a very complex word subsuming a wide range of experiences that are obviously difficult to classify or pinpoint with the accuracy and rigour of the scientific method. Hence, mysticism is defined in negative and metaphoric ways. Recognizing this problem, Antony Flew in his *Dictionary of Philosophy*, states that mysticism "is claimed to be direct or unmediated experience of the divine in which the human soul momentarily approaches union with god" (239). Another comparable definition of William Reese is,".....as a spiritual and non-discursive approach to the union of the soul with God with whatever is taken to be the central reality of the universe" (374).

In the quest for the Absolute, the mystic discards the senses and the logical mind. Intuition tells him that there is more to be known that is communicated to him through his senses more than his analytical mind can comprehend. This aspect of mystical experience, rendered ineffable, can be understood only through extraordinary level.

A mystic has no proper adherence to rituals and practices of religion; he takes a sudden shortcut to realisation, speaks an esoteric and symbolic languages in communicating his experiences. He lives in an elusive and always in camouflaged surroundings. He leads a secretive life and does not interpret and communicate his experiences. He never shares his joy with others.

In other words, the mystic feels that the Supreme Soul or God is one and the same, but it assumes different forms. It animates Man as well as the different objects of nature. Thus the mystic believes not only that all Nature is alive, but also that there is essential identity of Being among Man, Nature and God. He believes that all things in the visible world are but forms and manifestations of the One Divine life and that these phenomena are changing and temporary. While the soul that informs them is eternal. A study of some of Aurobindo's shorter lyrics will reveal Sri Aurobindo is a true mystic in all respects.

A mystic is also convinced that the human soul is eternal. It is the body, which dies; the soul lives on. As Shelley puts it, death is merely a transformation. The soul comes to this world from the Eternal and assumes a particular form: after death, it still lives on in the eternal and may assume some different forms.

One may know that Mysticism is ineffable and inexplicable, but it is communicable through language. Especially poetic language is frequently the vehicle of expression. This is true and one can witness this in Sri Aurobindo's minor poetry.

In the poem, '*To Weep Because a Glorious Sun*' (p.129) the poet asks others not to weep for the glorious sun, which is going to set. The reason is, the sun will arise freshly in the morning. The setting sun doesn't indicate that, it is going to die or it has died. But it shows that it is going to be born again brightly with fresh life. Likewise, death of a person doesn't confirm that he or she is dead. Even though death swallows or devours them, the destruction is only to the physical not to the soul. The soul like the glorious sun takes several births in order to freshen it for each birth. The sun, which comes in the morning and evening, is the same. Likewise the death and birth are the same. They are the two sides of life like two sides of a coin, one and the same. So one should not weep for the arrival of death, instead they should treat both birth and death equally. "To weep because a glorious sun has set/which the next morn shall gild the east again" (129). Regarding this poem, Syamala Kallury comments:

Man should not feel sorry for his misfortunes, for, there is always the hope of a new dawn, which is the sign of happiness and joy. Man, who fails to recognize that the brief spell of life is only a prelude to a brighter day, weeps at the sorrows and agonies of life. (20)

Aurobindo describes dawn as the power, which takes man to Eternity and Infinite in the poem, '*Moon of Two Hemisphere*' (p.583). The moon, which pervades the height, leads, "To the Dawn, their harbour home, to the light unsealed / To the sun face Infinite-the untimed revealed."

It brings unsealed and unconcealed light and leads to the Infinite, bright and glorious, and reveals the 'untimed'. According to Dwivedi, "this poem is surcharged with the poet's spiritual yearnings. Here, the moon itself is a symbol of spiritual light" ("Sri Aurobindo Meditative and Mystic Poetry" 105):

In the poem, 'To the Sea', Sri Aurobindo says that the sea has a message to tell him. The poet, who stands near the sea, looks a small pale boat fluttering over the waves. The roar of the sea seems to ask ".... why dost thou linger on the shore with fearful eyes" (45).

Thus the sea calls out him and asks when the small boat dares the night of the sea, why should the poet linger behind. It exhorts him to come forward and dare the wide roar of the sea. There is rapture and ecstasy, for, the poet is facing the danger. The poet, inspired, asserts himself and claims that man is mightier than the sea. The river of human mind thus seeks to reach the height of heaven through the ocean of Divine Consciousness. He realizes that to linger on the safe lands is to miss what God has planned for his soul. If Eternal God-Head is the goal of man, the sea is the way through which he can reach the Divine Abode.

The path to reach the Divine Abode is not an easy one to tread. What is involved is a yoga and a sadhana; pain, difficulty and danger are the barriers that man must cross to reach his destination. The thunder and the clouds are only the means through which God trains man to overcome pain:

> The cloud He informs
> With thunder and assails us with His storms,
> That man may grow
> King over pain........(45)

In 'To R' (pp.75-76) he says that human life is a wave upon the crowded sea pushing towards the shore with regular rhythm. The power and force of the sea is the driving spirit that guides human life. Here also the sea stands for yoga or sadhana, which always beckons man to join it and through it reaches the Divine. Man has to trust the force of the ocean (human consciousness) and be sure that he will be guided safely. Even he goes further and calls ocean as a pilot and God as a captain. So there is no doubt on captain's work, because he will not sleep. He further states that he doesn't need to be afraid because even those who sink, sink only into his breast. Thus he assures the soul:

> Rejoice and fear not for the waves that swell,
> The storms that thunder, winds that sweep;
> Always our captain holds the rudder well,
> He does not sleep. (75)

In another poem, '*The River*' (p.560). Aurobindo describes the wild river. Here also the river is used symbolically. In this poem, he assures that the longing for union is not attained in a short period, but it takes millions and millions of years.

Thus he suggests that the stream of human consciousness has started millions and millions of years back proceeding farther and farther to reach the sea of Divine consciousness. The loud-thundering, fast galloping mighty waters of the river flow with a mass movement. The speed itself suggests the questing spirit of human soul travelling far and wide towards its destination. It is "a heart's hunger on God's barriers". After this, it reaches its certain goal.

In the '*Ocean Oneness*' (p.557) also he speaks about the union of the soul with the over soul. In this poem, the spirit of the poet widens, clasping the universe as soon as it associates itself with the silent and boundless sea. The horizon of his consciousness goes on widening until all that seemed becomes Real, one is mighty and simple vastness, there he feels the presence of someone deeply in thought. "Some one broods there nameless and bodiless, conscious and lonely, deathless and infinite" (557).

Thus, these poems '*To the Sea*', '*To R.,*' '*The River*', '*Ocean Oneness*' are highly suggestive and mystical. In all these poems, river stands for human consciousness, sea stands for yoga or sadhana and ocean stands for Infinite or Eternal Existence. These symbolic elements expose the mystical elements employed in these poems. Thus, the ultimate goal of man is getting union with the Divine. This mystical idea is aptly presented using symbols such as river, sea and ocean. Aurobindo presents the idea that the human consciousness, which attains its salvation through sadhana or yoga by joining the ocean of Eternal Existence.

In the sonnet, '*The Golden Light*' (p.146) he reveals the secret, the secret about his poetic creation. His saying, the true creator of poetry is the soul and the true enjoyer too the soul (Dwivedi, 'Sri Aurobindo as a Poet' 119) is apt to him, because his mystical poems all come from his soul. And his soul is able to produce such poems with the help of the Divine Light. He says that Divine Light, which has enveloped him, helps him to create poetry. That Divine Light is nothing but only the Divine Wisdom, which comes from God to him. Here "The Golden Light" suggests "The Divine Wisdom."

When light is there, there is no room for darkness. '*Light*' (p.160) is another sonnet in which Sri Aurobindo says that life's ignorant gulfs give up their secrecies at once as soon as the light of Divine Knowledge touches it. It opens the mysterious doors of the holyland.

Sri Aurobindo says that man is caught under the ignorance or maya. Ignorance turns a man into evil. If darkness fills a person, a person forgets his ethical life, his native mansion. Soon he is engulfed with pride, ego, envy, jealous and greed, etc. He totally forgets the root where he comes from and gradually starts to move away from Him. According to Aurobindo, the main motto in man's life is to seek for perfection, freedom and mastery of the unknown. In short, Man's highest aspiration is the preparation of a higher life upon earth.

In order to get higher life, a man needs to know about himself. If a man comes to know about himself, at once his/her ignorance will start to run away from him/her. All will be possible, only if Divine Light enters his body. Here too, "Divine Light" once again refers to "Divine Knowledge."

'*A Tree*' for Aurbiondo is the soul of man, rising upwards to reach the heavens. The earthly body obstructs man from his heavenly pursuits. In this short and simple poem, '*A Tree*', the poet weaves a great philosophy of life. The top of the tree always looks at the sky with some longing to touch it. The tree itself is earth bound but it always aspires to reach the impossible sky. In the same way, the task of achieving God's love becomes impossible to man, when his brain and body get involved in worldly pleasures. Actually one's heavenly flight is delayed when he becomes needy or greedy. Thus, this poem suggests the essential duality of human nature—"earth-bound; heaven amorous."

In a more effective manner, the poet speaks of the flight of the human soul in *'Liberation'* (p.159)

> My mind, my Soul grows larger than all space;
> Time founders in that vastness glad and nude:
> The body fades, an outline, a dim trace,
> A memory in the spirit's solitude. (159)

The soul's adventure is suggested through the flight of the bird. His mind and his soul grow larger than the space and time. The soul is separated and seen flying upwards. The body fades into an outline, a dim trace and lastly into a memory. The white radiance of eternity touched by the bird's soul makes this universe a vanishing circumstance. The thought gets lost in the light and passion of the Eternal Bliss obeying the edict of eternal peace. Life thus becomes the dwelling place of the Ineffable. One's life on the earth ends and the spirit is now alone with this Divine Bliss.

How to turn fragmented existence into Divine Existence is a mystical idea, which pervades in his poems. Thus, his lyrical poems are very short and they express the writer's personal mystical thoughts and feelings. The lyricism is spiritual, mystic and psychic. Sonnets represent Sri Aurobindo's highest achievement in spiritual, mystical and yogic poetry. Thus, most of his lyrics and sonnets are reflections of the highest term of life, joy of being, delight of realization and correspond in thought and substance to the philosophical concepts expounded by him in his *The Life Divine.*

To conclude, Sri Aurobindo is no doubt an excellent mystic poet. His poems are all epitomes of Indian mysticism. Since Sri Aurobindo held his early studies in the western countries, it is but natural for him to spell out his mystical ideas in proper language especially through poetry. Thus, the element of mysticism is strung like pearls on a silken-thread.

Works Cited

Aurobindo, Sri. *Collected Poems*. Pondicherry: Sri Aurobindo Ashram, 1972.

______________ .*Collected Poems and Plays*. Vol. 3. Pondicherry: Sri Aurobindo Ashram, 1972.

______________ . *The Future Poetry*. Vol.1. Pondicherry: Sri Aurobindo Ashram, 1953.

______________ . 'Sri Aurobindo as a Poet.' *Four Indo-Anglian Poets*: op.cit., A.N. Dwivedi Bareilly: Prakash Book Depot, 1981.

Dwivedi, A.N. 'Sri Aurobindo: Meditative and Mystic Poetry.' *Four Indo-Anglian Poets*: (Study of Toru Dutt, Rabindranath Tagore, Sri Aurobindo and Sarojini Naidu). A.N. Dwivedi. Bareilly: Prakash Book Depot, 1981.

Flew, Antony. *Dictionary of Philosophy*. London: Macmillan, 1984.

Gokak, V.K. 'The Meaning and Appeal of Indo-Anglian Mystical Poetry.' *New Perspectives in Indian Literature in English: Essays in Honour of Professor M.K. Naik*. Yaravintetimath C.R., G.S. Balarama Gupta, C.V. Venugopal, and Amritjit Singh. New Delhi: Sterling Publishers, Pvt. Ltd. 1995.

Gupta, Nalini Kant. *Poets and Mystics*. Madras: Sri Aurobindo Library, 1951.

Hornby, A.S. *Advanced Learner's Dictionary of Current English*. New York: Oxford University Press, 2000.

Iyengar, Srinivasa K.R. 'Lyra Mystica.' *Adventures of Criticism*. New Delhi: Sterling Publishers Pvt. Ltd. 1985.

Kallury, Syamala. Symbolism in the Poetry of Sri Aurobindo. New Delhi: Abhinav, 1989.

'Mysticism.' *The New Encyclopaedia Britannica: Micropaedia*. 1968 ed.

Reese, William. L. *Dictionary of Philosophy and Religion: Eastern and Western Thought*. New Jersey: Humanity, 1980.

12 The Poet as Social Chronicler and Reformer: A Study of Basavaraj Naikar's (Trans). *Musings of Sarvajna*

— Dr. S. John Peter Joseph

> Good translations can and should recreate an inner music and inner form in a new medium and while doing so, there is a surrender and a synthesis, a deviation which is extension, but still pointing to the archetypal idea and form common to both (K. Chellappan 168).

Of all the forms of literature, poetry is considered the most magnificent form of literary expression. As an art form, it manifests man's emotions and aspirations in a musical cadence. Good poetry is not only a 'finer spirit of sublime knowledge', but also a great and valuable source of inspiration and aesthetic pleasure. Despite different interpretations offered by eminent people, poetry is fundamentally an imaginative and emotional interpretation of life. The poet with his poetic vision and creative imagination not only "sees eternity through the limiting veil of time" but also undertakes "a comic adventure undeterred by geographical boundaries imposed by time and space!" (Sadani 445).

Poets depict human experiences, thoughts and emotions in rhythmic cadences in their immortal poetic compositions. The musical quality and melodious nature of poetry expresses the imaginative depths of man's true and essential being. Though poetry has the intrinsic qualities of inspiring and illuminating the readers, it never fails to communicate certain fundamental human values. The moral and aesthetic values conveyed in great poetry never cease to touch the very core of humanity. What is more precise and significant is that splendid and exquisite poetic compositions portray the universal dimensions of life. The noble thoughts and inspirations of poets leave behind a rich heritage and legacy not only for their nations, but for the whole mankind. Undeniably poets with their immortal thoughts and eternal notes of wisdom are the apostles who put together the hearts and souls of human beings all over the world in a bond of common brotherhood. What Dr.S. Radhakrishnan has stated holds good in this context. According to him, "Poetry is the echo in the human heart of the melody of the universe" (quoted in Sadani 465).

Kannada is one among the Dravidian languages, which have an ancient and a very rich literary history. The literary history of Kannada not only depicts the political, the social and the religious history of the Kannada-speaking people but also reflects the cultural greatness and the resplendence of the respective periods. Available works of early period indicate clearly that literary activities in Kannada might have begun from the beginning of the Christian era. The tenth century is considered to be a remarkable and a splendid period of Kannada literature. Pampa who lived during this period truly represents the spirit of the age. During the twelfth century Karnataka bore witness to a momentous socio-religious reformation initiated by Veerashaiva Sharanas like Basaveshwara, Chennabasaveshwara and Prabhudeva who envisaged a society based on values such as liberty, equality and brotherhood. They had a strong notion that people should not be discriminated against one another based on caste, creed and religion. These Shiva Sharanas began their movement through literature which was distinctly known as *vachana* literature or *lingayata* literature. They propagated through *vachanas* their doctrines of the unpredictable nature of life, the vanity of affluence and ostentation, the meaninglessness of rites and rituals either domestic or religious. They also urged the people to abandon the desire to hoard riches or wealth, to live a life of sobriety and finally to attain the spiritual enlightenment of Shiva. Apart from these poets with their socio-cultural and spiritual ideologies and viewpoints Kannada language abounds in the literary works created by Pampa, Ranna, Nagaverma, Basavanna, Mahadevikka, Harihara, Raghavanka, Naranappa, Lakshmeehas, Sarvajna, Ratnakaravarni, Kempunarayana, M.K. Srikantesha Gowda and Muddanna. The works of these literary giants are comparable to the works of the illustrious and eminent writers of other literatures in the world.

Musings of Sarvajna (1990) is a pioneering work of Basavaraj Naikar who happens to be a front-runner in popularising Sarvajna, one of the genuises of Kannada poetry to the English-speaking world. Though there are plenty of books and scores of research articles and erudite commentaries on the poems of Sarvajna in Kannada language, they have failed to make the fame and the stature of Sarvajna known to the people outside the State of Karnataka. Basavaraj Naikar, a well-known novelist, an accomplished short story writer and a renowned critic, introduces the poetic genius of Sarvajna not only to the oriental literates but also to the learned in the West. Naikar, known for his bilingual scholarship and profound knowledge in the fields of culture, philosophy, religion, music, mysticism and literature of different kinds, has endeavoured to bring to light the enlightened spirit, the encyclopaedic knowledge and inimitable wisdom of Sarvajna. Commenting on the erudite scholarship of Naikar, S.R. Gunjal rightly observes:

> Mr. Naikar's attempt to offer a sustained and systematic critical picture of Sarvajna's poetry is very commendable because it requires the critical skill of selecting the salient thoughts, rejecting the repetitive ones and yet retaining the native imagery employed by the poet. His discussion of Sarvajna's varied themes, images and language is ideally matched by his sharp analytical approach, clarity of thought and lucidity of style. One might say without any hesitation that Mr. Naikar has built a cultural bridge between the East and the West and given the right place for Sarvajna in the world- literature *(Sarvajna: The Omniscient Poet of Karnataka, Preface).*

Kannada literature is simply desiccated and spiritless without the incomparable poetic works of Sarvajna. As a unique and exceptional phenomenon, he has been enthralling and enlightening readers for centuries together. What is quite significant is that one cannot easily find a similar stature of poetic genius in other literatures. The universal appeal of his poetry is so great and tremendous that it cannot be easily restricted to any particular race, caste, creed and sex. The vachanas of Sarvajna have become quite familiar with both the educated and illiterates in every home in Karnataka. Kannadigas believe that without imbibing the edifying and illuminating principles of Sarvajna they can never become truly cultured and refined. The influence and the impact of Sarvajna are so great on Kannadigas that Kannada poetry without Sarvajna is "like Telugu poetry without Vemana; Tamil poetry without Tiruvalluvar; Marathi poetry without Ramadas; Hindi poetry without Kabir; Sanskirt poetry without Bharathari; English poetry without Ezra Pound; Italian poetry without Dante; and Japanese poetry without the Haiku" (Naikar, *Sarvajna: The Omniscient Poet of Karnataka* 1). Though *Sarvajna* happens to be a regional poet of the Indian subcontinent he shares certain universal concerns with the poets of the world who belong to different regions, climates, time and *milieu.*

The biography of Sarvajna like the great poet saint of Tamil-Nadu, Tiruvalluvar, is quite fascinating and interesting. He is believed to have belonged to the later half of the sixteenth century and to have lived during the regime of Sri KrishnaDevaraya. He is supposed to have hailed from a small hamlet namely Madagamasuru of Hirekeru taluk of Dharwad district in Karnataka. Though the exact date of his birth is not clearly known one could get details of his parentage and the place where he was born and brought up from his own *vachanas.* Born to Basavarasa and Mali of the potter community, Sarvajna was a self-taught man. He not only remained a bachelor but also led a life of a sanyasi. Furthermore, he was a strong proponent of Virasaivism though he loved the positive aspects of other religions. His own *vachana* describes the kind of life led by him:

> A begging bowl in hand and a large country to wander forth
> And a God like Hara to depend on
> Who is there richer than I? *(Musings of Sarvajna 2)*

The traditional portrait of Sarvajna illustrates a man in "a loin cloth and wollen blanket across his shoulders, chappals under his feet, a distaff in his right hand and a begging bowl in his left, horizontal triple ash-marks on his forehead, an isthalinga tied in a cloth and a rosary of rudraksi around his neck" *(Naikar Sarvajana: The Omniscient Poet* 2). To Sarvajna, life was nothing but journey. As a holy pilgrim, he went in search of knowledge and wisdom. Emphasising Sarvajna's thirst for knowledge, C.N. Hiremath observes:

> He had also the insatiable hunger for knowledge and learning. From house to house, from door to door he went, gleaning golden grains of knowledge and wisdom, accumulating, digesting and assimilating whatever he gathered. He went on gleaning and garnering grains of wisdom with the diligence of a squirrel and the assiduous industry of an ant (*Musings of Sarvajna* xi-xii).

While answering the question whether the readers consider him as a man of conceit, Sarvajna himself observes:

> Thinkest thou Sarvajna a conceited man?
> Nay! Learning a word of wisdom from one and all
> Lo! he became the veritable mountain of wisdom (2).

As a poetic wayfarer, Sarvajna sang songs extemporaneously. His songs undoubtedly reveal his pensive, reflective and analytical bend of mind. His poems abound in humanism, melodiousness and soothing features. As a moral teacher, he does not fail to give the readers and the listeners the ideals to be followed in one's life. As the greatest personification of freedom of thought, expression and deeds, Sarvajna exemplifies truth in his songs, which were actually a source of inspiration and moral guidance to both the learned as well as the laity. His songs were composed in the form of tripadi or triplets, i.e., "a three-lined form, which roughly corresponds to the terza rima of Italian poetry". Every tripadi consists of "twenty mantras or digits in the first line; eighteen in the second; and thirteen in the third. The second syllable of each line rhymes with the corresponding ones of the other lines and contributes to the alliteration" *(Naikar, Sarvajna: The Omniscient poet 3)*. Illustrating the effective use of the poetic form by Sarvajna, Naikar states:

> Although Sarvajna was not the originator of this poetic and metric form, he gave a new currency to it by his exclusive and powerful use of the same in the manner in which Dante gave a new currency to terza rima although he was not the originator of that metre". (3).

Since the *tripadi* form is short, it is always easy for people to remember the songs and sing them whenever they want to. Moreover, its musical cadences and epigrammatic nature enable people to treat them as valuable quotations. Because of the forthright manner, relevance and memorableness of the poems people recite them spontaneously on various occasions.

Though Sarvajna is believed to have sung 70 triplets, only a few hundred of them are available now. *Musings of Sarvajna* is an English translation of 188 triplets from the Kannada language. The poems included in the collection illustrate the universal perceptions and the variegated themes of Sarvajna. While translating the poetical compositions of Sarvajna, Naikar took into his consideration the translatability of the poems into English language. The author himself admits that he has not attempted word-to-word translation. What he precisely aims at is literal translation, apart from placing special emphasis on the imagery, metaphors, similes which are specifically related to the North Karnataka region.

The poetry of Sarvajna is distinctly known for its all-encompassing and comprehensive nature. True to the meaning of his name, i.e., the all-knowing or the omniscient, Sarvajna is endowed with a vast knowledge of human experience. With his exalted wisdom and phenomenal vision of life, Sarvajna happens to be an extraordinary poet who could sing songs on any theme under the sun. The heterogeneity and multifariousness of his themes are not only remarkable but also quite incredible. In his poetry he dealt with themes ranging from "the mundane to the metaphysical; politics to religion; sexology to astrology; agriculture to alchemy; prostitution to mysticism and so on (Naikar, *Musings of Sarvajna* xviii)."

While talking about alms and charity, Sarvajna makes it clear that alms and things given in the form of charity to the poor and the needy will certainly be reserved for the alms-giver himself. And he does not hesitate to say that the riches hoarded by self-centered rich people are meant for others. He continues to say:

> Those who feed the hungry and speak the truth
> And love others as themselves
> Are indeed invitees to Kailasa (3).

Emphasising the true spirit of giving alms to the needy Sarvajna observes:

> Say not 'come tomorrow' or 'the day after'.
> Give alms to the needy today
> And that indeed is true religion (4).

Feeding the hungry and helping the needy, according to Sarvajna, will enable one to find a place in heaven. The concerns shown by the poet for the poor and the needy finds a parallel in the 'Sacred' *Kural* of Tiruvalluvar. While illustrating the essential features of domestic virtue Tiruvalluvar observes:

> Call that a gift to needy men thou dost dispense,
> All else is void of good, seeking for recompense.
> ('Sacred' *Kural* 31)
>
> 'I've nought' is ne'er the high-born man's reply;
> He gives to those who raise themselves that cry (31).
>
> Let man relieve the wasting hunger men endure;
> For treasure gained thusfinds the treasure-house secure. (32).
> 'Tis bitter pain to die! 'Tis worse to live
> For him who nothing finds to give! (32).

Describing the significance of enlightenment Sarvajna observes:

> Why should the one who has realised
> The light within himself bother about
> The business of living? (*Musings of Sarvajna* 5).

Differentiating the enlightened from the benighted Sarvajna sings:

> Enlightened indeed is he, who has realised his own self,
> But the one who knows not
> Is like a dog of a deserted village (5).

Sarvajna sang about the sagacity of the men of illumination. He states:

> The enlightened man is supremely silent
> Though blamed and criticised by the wordly fools
> Like an elephant regally moving along the path unmindful
> of the barking dogs (6).

He continues to say:

> The enlightened man laughs at the benighted one
> Like an adulteress laughing at her own husband
> Who thinks the lover's child his own (6).

Speaking more about the benighted man the poet observes:

> A benighted man eats only the husk
> And tastes not the core of Truth
> Like a sheep nibbling at the leaf but not tasting juice in the cane (7).

While bringing out the distinction between the men of knowledge and the ignorant Sarvajna remarks:

> The face of the learned is pleasing to watch
> And that of the illiterate is detesting
> Like a kite of a deserted village (9).

Like a true philosopher, Sarvajna has written much about the significance of the Guru and the essential nature of spirituality. In Virasaivism the Guru is a living manifestation and epitome of God himself. Being aware of the importance of the Guru in one's life Sarvajna says:

> Guru's grace can transform
> A log into a wish tree and a barren cow into a milch cow
> And benighted fools into enlightened reciters of *Pranva* (15).
>
> Your kith and kin will come and dine with you at home,
> But will they release you from the cycle of birth and death?
> Realize, oh ignorant one! The Guru alone can free you from the chain of *Maya* (16).
> If you fall at the feet of the Guru
> Your accumulated sins would dissolve
> Like a mountain of camphor touched by the spark (16).

Sarvajna points out the meaninglessness and futility of worldly prospects and material accomplishment, which are devoid of spirituality. According to him, the Guru is an exemplary and ideal human being who illuminates the entire cosmos. Man can understand the essence of God or the divine principle only with the help and the guidance of the Guru. For disciples the words of the Guru are quite indispensable to tread the path of spirituality.

Pointing out the advantages of associating oneself with the righteous and noble men the poet says:

> Friendship with the virtuous is like tasting honey
> But the company of the vicious
> Will bring you the excruciating pain of breaking your kidney bones (13).

Several poets both in Kannada language and other languages have written much about *karma,* which is one of the fundamental beliefs or doctrines of Hinduism. *Karma* is a precept and the doctrine of causes and consequences of human action. It also indicates the retribution received by a person as the fruit of the good or evil deeds he has done. Sarvajna has written a number of poems about the inevitable and the inescapable consequence of *karma.* He reflects and philosophises:

> The *karma* of your past life will chase you
> Be you in the heart of Varanasi or at the bottom of the sea
> Or even by the side of Lord Virabhadra (17).
>
> You cannot escape from the clutches of death even if you visit
> The sacred shrines or hide in the rocky caves
> Or seek shelter with the wise (17).
>
> Does the tick in the udder taste the frothing milk?
> Much worse indeed is the lot of the person
> Who does not savour the fruit of his past merit (19).

Tiruvalluvar also has written ten couplets on *karma.* Some of the couplets, which find similar veins of thought are:

> Wealth-giving fate power of unflinching effort brings;
> From fate that takes away idle remissness springs.
> ('Sacred' *Kural* 52)

The fate that loss ordains makes wise men's wisdom foolishness;

> The fate that gain bestows with ampler powers will
> wisdom bless (52).

> What powers so great as those of Destiny? Man's skill
> Some other thing contrives; but fate's beforehand still (53).

While talking about the inevitable nature of destiny, the poet of *Naladinanuru* observes:

> To avoid those things which are to happen or to detain those which are to depart is alike impossible even to saints; even as there is none who can give rain out of season, or prevent its falling in season (quoted in F.M. Eills 12).

Sarvajna strongly believes in the true spirit and the essence of religion. He openly criticises the meaninglessness of the external rituals of religion especially the ritual of taking bath in the holy rivers without realising the significance of God. Hindus firmly believe that bathing in holy rivers will dissolve all their sins and purify them. The poet asks:

> Why you dip and leave into the flowing waters of the Ganga
> The Godavari, Tungabhadra and the Krishna
> Without realising God deep down in your own heart?
> (*Musings of Sarvajna* 20)

> Religions preaching violence and bloodshed!
> Throw them all into the fire.
> Lo, I would place on my head Jaina religion forbidding
> violence of any kind (22).

Sarvajna does not fail to glorify Jainism, which gives importance to peace and non-violence in life.

While trying to describe the unique and the phenomenal significance of Linga which is obviously a Virasaiva equivalent of the absolute or Lord Siva, the poet draws the attention of his readers to the idea that God is one who has genuine concern and veritable compassion for all the living beings in the world. His illustration of such a difficult concept through simple and vivid metaphorical language will be understood by both the educated and the uneducated.

> Immanent and omnipresent is the Linga in all things conceivable.
> Rocks, breasts, measuring cans and even sheep's droppings!
> Do the nigamas realise this? (23).

Who could put inebriating aroma in asofoetida;
Milk in coconut, music in the throats of the bumblebee and the cuckoo?
Tell me if ye know. (23)

Invisible like ghee in milk,
Like particles of dust in water
Lord Siva dwells in our hearts.(25)

Like Sivaratri among all nights,
Like Srisaila Fair among all others, like Srikasi among all holy places
Our Siva-doctrine is the crown and glory of all doctorines.
(27)

One and only one is the Lord for the Universe,
One and only one is the creator for the cosmos.
Know ye fool, there are not two. (27)

To Sarvajna, inner purity is very important for people in this world. He teaches that one cannot achieve spiritual bliss without inner devotion and purity. He also advocates the devoted practice of yoga for the accomplishment of spiritual enlightenment. For him, to attain inner purity, self-discipline or inner discipline is very important.

Though the poet is a staunch upholder of the values of Hinduism, he gives special importance to the Virasaiva method of salvation namely Sivayoga. He is of the view that a Sivayogi should conquer the negative feelings like lust, greediness, desire, anger, covetousness, self-centredness and cruelty. About the Sivayogis the poet observes:

He is indeed a *Sivayogi*
Who shuns food and water;
Woman and gossip (35).

Burning himself the Sivayogi enlightens mankind
Like the oil of a lamp burning itself
To illumine the world? (35).

Sivayogi renouncing the world.

What need has he for pelf or a female;
Pomp or power? (33).

The poet states that it is not easy to comprehend the complex nature of Brahmarandra but a Sivayogi can become Lord Brahma if he dispenses with his egocentric self.

None could understand the secret of Brahmarandhra overnight.
Could a Sivayogi become Lord Brahma?
With his self smothered with the smoke of egotistic vanity! (36).

While criticising the Sivayogis who lack noble qualities, Sarvajna observes:

What use is anger for a recluse?
Divine principle for the wicked, sight of other men for a faithful wife
And scandal mongering for a yogi? (36).

The poet warns that if the Sivayogi is lustful and enjoys the company of women, he will be certainly ruined.

The butter melts in the vicinity of fire,
How could the *Sivayogi* remain inviolate
In the company of a woman? (40).

Sarvajna emphasises the point that inner discipline is more important for a yogi than the external one. He is of the opinion that a yogi should be able to control his senses rather than indulge in smearing his body with sacred ashes and boasting about his saffron garments.

Reading countless books, smearing the body with *vibhuti*
Donning saffron robes, nay, you will not be a yogi!
He alone is a yogi who has conquered his senses (41).

The poet reveals the frivolous nature of the fradulent yogis. He digs at the incongruity and discrepancy between the true ideals of spirituality and the sensual nature of false yogis. He questions the integrity of the yogi who dresses himself in a tiger skin, sits upon a rock, chants mantras but lives a lustful life.

Clad in a tiger skin and sitting upon a boulder
Chanting mantras, the yogi
Is still obsessed with the vagina (31).

The poet continues to question the probity and the truthfulness of the yogi who, despite his external appearance, has not understood or realised the true meaning of the divine principle. He makes it very clear that such a one is similar to a fig tree burdened with several unwanted fruits.

What does it avail if you wear *rudraksa*
Knowing not the principle!
You have become a fig tree saddled with numerous
fruits (30).

Pointing out the potential nature of the yogis, the poet rightly observes:

Yogi is he who leads the swan
From the eight petals
To the focal point of the lotus (38).

Could one riding an elephant be ever frightened by a dog?
The Sivayogi enlightened as he is,
Is not frightened by worldly fools (40).

Making pertinent observations regarding the difficulties in conquering one's senses and desires, Sarvajna states:

One can braid one's hair, wear saffron robes, and reside in a temple, But most difficult it is To control one's senses (37).

Similarly,

One could be a recluse in the forest, forsake the spouse
And meditate all through the night and day
But lo none could conquer desire! (34).

The poet continues to say that one will find heaven on earth if he is able to conquer his desires. Otherwise, the present life will become a hell to him.

When one, renounces desire, one attains heaven here and now
When one nurses desire
One suffers hell here and now (41).

Sarvajna always appreciates people with noble qualities. Comparing the virtuous and men with pure conscience to pearls, the poet never hesitates to criticise people with false pretensions and attitudes. Commenting on the Brahmin who spends a lot of time in arguing about *Vedas* without realising the experience of God, the poet states:

If by dipping in water a Brahmin could ascend to Heaven
Why not then a frog always in water
Go to Heaven? (42).

If a Brahmin wearing a triple thread could rise to Heaven
Why not a shepherd swain wearing a blanket
Of countless threads go too? (43).

Why do you argue the written Veda is great?
What, after all, is Veda
If not an experience of God? (44).

Sarvajna talks about sex in a frank and uninhibited manner. He seems to believe that sex plays a dominant role in one's life and says that even gods are no exception to this.

The entire animate world is born
In the fleshy palace of Lord Smara
Located at the meeting of thighs (45).

The slushy hole between the thighs is the centre of the world.
That is the reason why
Nandivahana, Aja and Hari cling to it (46).

When the gods themselves are drowned
Head over heels into the big tank of the City of Desire
What shall we say of poor mortals? (47).

Sarvajna has sung excellent riddle poems which are said to have enriched the already existing riddles of the folklore of North

Karnataka. He even challenges the learned readers or the poets to interpret his riddles.

> Three hundred and sixty nuts are there and twelve fruits;
> Three bunches and a stalk.
> Let the learned then elucidate the meaning (48).
>
> Horn has it but no legs, a tail too and flies in the sky
> But bird it is not.
> Let the poets tell us what it is (49).

The poet's acquaintance with the knowledge of astrology is highly extensive and encompassing. His picture of mathematical astrology is quite accurate and comprehensive. He points out:

> The moment the Jupiter enters the House of Taurus
> Countless clashes, famines and homicides
> Will be the consequence in the world (50).
>
> When the Jupiter enters the House of Acquarius
> Wells and tanks will overflow,
> A rich harvest and the joy and jubilation (51).

Sarvajna is unquestionably a staunch critic of caste discrimination and the practice of untouchability. He strongly believes that the deeds of a person should be judged not by his caste but by common ethics. To him, caste discrimination is only man-made and is the result of the degenerated and evil intentions of man. He feels that God has no hand in the creation of castes, which eventually has set one against another. He, therefore, astutely asks whether the yogi has any caste or the spiritually enlightened man has arrogance or the sky has beams and columns. He also states authoritatively that the untouchables do not have separate places in Heaven. He further insightfully questions the origin of caste when basic instincts like thirst, hunger, sleep and sex, are universal to all men, birds and beasts. He also wonders how the light in the houses of the untouchables is inferior to the light found in the houses of others. He finally concludes that those who are virtuous and dear to God are indeed superior human beings.

> Has the yogi any caste; the enlightened, obduracy;
> The sky, beams and columns?
> But Heaven has no castaway untouchables (52).

> Common are hunger and thirst; sleep and sex
> To man, bird and beast.
> Where, then, did caste originate? (52).
>
> The earth we tread, the water we drink, the fire we use,
> Are they not one and the same?
> Why then caste and subcaste? (52).
>
> Is the light of the lamp at the house of the lowcaste damnable?
> Discriminate not among castes.
> Only he dear to the almighty is indeed highborn (53).

Though a bachelor, Sarvajna has sung several songs about woman and sexology. His knowledge about subtle matters of sex and sensuality is quite thrilling and exceptional. While talking about man's inability to understand woman and trust her fully, the poet remarks:

> The music of the ocean, the mystery of clouds and the sublime grandeur of Sambhu
> And the heart of woman
> Is there anyone who has understood them? (56).
>
> When ginger and neem become sweet
> And statues begin to dance
> Then dost thou trust woman (56).
>
> When woman is pleased
> She would help and pave the way for Heaven
> But rue the day she frowns, she will bring ruin to all (56)..

Sarvajna strongly believes that woman plays a vital role in man's life. Man enjoys peace, happiness, harmony, pleasure and spiritual enlightenment only through woman. A home without woman is empty and useless. Even gods cannot exist without women. That is why gods take different forms to attain the women of their liking.

> A cozy house, gold for expenses,
> An understanding wife responding to the will and wish of her lord
> Set fire, then, to Heaven (54).

Woman and gold and a tree with juicy fruits
Is there anyone who desires not
When he sights them? (55).

A thin string bending a string bow of bamboo.
Woman though helpless and weak
Bends the powerful man, nonetheless (55).

Harmony here, happiness hereafter
All wealth and prosperity are possible only through woman.
Is there anyone who wants not a woman? (55).

One may find similar views about woman in *Tirukkural* also. Tiruvalluvar discusses the role played by a woman in man's life quite extensively.

If wife be wholly true to him who gained her as his bride,
Great glory gains she in the world where gods in bliss abide

('*Sacred*' *Kural* 11).

If woman might of chastity retain,
What choicer treasure doth the world contain? (10).

Sarvajna's ideas of about adultery and prostitution are indeed candid and forthright. He elaborates on the susceptible and vulnerable nature of the prostitutes and adulterers in the most striking and uninhibited fashion. Commenting on the typical characteristics of harlots the poet aptly remarks:

A woman wearing immaculate pearls and big ear-rings
Letting loose the hem of her saree
Is willing for amours (*Musings of Sarvajna* 58).

He further adds:

A woman doffing and donning her saree on and off
And scratches her teeth
Is an easy and willing lay (59).

Smiling and giggling, showing the teeth, leaning against a pillar
With style and diaplay
Is an open invitation to meet and mate (59).

The poet describes the professional art of the prostitutes by employing similes and comparisons. He compares a prostitute to a boat, which is boarded by a new customer as soon as the old one gets off.

> A boat and a whore are of the same stuff
> The moment a passenger disembarks
> Another boards (58).

The poet seems to suggest through various similes how dishonourable and unsavoury for men to have association or acquaintance with women of ill reputation. He states explicitly that the prostitute has no mercy just as a fig tree has no flowers, the monkey has no curls and death has no medicine.

> The banyan tree has no flowers and the monkey, no curls;
> Death has no medicine to conquer
> And the whore has no mercy (65).

The poet has sung several songs on miscellaneous themes. He exhorts men not to borrow money from others. The borrower will find it hard to face the consequence in case he is unable to pay back the debt in time.

> Borrowing money from others is delectable like rice and curds,
> But when repaying the loan
> You smart under the scorpion sting on your buttock (61).

Similarly the poet is quite outspoken about the merchants in general. He asserts that the oil-maker knows fully about the sesame; the tailor the knack of telling lies; the watchman the stealthy movements and activities of thieves but the merchant is an adept in all these activities.

> The oil-maker knows the sesame; the tailor, the art of lying;
> The watchman knows the thieves,
> But the merchant knows all these three (69).

Sarvajna as a poet of common man expatiates the truth of life admirably through simple and understandable metaphors and analogies. He enumerates certain things to be deliberately spurned and avoided in life.

A mind with evil thoughts, a soldier not killing the enemy
And a wife who is frigid in bed.
Shun them all forever (62).

Flee from the house that leaks,
The whore that has no teeth
And the king who lies (65).

The poet also renders a list of things, which should be detested and abhorred by people in general.

Detestable indeed like a cot with tattered strings,
A monastery without a Guru; a family without elders
And a capital without a king (62).

Similarly, he points out frankly:

A meal without savoury dishes, sex without love;
A king not loving his own subjects
Are as detestable as camping in a cave with a tiger (63).

Undesirable indeed are blemishes on one's reputation;
Sagging women's breasts and loose beams in a house
And surely parting from the virtuous (66).

Sarvajna's songs not only describe common human experience impressively but they also acquire epigrammatical status. His forcible and convincing explication of moral truths and absolutes, which are experienced by people everywhere are quite striking and admirable. For example, while talking about filial son, homely wife and a virtuous Brahmin he observes:

A son with filial piety, a wife humble and courageous;
A Brahmin who is the embodiment of virtue
Are indeed the lights of the world (67).

Likewise, when he talks about the causes for painful experience in one's life the poet remarks:

Blackmailed by people and cheated of peaceful slumber,
Scoffed at by your own people and children
You will surely experience death (66).

Sharing his thoughts regarding the role played by gold and money in the lives of people the poet observes:

> Gold could bring friends together
> Gold could drive a wedge between cronies
> Gold again makes friends bitter foes (60).

> You are resplendent like the sun with gold and money.
> You will be a dog of the deserted village
> The moment you lose your wealth (61).

While stressing the need for acquiring the company of the noble Sarvajna says:

> The humming of a bee is good to hear; the jay, pleasant to watch;
> Heart-warming words are good to hear;
> The company of the noble is indeed good for the soul (69).

Illustrating the evil and the poisonous things in life Sarvajna points out:

> The fangs of a snake, the tip of a sword;
> The words of the ruthless and the life of the vicious
> Are surely all poisonous (67).

The poet expounds on the transcient and the ephemeral nature of life in this world. What he has said about the meaninglessness of accumulating wealth, gold and money is quite convincing and acceptable to one and all.

> Delude not yourself that riches will last long.
> Life is but a big fair lasting for a while
> And vanishes thereafter (69).

What Sarvajna has stated about the fleeting and the impermanent nature of life can be compared with Shakespeare's philosophy of life, which is shown in *Macbeth*. Philosophising over the futility and the hollowness of life Macbeth sums up:

> Life's but a walking shadow; a poor player
> That struts and frets his hour upon the stage

And then is heard no more: it is a tale
Told by an idiot, full of sound and fury,
Signifying nothing.
(*Macbeth* Act V Scene v 11. 25-29)

Sarvajna is thus a social analyst and critic. As a chronicler and reformer he censures human foibles and fallibilities with unflinching determination and undaunted courage. He expresses his ideas effectively by using striking imagery, suitable metaphors and impressive analogies. The use of colloquial language, interrogative sentences and aphorisms make his poetry more illustrious and unforgettable. Being aware of the true dimensions of the social evils of his times, the poet with his unswerving resolution and commitment to mankind strides to bring about healthy transformation in society. As a poet with a genuine catholicity of mind Sarvajna not only strove hard to establish the principles of love, peace, communal harmony, secularism, and religious tolerance but he also practised them in his own life. The values of life preached and practised by Sarvajna truly reflect the long-cherished traditional, social, cultural, religious, moral and the ethical standards of India. Like the immortal poets of India such as Tiruvalluvar, Kamban, Vemana, Ramadas and Kabir, Sarvajna has carved a niche for himself among the renowned poets of the world. Commenting on the universal appeal and immortal fame of Sarvajna, C.N. Hiremath pertinently remarks:

> Such bards and ministrels like Sarvajna are not of one age, clime, country or community. They belong to all ages, all countries and all mankind. They are citizens of the world. They are not only 'the uncrowned legislators of mankind' as Shelley claims but also the unanointed mentors of mankind (*Musings of Sarvajna* xv).

Translation is, no doubt, a commendable art. A good translation is a proper understanding and appreciation of the original text of the source language by the translator himself. It is also "a recreation and reincarnation of the poetic experience" (Chandrashekhara Patil 177).

While talking about the essence of translation J.P.Postgate in his work, *Translation and Translations* aptly observes:

> "Translation of literature is the art of rendering the writing of one language into another language. The art of translation lies not merely in translating the literal sense of one language into another but of translating also the feeling, thought and character of the work, so that the finished translation is equal in quality to the original". (qtd in Mallikarjun Patil 12).

In the words of K. Chellapan the translator's "originality lies only in 'original' recreation of the original" (159). Moreover, good translations assume the status of creations or transcreations. An expert in the art of translation, Basavaraj Naikar has successfully endeavoured to introduce the immortal songs of Sarvajna to the English-knowing global community. As a bilingual mediator, Naikar reveals his remarkable ability as a translator by maintaining the poetic essence and the spirit of the original text. Known for his dynamism, Naikar brings out in the translation the creative impact and the aesthetic unity of the original text. The difficulties of translating poetry are undeniably enormous. While discussing the problems in translating poetry Mohit K. Ray rightly points out:

> Poetry, we know, is notoriously untranslatable. While the semantic content of a poem can be translated into another language, its sonic content can never be transferred. Every poem has a definite sound-pattern and in good poems the sound-pattern is integral to the poem. It contributes to and reinforces the poieisis of a poem, because a good poem is always an organic whole in which the music and the meaning, the sound and the sense, the images and the metaphors, in fact, all the poetic elements are inextricably interlinked (iv).

The translation of the imperishable and everlasting poems of Sarvajna must have posed several problems to Basavaraj Naikar. Moreover, translating the Kannada poetry itself involves several obstacles because it "abounds in recurring sound patterns which have definite lexical meanings. These sound patterns evoke sensations of sound, sight, touch, movement etc., in addition to creating internal rhyme pattern" (Chandrashekhara Patil 175).

As a committed writer with deeper roots in the basics of translation, Naikar has followed the original text carefully and rendered the translation in English in simple and effective prose. Though he understands that 'it is impossible to transmit the subtle shades and nuances and the inimitable idiom of one language into another language which is nurtured in a different clime and a different culture (Hiremath, *Musings of Sarvajna* xvi). He with an exceptional imagination and true scholarship tries his best to recapture the rhythmic design, the music and the melodious structure of the Kannada language in his translation. As a true promoter of cultural and social synthesis, Naikar reveals his unique ability to carry the message of Sarvajna and to spread the social, the cultural and the literary wealth and heritage of Karnataka through his translation to the entire globe. Undeniably, his translation with his appropriate language proprieties and subtle nuances and artistic integrity and unity will certainly have an appeal to various minds with different social, cultural and historical backgrounds.

On the whole, Basavaraj Naikar's book, *Musings of Sarvajna* in translation is undoubtedly a rich and valuable addition to the corpus of Indian Poetry in English Translation.

Works Cited

Chellappan, K. 'The Paradox of Transcreation'. *Literature in Translation: From Cultural Transference to Metonymic Displacement*. Ed. Pramod Talgeri and S.B.Verma. Bombay: Popular Prakashan, 1988.

Eills, F.M. *Tirukkural*. Ed. R.P. Sethu Pillai. Madras: University of Madras, 1955.

Naikar, Basavaraj. *Musings of Sarvajna*. Dharwad: Sivaranjani Publications, 1990.

______________, *Musings of Sarvajna: The Ominiscient Poet of Karnataka*. Dharwad: Sivaranjani Publications, 1984.

Patil, Chandrashekhara. 'Rhythm in Translation: Between Words and Beyond Them'. *Literature in Translation: From Cultural Transference to Metonymic Displacement*.

Patil, Mallikarjun. 'Literary Translation: Its Importance, Ways and Difficulties'. *Studies in Translation*. Ed. Mohit K. Ray. New Delhi: Atlantic Publishers and Distributors, 2002.

Pope. G.U. *Sacred Kural*. Asian Educational Services, New Delhi, 1980.

Ray, K. Mohit. Preface. *Studies in Translation*. Ed. Mohit K.Ray. New Delhi: Atlantic Publishers and Distributors, 2002.

Sadani, Jaikishandas. 'Indian Images in English Poetry'. *India and World Literature*. Ed. Abhai Maurya. New Delhi: Indian Council for Cultural Relations, 1990.

Shakespeare, William. *The Complete Works of Shakespeare*. Scotland: Geddes & Grosset, 2001.

13 The Post-Colonial Interpretation of Bharati Mukherjee's *The Tiger's Daughter*

— Dr. M. Thaiyyal Nayaki

The term "colonial" broadly signifies a political subjection but it can also be extended to include ingrained cultural and literal marginalisation, thus making colonials a rootless throng in their own homes. Though the British rule ended in India in 1947, the impact of colonial imperialism still persists; they "rule us"; our normative patterns are derived from them; they influence our intellectual traditions. By influencing us deeply at a psychological level, they have converted us into "fractured selves" which Nayantara Sahgal referred to as the schizophrenic self. Bharati Mukherjee is "hyphenated self" while Jasbir Jain calls "the bicultural self". As Ashis Nandy puts in his The Intimate Enemy; Loss and Recovery of Self under Colonialism, colonialism is an attitude of mind and does not necessarily coincide with political control. This kind of 'bicultural self' is what rocks the personality of the heroine of *The Tiger's Daughter* by Bharati Mukherjee. The portrayal of her heroine Tara by Mukherkee is autobiographical because both underwent the same problem of split personality.

In other words, Mukherjee's writings can be identified as diasporic because she has stayed away from homeland but lived with the longing for homeland and its traditions and beliefs. Mukherjee, a native of Calcutta lived in Canada from 1966 until 1978 and was disillusioned with Canada where she felt marginalized by racism and so immigrated to the United States. The diasporic consciousness preoccupies Mukherjee. What she emphasizes is not so much the nostalgic yearning for the homeland but the "exuberance of immigration" which fosters new beginnings. She is aware of the challenges and difficulties immigrants face but feels that these are exacerbated if they are constantly vacillating between two worlds. Mukherjee is for mutual assimilation and acculturation of the dominant and the immigrant communities, seeing the process as "a two-way metamorphosis" and advocating what she calls "Mongrelization" of peoples and cultures.

An important concern of the post-colonial literature is related to place and displacement. The concern with identifying a relationship between self and place leads to a crisis of identity. Ethnic women in America are clearly twice marginalized by virtues of their ethnicity and their gender. The central figures in Mukherjee's novels, *The Tiger's Daughter, Wife and Jasmine—Tara, Dimple and Jasmine—flight* two battles simultaneously against marginalization during their early expatriate experiences in America; coming as they are from the other world their very identities are in question in America, calling out for a re-visioning and re-defining at the start. The identities that Mukherjee's women eventually emerge with exemplify the characteristics of a whole new breed, the 'ethnic' who is also 'American'. The process of finding their identities must be a matter of intense struggle; with the self, with tradition, with the wonders and horrors of a new culture, with growing aspirations, hopes and desires.

Mukherjee's women eventually find their distinctive voices, but not before they have battled violently with the images of their own selves as representations of 'otherness'—exotic yet silent, capable yet suppressed. More often than not, these women have grown up in Indian families whose cultural roots retain their hold in insidious ways; though in times of fear and indecision Mukherjee's Westernized Indian women return to seek the comfort of traditional faiths, they increasingly discover it to be cold and so the quest for a new identity continues.

Apparently Mukherjee's growing concern is that their newborn identities should not suffer from the terror of marginalisation, a concern that is probably legitimate to immigrants everywhere. Tracing a development through Mukerjee's novels, one finds that this community is, ever increasingly a celebration of what the author obviously considers the spirit of America, a spirit that defies homesickness and nostalgia in order that one may favour "the exuberance of immigration."

The greatest interest of these stories lies, however, at those critical junctures when decisions need to be made, when old habits and beliefs have to be discarded for more daring fancies. *The Tiger's Daughter* is primarily a prolonged tale of this conflict.

Duality and conflicts are features of immigrant life in America. Mukherjee's women are brought up in a culture that presents them with such ambiguities from childhood. The breaking of identities and the discarding of languages actually begin early, their lives being shaped by the confluence of rich cultural and religious status on the one hand, and "the new learning" imposed by British colonialism in India, on the other. These different influences involve them in tortured process of self-recognition and self-assimilation right from the start; the confusion is doubled upon coming to America.

The heroine of *The Tiger's Daughter* suffers a cultural shock by going to the United States. Basically the novel is an immigrant rendering of Mukherjee's personal experience in going to the West and the after effects of the cultural shock felt by her.

The protagonist Tara Banerjee Cartwright is the author herself who is also married to an American. Tara's habit of retaining her maiden surname after marriage symbolically reflects her subconscious mind, which is still deeply rooted in her native land.

There is a strange fusion of the Americanness and Indianness in the psyche of Tara and they are always at a note of confrontation with each other. Sometimes she makes futile effort to establish her American self but it clashes with the pulse of Indian life on her visit to Calcutta. She can neither take refuge in her old Indian self nor in her newly discovered American self. Being depressed and disgusted with the deteriorating situation in India and with her new personality, she finds it difficult to adjust with the situation and finally wishes to go back to the USA to her husband but becomes a victim of violence in India. During those moments when she is caught up in the violence, her mind is preoccupied with her husband David in America.

Tara is the daughter of a Bengali Brahmin industrialist known as Bengal Tiger. While she was in school at New York, she sensed discrimination if her roommate did not share her mango chutney. She defended her family and country vehemently. She created an

Indian atmosphere at New York: "On days when she had thought she could not possibly survive she had shaken out all her silk scarves, ironed them and hung them to make the apartment more Indian" (p. 34)

Her husband David Cartwright was painfully American as to ask naïve questions about Indian customs and traditions. She felt completely insecure in an alien atmosphere. "Madison Square was unbearable and her husband was after all a foreigner" (p.38).

When Tara returned to India, the clash between her American and Indian selves was deeply felt in her inability to adjust with her friends and relatives. The greatest irony of her return to India is that she felt lonely even in her homeland; her new identity was mainly responsible for this discomfort, which was further aggravated by the deteriorating social changes in India.

To her, Bombay railway station was "more like a hospital; there were so many sick and deformed men sitting listlessly on bundles and trunks" (p.14) She immediately thought of her husband; this symbolizes the developing new self in her; she repented to have come to India without her husband. "Perhaps I was stupid to come without him... I was impulsive, confusing my fear of New York with home sickness..." (p.16)

The Calcutta she visited now was disgustingly in the grip of violence due to communal riots. She was disappointed and that made her a misfit in the company of friends like Sanjay, Pronob, Nilima and Reema and she became an outsider even at home where she could not participate in the domestic rituals. In India she felt marginalized as she felt once when she first landed in America. "In Calcutta her alienation is deepened as she is welcomed by her relatives as Americawali" (p.50).

Her marriage with an American was the main cause of her sense of alienation: "In India she felt she was not married to a person but to a foreigner, and this foreignness was a burden" (p.62).

Tara is torn between mutually contradictory emotions on seeing her aunt, Jharna. On the one hand, she cannot sympathize with the aunt's religious attempts to heal her child and on the other hand she thinks, "I don't hate you, I love you and the miserable child, the crooked feet, the smoking incense holder, love you all" (p.38).

Tara feels similar antithetical feelings in the company of her friends too. During such conflicting moments, she felt like going back to her husband. Caught in this gulf between the two contrasting worlds, Tara had forgotten many of the Hindu rituals of worshipping which she had seen her mother performing since her childhood. This was not a simple loss; it was a little death, a hardening of the heart, a cracking of axis and centre.

Tara was caught in a similar antithetical tension when she realized that admiration did not come from either quarter. While the Indians considered her marriage "an emancipated gesture" (p.86), her husband David did not appreciate her for "cleaning bathrooms."

When everything about India was so 'frustrating' and horrible including her trip to Darjeeling, she booked a seat on a flight to NewYork but unfortunately and ironically, she was victimized by the Indian mob whom she wanted to see as a source of consolation. Locked in the car, she thought of her husband David in whose arms, the Indian young girl realized greater love and security; her trip to India "was so vague, so pointless" (p.201).

To conclude, Bharati Mukherjee's message to the readers through *The Tiger's Daughter* is "mongrelization" and not just the conflict between two selves. The title of the novel and the name of the heroine are symbolic of the standpoint of the author. "The Tiger's Daughter" is a rate combinaton of two races—'the tiger' representing the animal species and 'daughter' the human race. The name, Tara Banerjee Cartwright, is again a rare combination with an Indian maiden name and a European surname. This rightly symbolizes the conflict in Tara between the American and Indian selves. It is quite uncommon retaining the maiden name when one attaches her husband's name to hers. This is an example of "mongrelization" -a mixing and mingling of two races-Indian and American. In resolving the question of conflicting identities, Tara prefers her newly found identity because neither Tara nor the old traditional Indian society is accommodative of the other. She has become more an American than an Indian. Mukherjee wants the immigrants to take deeper roots in the foreign soil and become global or international citizens to avoid the psychological conflicts, which she herself experienced intensely.

Works Cited

Carb, B. Alison 'An Interview with Bharati Mukherjee.' *The Massachusetts Review*. Winter 1988.

Dhawan, R.K.ed, *Explorations in Modern Indo-English Fiction,* New Delhi: Bahri, 1982.

_____________ .*Indian Women Novelists,* Set 1, Vol. 1, New Delhi: Prestige, 1991.

Eldery, B.R. ed. *The Realistic Movement in American Writing*. New York, Oddyssey, 1965.

Elliot, Emory, ed. *The Columbian History of American Novelists.* New York: Columbia University Press, 1991.

Jain, Jasbir. 'The World of Bharati Mukherjee's Novels.' *The Journal of Indian Writing in English*. Vol. 13, No.2 July1985.

Joshi, Arun. *The Foreigner*. Delhi: Hind Pocket Books, 1968.

Mukherjee, Bharati. *The Tiger's Daughter*. New Delhi: Penguin Books, 1976

Nelson S. Emmanuel. ed. *Bharati Mukherjee: Critical Perspectives*. New York: Garland Publishing, 1993.

14 Situations of Incomprehension: Arun Joshi's *The Strange Case of Billy Biswas*

— Dr. V.B. Vinod

Writers have time and again, romanced the individual's quest for the meaning and purpose of Existence. A Jason in quest of the Golden Fleece or a Pure Knight in search of the Holy Grail has been expansively reworked by novelists. The twentieth century novelist has added yet another dimension to the Classical and the Christian quests. While the Classical frame privileges the physical and the Christian frame privileges the spiritual, the twentieth century individual's search is informed by the absolutely rational.

The riddle of Existence harasses but the thinking man. Writers like Andre Gide, Thomas Mann, Dostoevsky, Herman Hesse, Sartre, Pasternak and Camus have made telling forays into the philosophical terrain of Existence. Each of these writers has explored a different facet of Existence and, in the bargain, left his unique literary signature. One of the Indian English novelists, who, deserves to be in the pantheon of such writers is Arun Joshi. Coming from a country with a Himalayan corpus of philosophical discourse about Existence, it is surprising that, he is among the very few who have fancied the problem of Existence.

One can cite Raja Rao's *The Serpent and the Rope*, R.K. Narayan's *The English Teacher*, G.V. Desani's *All About H.Hatterr*, Kamala Markandaya's *A Silence of Desire*, as some of the widely discussed novels on the facets of Existence. Each writer has, in the consciousness of being moored in Indian Philosophy and Spirituality, examined the problem of Existence. Individuals have been located in typical situations that facilitate the critique of philosophical perspectives obtaining in India. *The Strange Case of*

Billy Biswas[1] is located within the frame of the problems of Existence. However, the narrative flourishes of Arun Joshi far exceed the above-mentioned novels both in expansiveness and in intensity. That is why R.S.Pathak calls him "an outstanding novelist of human predicament"[2] (105).

The Strange Case of Billy Biswas reminds the reader of several remarkable novels with remarkable individuals. Billy has his fictional counterparts in Hesse's Siddhartha, Harry Haller, Narcissus, Goldmund. He resembles Pasternak's Doctor Zhivago. There are aspects of the Stranger, Meursault of Camus in Billy. As an intellectual who is analytical about his existential situation, he resembles the Dostoevskian thinker, Raskolnikov. The kinship Billy shares with all the literary solipsists is in the persistence with which the purpose and meaning of Existence is interrogated. Paul C.Verghese in *Problems of the Indian Creative Writer in English* says Joshi is concerned with the "search for the essence of human living"[3] (124).

The characters mentioned above are thinking men. They have an evolved rational mind. They are also endowed with the dual qualities of skepticism and faith. They are skeptical about the givens in the situation of Existence. They have faith in their own intellectual nerve to work out rational constructs that would shore up their understanding of Existence. Their constitutional skepticism causes a restlessness and dissatisfaction with the given situation of life that is recognized as tradition, patriarchy, societal norms, polite behaviour, conformism. Their stout rationality about which they are, almost, narcissistic, enables them to construct a personal universe as a means to salvage the self that is constantly being assailed by the society of men at large.

It is, indeed, interesting to note that these characters are remarkable not because they have all realized success consequent to making crucial intellectual choices in life. On the contrary, in the eyes of the world, all of them, after a pattern, have failed in their attempts to arrive at a reasonable notion about life. Ironically, each of these characters, setting out to tackle one question or problem, generates a plethora of questions by problematizing the idea of Existence itself. Questions do not get rounded off into satisfactory answers. They move eccentrically towards more baffling situations that suggest to these characters, time and again, that conviction owing to rational answers is bound to be thwarted. What amuses the reader with regard to these characters is the inventiveness with which they persist with the quest for answers even when repeatedly thwarted. In fact, they are remarkable for this quality of keeping the hearth-fire of questions burning in the home of Existence.

The narrative of Arun Joshi holds interest even today for the manner in which the purpose and meaning of Existence is relentlessly interrogated. The narrative possesses an intensity not found in the other Indian English novelists who have pursued the theme under discussion. It uses a technique one recognizes in Hesse's *Narcissus and Goldmund* and Samuel Beckett's *Waiting for Godot*. The concept of man is presented as the individual differentiated: one, symbolizing the body and the other, symbolizing the mind; one symbolizing the sentimental entity and the other, symbolizing the sentient entity. The reader, who still finds his Modernist hat relevant, performs an act of integration to put together the concept of man.

The Strange Case of Billy Biswas, intensely persists with the WHY of human intentions and actions. And yet one does not feel that the novelist is performing a monotonous exercise. It is, precisely, the manner in which Arun Joshi persists with the WHY of intentions and actions that gives the narrative its piquant charm. Billy Biswas, the eponymous hero, is an exceptional specimen compelling attention and understanding: the desire to know. Every one wants to 'know' the real Billy: Billy, the man. Even Billy wants to know what kind of a man he is. Everyone comes far in his or her journey to know about Billy. And everyone, including Billy, has to smart under the frustration that the journey must go on with the destination always out of sight or reach.

Perhaps, no other Indian novel in English has PERHAPSE-D as much as *The Strange Case of Billy Biswas.* Every character: Romesh, Billy, Tuula, Meena, Rima, Dhunia, Bilasia, Rele, Mr.Biswas and Situ, has either asked questions in expectation of answers and been denied answers, or, they have themselves admitted that answers are not forthcoming. A cursory reading reveals that there are about sixty situations where characters admit to a lack of comprehension or the lack of sufficient knowledge. In a way, the charm of the novel lies in the ingenious ways in which Joshi presents situations of incomprehension and indecision.

Opening Premises

Romi (Romesh Sahay) is the narrator. He is about to relate Billy's story. To him, Billy is a man of "extraordinary obsessions" (7) and hence the fascination. Romi is the Collector who has just completed his official report about Billy. He admits that he cannot "claim to have understood him [Billy]" (7). He opens *The Strange Case of Billy Biswas* with the philosophical premise: As I grow old, I realize that the most futile cry of man is his impossible wish to be understood. The attempt to understand is probably even more futile (7).

He finds it difficult to believe that such a man as Billy could live in "the middle of the twentieth century, in the heart of Delhi's smart society" (7).

Romi, the sensitive narrator, is able to see the same sense of futility engendered by indecision in every situation in life. Even banal situations like leave-taking and casual badinage are tentative exercises. When Billy asks Romi to "come out after the roll-call" (40), the latter explains that a big-shot from Delhi is visiting the district. He replies, "I doubt if I can skip it". Later, when Billy announces that he is leaving the next day, Romi is taken unawares. He "did not know" (47). In another situation, in conversation with his wife, Situ, Romi tries to describe his New York days with Billy and the relationship between them. At the end of the day, he realizes that "he was not sure what exactly... [he] was trying to say" (72). Similarly, in a conversation, this time with Meena, they talk of an impending Cabinet reshuffle "about which... [they] knew very little" (72).

As the only trustworthy friend of Billy, Romi is a witness to numerous situations where Billy has to negotiate ticklish problems. One such crisis is the deep urge felt by Billy to respond to the pulls from primeval Nature. He is equally torn by his conscience, which compels him to commit on the side of family life and loyalty to his wife, Meena. Evaluating the situation by being sympathetic with both Billy and Meena, Romi feels that "all of us [are]... ignorant of the tortuous complexity of the situation (72)." The situation is perennial calling for a heroic spirit to grapple with the overwhelming problems of Existence.

Billy, the Man

The profile of Billy is constructed through a cobbling of impressions. It is ironical, that the only man who is sincere about understanding Billy (or, comes anywhere near real understanding) must describe the personality of Billy with "I do not know..." (8) and "I know no other...." (8).

Romi finds Billy to be a unique human being who sought "those dark mossy labyrinths of the soul" (8) and who "abandoned himself so recklessly" (8) to the call from within. Such a strange human being has a robust love for knowledge because he believes, as all rational men believe, that an intellectual conception of life needs a proper education. Billy's eclectic choice of books "made no sense at all" (13) to Romi. All the same, they are suggestive of Billy's appetite for life and the furious energy to pursue its meaning. The mélange of books include: "Old copies of *National Geography magazine,* latest pornography, learned treatises on black magic and witchcraft to a critique of the theory of relativity" (13).

Romi admits that he "did not know much about.... [Billy's] subject" (14). Billy's conversation with Tuula Lindgren reveals his interest in the Gond Kings, Verrier Elwin, concepts of rituals and taboo, religion, yoga and Gandhi. It is a deep-set desire to know more about man that he takes the route of Anthropology. Such a person who makes a conscious choice of his subject is unable to explain why the choice was made. He can only say, "I don't really know, I am afraid" (13). Everything that Billy is able to recall about his interest in Man as a subject, is the call he received about the age of Twenty One. With something barely better than absolute vagueness he tells Tuula, "I was twenty-one, but knew nothing of this great attempt of man to find himself" (19).

Billy is an anthropologist by choice: passionate and committed because it promises him a prospect of greater clarity about being situated in Existence. The aridity of an Academic position as lecturer of Anthropology does not help the cause. He feels "pinned down there like a dead butterfly" (47). Billy feels the manacles snap when he attends a performance of the Odissi along with Meena and Romi. He is transported by the "music, the dance, the movement, the sonorous voice of the singers, the *ghunghrus,* the darkness of the auditorium" (56). Romi, who finds

Billy sitting entranced on the edge of his seat, senses a strange sensation on his face. However, he is unable to penetrate its inscrutability. He admits, "once again I could make neither head nor tail of it" (56).

If Billy's sensations were indecipherable for his friends, his own account of his dreams is not helpful either. During a picnic with Meena and friends, Billy falls asleep to experience one of "the usual abracadabra of dreams" (60) in which Tuula and George appear. He narrates this dream to Romi hoping to have an exegesis. Romi can only reply, "I don't know" (60). This is one of the many instances when others were aware of Billy's dark mood, "even if they did not know its origin or its cure" (71).

On one of the field-trips with the students of Anthropology, Billy announces that work would begin the following day. But when he is pressed by one of the students about the time when they would begin work, Billy replies, "I don't know" (133). This is the pattern about the actions of Billy. He almost completes; something always eludes his grasp. This acute consciousness of not knowing hounds him even when he reflects on the choices in his life. He understands that one thing has led to another. But he is never ever able to understand: "Why all this happened.... I do not know" (144).

Billy evaluates his married life on account of a hasty choice. He is constantly reminded of the experience in Bhubhaneshwar that had a lasting impact on his life. Trying to explain everything to Romi he stutters and fumbles with incomprehension: "I don't know how to begin... or where to begin. It is, precisely, this phantom that I myself have been trying to pin down all these years (180)." Finally, what he really manages to pin down is not a phantom but a real police constable for which crime he has to pay with his life. When Superintendent of Police, Rele conveys the message that Billy has speared a constable, Mr.Biswas asks Romi, "How did it happen?" (213). Romi, like many things about Billy which he does not sufficiently understand, replies, "I don't know" (213).

Billy and Friends

"Who is Billy?" This is the question any reader would want to ask. Arun Joshi works with the narrative spaces in such a way, as if the reader had asked "What is *Brahman?*" in the spirit of the Upanishadic quester epitomized by a Nachiketa. Billy's friends—Romi, Tuula and Situ—find themselves in situations where they do have occasion to know Billy. One supposes that in each of those situations, they frame the question: "Is this the real Billy?" They realize that they do not know enough. The question is persisted with till the next situation happens. Arun Joshi has achieved a rare feat by describing Billy through the eyes of the latter's friends, not as firm impressions but as a series of negations *(neti)* or a concatenation of incomprehensions in the manner of the *Upanishadic* quester.

Romi describes Billy (under the circumstances) most accurately by trying to know what drove the latter to "run the most terrible of perils that man is capable of" (8) and he says, "I am intrigued" (8). R.S. Pathak feels that "Billy's search for meaning, however, is conducted in a very hostile atmosphere and he has to pay a heavy price for it" (51). Tuula too finds Billy to be an exceptional person and wants to know from Romi, if such persons are common in India. Romi gives to Billy an exclusive status by replying "I [do] not think so" (22). Tuula herself suffers the paucity of philosophical terms to describe Billy's strangeness with "I cannot find the right words" (22). Her enquiry as to what Billy would do after returning to India is met with Romi's circumspect reply, "Teach, I suppose" (22).

Sometime later, sitting across a table, in a restaurant, Tuula and Romi bring up the subject of Billy. This time they try to describe the personality of Billy: they discuss the vital element of his personality that makes him stand out from the crowd. From the moment when Tuula lights the candles and then blows them out with an exaggerated flourish of theatre, to the moment when she articulates the vital force *urkraft,* there is a series of tentative brush strokes on either side to get the image of Billy right.

Tuula lights the two candles that stood on their table which she blows out presently. She wants Romi to respond to the meaning of the gesture. Romi says, "I think, I do... feeling vaguely uncomfortable" (23). Tuula, at this point, leans forward and says, "No, you don't [understand]" (23). Tuula realizes that "Billy feels something inside him, but he is not yet sure" (23). To her, that something is "a great force", *urkraft,* a... primitive force" (23), waiting to explode within him. She is convinced that, that is why Billy is afraid and tries to suppress that feeling inside him.

Romi makes several attempts to know about Billy and his predicaments. His intense desire to know the man takes the shape of several ploys: direct and oblique, well-disguised and well-stated, at different times in different situations. Billy's wit is too much for him to handle that he feels that "there had been some great error of judgement" (82). Earlier, at a luncheon conversation, hoping to eke out as much knowledge out of Billy as possible, he has to admit, "If my intention had been to obtain information about his 'problems, I could not have more abundantly failed" (81).

So, Romi settles for the next best option of scrutinizing the letter from Tuula with an account of Billy's transformation and his perception of the pulls of destiny. The letter is interspersed with Billy's own words about how the transformation came about. The experience of the sense of vacuity and incomprehension in the temple when the rituals were going on is vividly narrated by Billy: "What I had hoped to achieve by my visit I do not know" (98). He discusses the institutionalized gods during this momentous visit and realizes that what really awaited him at that point of time is "Fate" (98).

Romi understands that Billy is endowed with a unique vision. He is capable of seeing beyond the common vision and looking into the uncommon sights. Romi recalls "the almost inhumanly sharp eyes" (43) of Billy with which he could see "those pine trees each from the other" (42) while Romi "could see nothing" (43). It is this capacity to see beyond the ordinary that takes Billy into the forests around the Maikala Hills. Romi, though is told by Billy about the existential choice of life with the tribals and integration into forest life, he admits resignedly: "I knew enough of life to realize that the full answer would never be known" (152). What intrigues the reader is what Billy himself says when asked by Romi what he had been doing with himself in the past ten years. Billy guffaws and replied enigmatically,

Well, the fact is that I don't know. At times I put the question to myself and find that I haven't really got much to say for myself. (190)

Compared to Romi and Tuula, Situ's acquaintance with Billy is but fleeting. She has only a couple of occasions to meet Billy. Romi does bring her up on their New York days and their relationship. Situ listens attentively. Romi's inability to know how much Situ has registered is evident when he says, "How much she understood of what I was trying to say I do not know" (72). Yet the most meaningful response, in a chain of incomprehensions framed in I-don't-knows, comes from Situ who, after meeting Billy for the first time says, "I suppose I did [like Billy]. I hardly know him" (71).

Billy and the Family

Family entails commitment and duties. It means, submitting oneself to the demands imposed by others. A free radical like Billy would find such a dispensation preposterous as it amounts to admitting impediments in the free flow of the questing spirit. Billy does make a conscious choice of marrying Meena. Billy, the householder comes through the futile attempts of Meena to keep him by understanding him and Billy on his part suffers the agonies of playing the proper householder.

What these family situations suggest is Billy's frustration at the thought of being located. When Romi meets him and Meena in Delhi after a long interval, Romi wants to know how long Billy would be staying in Delhi. Billy's reply is "I don't know" (38). Meena's reaction to this reply carries a dramatic irony with profound significance: Even without realizing the fact that Billy is uncomfortable in being located, she hits the bull's eye, "Billy never knows how long he is staying" (38).

This piece of dialogue is followed by Billy's staring "absently at the darkening sky. A thunderstorm was obviously building up. The smile in his eyes had gone out again" (38). These are early suggestions that destiny has reserved for Billy a different and unexpected turn to which he must submit in a state of incomprehension. From this moment on, Meena's hold over Billy weakens till her knowledge about his whereabouts is a clutch of suppositions. Even to an enquiry as to when Billy would come and from where, Meena replies, "I don't know. The University, I suppose" (73).

Meena finds her family life in disarray. Discussing Billy's credentials as a family man with Romi, she struggles to keep her composure. She, finally, breaks down inconsolably in front of Romi saying, "I don't know. Things are falling apart" (74). She does try adventurously to shore up her fortunes by asking Romi to throw more light on the character of Billy. "The profoundest thing" Romi could think of saying is that Billy is "a difficult person to understand" (76). On being prodded by Meena that he is perhaps the only one who has known Billy so much longer, Romi's studied answer is, "Hardly" (76).

Billy and the Call of the Wild

The Call of the Wild is a literary archetype. Conrad has worked that theme touching a mystical realm in *The Heart of Darkness*. Arun Joshi comes close to Conrad by working on Billy's response to the call of the Wild. R.K.Dhawan says that "Arun Joshi's fiction conforms to Conrad's conception of the novel [because it]... recognizes a reality beyond the merely phenomenal world"[4] (17). *The Strange Case of Billy Biswas* begins on a day in New York when Billy is drunk. The reasons for Billy's unusual behaviour "were only partly understood" (20) by Romi and others.

The next occasion when Romi and friends get to see the change of the rhythms of Billy's life is when he plays on the drums in a frenzied manner. It was a session that lasted for a quarter of an hour. It was not skilful or sophisticated. All the same, there was "a mesmeric pull" (21) and "sheer vitality" (21) to it. Romi was a witness to this freak incident. He realizes that the patterns of sound were dictated by a metaphysical energy beyond the rational mind's capacity to define or comprehend. All that Romi could infer was that the patterns of sound carried "a more fundamental message although what it was I, [Romi] or Billy for that matter, could not have said" (21).

A similar situation recurs later on in the narrative. Both Billy and Romi are inside the temple. Romi feels that they are not alone and that there was "another presence" (192). When they are in the temple, Romi, feels that the temple was passing on a piece of message: "Beware it seemed to say. There are things that the like of you may never know. There are circles within circles, and worlds within worlds. Beware where you enter" (192).

It is not the first time that Romi experiences an uncanny sensation. Beholding Billy ten years after he had disappeared into the forests, Romi describes the moment: "I looked at him as one might look at a spectre, quite unable to grasp the events of the day" (99).

Once in the lap of Nature, both Billy and Romi are equally childlike: helpless and in need of light of one kind or the other. While there are situations where the individual is wanting in the capacity to see, in other situations the individual is found wanting in the capacity to know. Billy points to a cliff face of the Maikala Hills that glows when the moon comes up. It is called "Chandtola" (106) by the tribals. He points out the hill to Romi and asks if he is able to SEE it. Romi replies, "No" (106). Later, Romi, his curiosity aroused, wants to know from Billy why Chandtola glows when the moon comes up. Billy replies, "No" (107).

Dhunia's words to Billy, You don't know. How could you? (145) could be dovetailed here. It suggests that the Wild did hold for Billy an irresistible pull. But he was, in choosing to answer the call of the Wild, not absolutely conscious or totally convinced of the reasons informing the choice. Dhunia understands that Bilasia has cast a spell on Billy and that the latter is enchanted. Dhunia confirms his inference by asking Billy who had done love magic on him. His native wisdom enables Dhunia to see Billy's incomprehension.

Dhunia and Bilasia represent experiences that are beyond the pale of the civilized society. They are denizens of a different universe where a different harmony prevails. It takes the extraordinary courage of Billy to choose to integrate with that universe. Romi, as the Collector who comes to Bilasia's hut after the killing of Billy recognizes in Bilasia, "the embodiment of that primal and invulnerable force that had ruled these hills, perhaps this earth, since time began" (226). The visions about Bilasia that Romi was receiving, caused in him "a fearful disturbance, the full meaning of which [he had] yet to understand" (226).

As a person of extraordinary sensitivities, Billy sees much more meaning into his existential situation than the others. In a mood of retrospection, he wishes the script of his life were revised a little. He tells Romi many years after the party in Delhi: "Things might have been different... if that wretched storm had not come up when it did. You see what I mean, don't you?" (39). As expected Romi does not know what Billy meant. He only manages to understand that it is Billy's great capacity for seeing which, "step by step, led him to the only end that awaits those who see too much" (39).

Closing Time

The thread of incomprehension does not snap till the end of the narrative. Situations where characters act in a sort of half-light are dexterously sequenced. Rele, the Police Superintendent hopes to draw more knowledge about Billy by trying to understand the relationship the protagonist has with Romi. The latter says that Rele and every one like him who looks at Billy "won't understand" (218): both the man and the relationship of that man with Romi.

The havildar who shoots Billy down could not have acted in a greater fit of incomprehension. To his eyes, Billy was a renegade who had to be restrained. He was conditioned by his duties as a policeman. But after having committed the act of shooting Billy dead, the havildar is contrite and apologizes to Romi. The havildar's response is phrased exactly like the responses of the other characters, when they had been placed in similar situations where an account of personal realization, knowledge and intelligent conception were called for. The havildar tells Romi, "I did not know who he was, Sir. I did not know who he was" (236).

Romi, in his capacity as the District Collector, is responsible for filing the official report: The Case of Billy Biswas. As the Collector of the District who is in possession of the 'known' facts, he is in the best position to tell the truth. As the confidant of Billy, he is in the best position to reveal the dark mossy labyrinths of the soul. Yet, when he finally gets down to the actual job of reporting the developments leading to the death of Billy in a police firing, Romi philosophizes: "who... has ever succeeded in putting into words what is truly wondrous and fearful about men" (240).

References

1. Joshi, Arun. *The Strange Case of Billy Biswas*. Delhi: Hind Pocket Books, 1971. [All citations pertaining to the novel are from this book].

2. Pathak, R.S. 'Human Predicament and Meaninglessness in Arun Joshi's Novels.' *The Fictional World of Arun Joshi*. Ed. R.K. Dhawan. New Delhi: Classical Publishing Company, 1986. 104-142.
3. Verghese, Paul.C. *Problems of the Indian Creative Writer in English.* Bombay: Somaiya Publications, 1971.
4. Dhawan, R.K. *The Fictional World of Arun Joshi.* New Delhi: Classical Publishing Company, 1986.

15 The Paradoxical Psyche of an Archetypal Indian Woman: Sita in Anita Desai's *Where Shall We Go This Summer?* — A Feminist Study

— Dr. V. Ramesh

Intolerance is instinctive to human nature and Sita of Anita Desai's *Where Shall We Go This Summer*? is no exception. A hyper-sensitive and out of ordinary character, she symbolizes a distinct dimension to the image of woman in family and society. To empathize or appreciate her delineation, a study of woman's position in society through historical standpoint is desirable.

Feminism and feminist movements are neither novel nor exceptional. "It (Feminism) emerged to be a world-wide cultural movement to secure a complete equality of women with men in the enjoyment of all human rights—moral, religious, social, political, educational, legal, economic and so on."[1] And literary texts lend authenticity in creating an awareness or making a powerful analysis of the society's working against the interests of women. But the positive exposition of women's plight and struggle can bring about a radical transformation in public attitude towards man-woman relationship and boost their self-esteem and lend credence to their just and long-pending demands. The evolution of the 'New Woman', signifying a new realization of her duties and responsibilities in family and society, is mainly aimed at the assertion of her rights as a human being and her determination to attain gender equity with man.

A silent sufferer, a showpiece of Indian culture and a cog in the family wheel and without an identity of her own to accomplish self-gratification and self-fulfilment, the ethnic Indian woman is depicted in a multiplicity of roles—mother, wife, daughter and sister. A monument of endurance and loyalty, she takes pride in service and self-sacrifice and enjoyed an enviable status during Vedic age. Manu lays down the rule: "Where women are honoured, there Gods are pleased; but when they are not honoured, no sacred rites yield rewards." *Rig Veda* decorates woman with compliments like *jaya, jani* and *patni*. But slowly, the woman's position lost its significance and charm. The *Maitrayani Samhita* equates women with dice and drinks and daughters become encumbrances. But there were people who stood for the cause of women. Some among them are Swami Vivekananda "educate your women first and leave them to themselves" and Annie Besant "the rising of India as a nation depends on the education of Indian women." The adoption of the new Indian Constitution brought enfranchisement to all women. The University Grants Commission advocated that "there cannot be educated people without educated women." The slow but steady changes in cultural, social and economic patterns of life have expanded and altered the nature of actuality for women.

The spotlight and stress on women and their struggle for survival in the current conglomeration of standards in society stem from the legality of gender equality, the new found freedom through constitutional rights, the empowerment and discernment attained through education and the strong tide of unity realized through organizations and forums serving their cause. But the modern Indian woman is torn between two extremes of emotions the traditional submissive role and the modern liberated: independent status.

An analysis of the above factors narrows down the deliberation on women's quests as the exploration for identity and defining the self. The voluminous feminist literature has assorted tones and standing—placid, leading and voluble. The confrontational issues are male chauvinism, sexist bias, psychological and physical exploitation, hegemonistic inclinations of not only male but also even some female sections of society and the neglect and disdain for the woman's psychological, cultural, familial and spiritual quests. Some of the remedies suggested for the resolution of these issues are: recording the protest in the mildest form, searching for a compromise through mediation or moderation, love and persuasion or burying oneself in a self-made exclusive environment, mostly escapist in style.

Any dialogue or investigation of feminism is inconclusive without a corresponding scrutiny of the 'paradox' of feminism. The clarion call that the 'new', 'enlightened' and 'modern' woman is intellectually on a par with man and economically independent, discarding all fetters and pulls off appreciable status in society on the levels of security, dignity and freedom is an understatement. Expectations and specifics of truth diametrically differ. For instance, the gender factor wields a greater pull to the inconvenience of women.

A study conducted in the Indian subcontinent shows the existing predicament of women, being pulled below the poverty line instead of achieving economic parity with men, as 'poverty within poverty'. The modern woman is not guaranteed of emancipation from male dominance even if she attains economic independence. Ajita Garg dubs it "enslavement on two fronts: domestic and employment."[2] This justifies the Communist Manifesto that "the bourgeois sees in his wife a mere instrument of production, echoed glumly in bride burning and dowry deaths."

Even outside the family, she is reduced to the level of an article of trade, exploiting her flesh obsessively in advertisement and sales promotion and thereby taking away the last shreds of the dignity of her person. Engels declares: "The social status of the lady of civilization, surrounded by sham homage and estranged from all real work, is socially infinitely lower than that of the hard-working woman of barbarism."[3]

Indo-Anglian fiction falls easily into two conspicuous segments: the pre and post independence group of writers. The pre-independence Indian Writing in English mainly stimulated the native literature and also signalled the fusion of the highest ideas of the East and West. Pioneer men novelists of the India in transition like K.S. Venkataramani, Mulk Raj Anand, R.K. Narayan and K.A. Abbas dealt with questions relating to socio-economic and political truths in their novels. After independence, women novelists of significance emerged elevating the genre with their centre of attention on the real predicament of women in the male chauvinistic society. Chief among them include Kamala

Markandaya, Ruth Prawer Jhabvala, Nayantara Sahgal, Santha Rama Rau and Anita Desai.

Among them, Anita Desai stands apart with her emphasis on the exploration of the troubled sensibility of woman. This is a neo-concept and a typical neo-Indian phenomenon. For instance, in Jhabvala's work, social background has remarkable attention, whereas Kamala Markandaya is bifocal in presentation—characters and also themes relating to financial, political, social and cultural. Hariprasanna has this to say about Anita Desai's novels: "Her novel is concerned with the emotional world of women, revealing a rare, imaginative awareness of various deeper forces at work and a profound understanding of feminine sensibility."[4]

The poignant race of women in Anita Desai's novels pictures the uncommunicative miseries and vulnerability of millions of married women, tortured and tormented by existentialist problems and dilemmas. "The journey within" her characters, the psychological discernment, reveal the trauma of existence in a hostile milieu, the conservative, straitjacket and taboo-ridden society.

The deep-seated ideas of Anita Desai's *Where Shall We Go This Summer?*, as also in most other novels of her, are the irreconcilable inner and outer worlds, the imponderable gulf between expectation and reality, leading to the anguish of the sensitive soul. Sita's articulated problems represent those of the inarticulate middle class people—universal and eternal. Some of the paradoxical, philosophical mysteries encapsulated in the novel are: the meaning or value versus vulgarity or monotony of life and prospects or unfeasibility of escape from the bondage of procreation for a woman. Anita Desai endeavours to offer her own solutions to these apparently unanswerable questions in a persuasive way.

Sita is a middle class married woman in her forties. She is the mother of four children and pregnant for the fifth time. She lives in a Bombay flat and her husband, Raman is an upper middle class factory owner. By all standards, she has a comfortable and even unperturbed lifestyle, dotingly yearned by women of her age and status. But her calibre is different. Her totally alienated and incongruous inner self, incompatible with the world outside, desires that the child should be 'kept' in her womb for ever and she could never even imagine of aborting it, as Raman misjudges her thoughts. This results in her hysterical outburst: "Mad", she gasped," you're quite mad. Kill the baby? It's all I want ..... I mean I want to keep it. I don't want it to be born" (*Where Shall We Go This Sun mer* 35).

This idea is really a phantasmagoria and clearly inconceivable in reality. Women have been traditionally brought up to esteem motherhood as the highest fulfilment of womanhood. Sita distrusts this notion. She frankly tells Raman, "Children only mean anxiety, concern, pessimism, not happiness" (20). Sita is stubborn. In the world in which her husband and children live, the one in which cruelty and inhuman tendencies form the core, creation is totally an aberration. Shanta Rangaswamy succinctly states: "She wonders whether she has gone insane or the world around her."[5]

Raman and Sita live on different planes. Raman could never fathom her mind's depth and its unusual and unilateral projections. They are temperamentally incompatible since Raman is pragmatic and outspoken, while Sita is an introvert with a sensitive soul and heightened imagination. For instance, Raman sees no meaning in Sita trying desperately to save a wounded eagle from the crows: "They have made a good job of your eagle ...... look at the feathers sticking out of that crow's beak. 'Perhaps it flew away', she cried, knowing it had not" (41). When Sita is psychologically affected by her life in Bombay, Raman could not decode her sensitive reactions to the happenings around: "But you're not leaving for such small incidents, Sita? They occur in everyone's life, all the time. If you're an adult, you know how to cope with them—they are only small incidents" (37).

It is only Raman, who rushes to the rescue of Sita, takes her away from the island, educates her and naturally marries her. But Sita's inner conflict, the boiling cauldron of emotions, misconstrues this as a resultant act of pity and lust. She strongly feels that she is forcibly evacuated from the theatrical era of her life (may be a ruined one) and violently led into the 'ordinary', 'empty', 'meaningless' and mundane married life, offering her no contentment.

But, sometimes, she becomes compassionate and genuinely anxious about her husband's troubles: "His boys at home must have worried him, while he was at work in the factory which was not without its problems either" (138). But she is inept, perhaps, disinclined to express her concerns and warmth: "It simply did not exist for her and should not make it exist. So she did not speak any words of love or reassurance to him. She looked away...."(41).

The discord and cavity between the mother and children are also paradoxical and full of dissonance: "All that mattered to her, they discarded" (137). Sita is attracted towards art but Menaka chooses science, especially medicine. "There are no dead-ends, now, in art. There is something, Menaka, and alive and creative." Menaka is for a life of "order, logic and sense" and averse to her mother's "disorder and nonsense" (116). The chasm is apparent: "Menaka lost interest—she had heard that argument too often. Arguments with her mother always ended in this kind of haze of obscurity and nonsense that her trim and practical self loathed instinctively" (69).

Distressing impact of her son's cry on her heart is rendered in the following words: "Each time it tore a fresh gash in her. It made her wild, it made her run" (141). The laceration of the mother's psyche is very true.

Her father is both grand and mysterious. "He had been ugly, grotesquely so as to arouse first notice, then pity and finally regard—a hypnotized kind of notice and regard" (66). He was a practical activist and self-educated in jails. "He looked very much like a saint, a mini Gandhi" (67). Thus Sita's father was more a man of the community than an affectionate father to his children. He was busy with his public activities as a social reformer. His children grew up with the crowd of people around him for ever. In fact, Sita is puzzled by her father's magic, miracles, cures and clinic. She admires, respects and adores him but cannot treat him as her father. She could not understand the mystery at all.

But Anita Desai is subtle in her suggestion that the life of Sita's father was the illustration of the magnifying quality of faith which made life ultimately meaningless. Sita had to face her dying father alone, because JeeVan had left the island a few days earlier and Rekha, within minutes of his death: "It was Sita, alone, who bewildered and confused, was left on the island for someone to arrange the funeral" (61).

Rekha, Sita's elder sister, is spiritually and devotedly closest to her father and helps him fulfil his devotional desire through hymns passionately sung in the large gatherings as she has the voice of a 'goddess'. But Sita is a small fly, because she is not endowed in any exceptional way. Rekha leaves the dying father in search of greener pastures and Sita is left alone to seek her own way of life. Even the description of her physical appearance such as dragging jaw, round shoulders and drooping eyelids liken her with down-to-earth personality, closest to the unexceptional and run of the mill person that everyone comes across in life. But Sita is a stubborn romantic dreamer trying to escape procreation, a very normal human phenomenon.

Sita's perplexing behaviour has another groundwork—her mother deserting them. Sita foolishly imagines that she is without a mother. She is greatly frustrated and becomes disjointed when she learns through her brother Jeevan that their mother has forsaken them and run off to Benares and is leading there a widow's life. She makes resolute attempts to trace her whereabouts but is unsuccessful as she neither knows her name nor remembers her face nor even in possession of a photograph to assist her in her search. This deprivation of motherly care and affection leaves a deep blemish and profound negative impact throughout: "Why had she left her husband whom they called the second Gandhi?" (6).

The intention of her visit to the village, Manori, is built on her repulsion with her immediate environment, her family and the deep abrasions made by the life in the city of Bombay. Her views of the merchant class flow like this: "They are nothing—nothing but appetite and sex. Only food, sex and money matter. Animals..." and again,

> It's all a madness—the boys acting out that scene from the film they saw, fighting each other on the floor; Menaka and her magazines and the way she's torn all those drawings of hers I'd kept so carefully; the ayah taking Karan to that—that roadside dump where all the ayahs sit and gossip and fight; the way you (Raman) laughed because I tried to keep the bird alive; the people here all around us, living here, all round... (36)

The merchant ladies are reminiscent of "elephants, she thought, eating grass, shifting from foot to foot, swaying their trunks, small-eyed, eating" (49). Incidents such as Menaka's destruction of new buds in a potted plant nauseate her.

R.S. Sharma brands Sita as an escapist: "Sita seeks to escape essentially from the cannibalism that is operative, unseen and unobserved, in contemporary city life."[6] Her flight from the mundane reality of her existence is to discover succor and serenity in her childhood home—a place of escape, a sort of dream land, a place of freedom and relief to the psyche of Sita buffeted by the complications of modern life—in the island of Manori. But that is not to be so. The atmosphere there of miracle, magic and spell has evaporated and Sita becomes cynical to the core.

Even the sea as a symbol of life represents adversity and the island is an escape from it. The unendurable and horrendous life is reflected in the feelings towards sea: "There's just the sea—it drowns us or strands us on the sandbar—and there's the island. That's all" (149). The rustling of the leaves of the palm trees, "the sound of battle and the sound of distress" (141), exemplify Sita's own offended and agonizing self, inconsistent between illusion and reality.

The very house, which has been once the seat of miracles, human service, cure of diseases, source of all relief to the despondents, the very temple of God, in the island of paradise, is now 'a waste of ashes', 'the cold remains of the bonfire' her father had blazed', and 'ashes white and waste'. The house is full of 'spider webs' and 'skeletal palm leaves', with the 'odour of bats and mild dew' (28) like undersea cave and discarded shell.

An analysis of Anita Desai's women characters, especially the protagonists, show their vigorous and fervent endeavours at setting sights on spiritual accomplishment which are made obvious through various metaphors—in the case of Sita, it is the metaphor of violence. The episodes or activities or essentials remain as backgrounds but the reactions of these protagonists—moral, spiritual and emotional—find more emphasis. They meddle with the idea as to whether it is possible to reconstruct the social order based on the psyche of women. Sharad Srivatsava is succinct in the assessment that "...in this regard, her novels are, in themselves, a metaphor of deconstruction, for in deconstruction, reconstruction is inherent."[7]

Sita and Maya in *Cry, The Peacock* rummage around for a life of gratification which they are unable to accomplish in the marital context. For them, this realization implies approval of their tender, delicate feelings and emotions and a throbbing life of consciousness and as such what they demand is an insightful approach in others towards them. Sita's retraction is exploratory of her great need for love, the kind of free and absolute love that would encase her.

To Sita, her identifiable ephemeral vision of perfect harmony between a man and woman is uncovered in her recounting to Raman a scene that she has observed of a young woman dying of tuberculosis and being earnestly attended to by a person who loves her. This kind of love transcends the self and makes no claims. It is a love in the face of death, the ultimate human certainty. This kind of communiqué is totally missing between Raman and Sita which stimulates her to retort thus: "What a farce marriage was, all human relationships" (105).

Her ineffective struggles to straighten out the two levels of her survival induce her to have the unrealistic longing of 'keeping' the baby in her womb for ever. At one level, she is a wife and mother. But she is also a person and woman. She discovers that in the structure of citation established by the society, she cannot be a wife and mother without conceding her existence as a person and as a woman.

Sita's return to Bombay after the 'escape' to Manori is not to be miscomprehended as symptomatic of her collapse and dismal surrender. She, in fact, returns with a new perspicacity, a new insight. The visual symbol is highly appealing: "The wind jumped up and buffeted her so that she could not stand still and she began to trail after him, knowing she would follow him, trail of foot prints he had laid out for her" (150).

Sita has become mellow, enduring and animated to cope with the trials and tribulations in life with all its ups and downs. Her tussle is investigative of the "intelligent and sensitive woman's revolt against the male smugness and philistinism trampling all finer values in marital life."[8]

Scrutinized from a feminist thrust of stance, Sita conquers 'personhood' but does not renounce family or society. She has traversed the "female phase in life" which is a phase of self-discovery, a turning inward freed from the dependency of opposition, a search for identity. She has now come to new terms with the family-"new terms with love and with work."[9]

There is categorically no swap or amendment in her assessment of her husband and society. Her return can never be connected with that of Prodigal son's return—a return with the ardent entreaty to be 'accepted'. Sita never conjures up the vision that such an acceptance is meaningful to a woman. Sita's lesson from her experience tells every woman that, in spite of the posture of the society, the new woman must not flee from it.

Anuradha Roy declares "novels however great they are, cannot change or destroy repressive social structures: but by posing questions, by suggesting re-assessment and re-definition, they can help in formulating a consciousness which can, perhaps, ultimately, bring about a constructive change."[10]

Thus Anita Desai undeniably divulges a commendable grasp of the quandary and dilemmas of woman and portrays her own vision of a variegated facet of woman in modern India and her fully stimulated feminine sensibility.

To conclude, Srinivasa Iyengar's prophetic words about Anita Desai's facility and its impact on readers is conspicuous through its manifestation in her works: "Anita Desai's is an original talent that has the courage to go its own way".[11]

References

1. G.D. Barche, 'Facets of Feminism in Indian English Fiction,' *Indian Women Novelists,* Set 3: Vol.1, ed. R.K. Dhawan, New Delhi: Prestige Books, 1995, 9.
2. Ajita Garg, 'Women Doubly Enslaved,' *Social Welfare* (M), Aug. 1988, p. 25.
3. Marx and Engels, 'The Origin of Family, Private Property and State,' *Selected Works,* Moscow: Progress Publishers, 1982, p. 495.
4. A. Hariprasanna, 'An Expression of Feminine Sensibility: Anita Desai's Bye-Bye Blackbird,' *The Indian Journal of English Studies,* Vol.33:1994-95, p. 81.
5. Shanta Krishnaswamy, 'Anita Desai: The Sexist Nature of Sanity,' *The Women in Indian Fiction in English,* New Delhi: Ashish Publishing House, 1984, p. 240.

6. R.S. Sharma, *Anita Desai,* Liverpool: Lucas Publishers, 1988, p. 95.
7. Sharad Srivastava, *The New Woman in Indian English Fiction: A Study of Kamala Markandaya, Anita Desai, Namita Gokhale and Shoba De,* New Delhi: Creative Books, 1996, p. 21.
8. Shyam Asnani, 'New Morality in the Modern Indo-English Novel,' *Indian Women Novelists,* ed. R.K. Dhawan, New Delhi: Sterling, 1990, p. 66.
9. Betty Friedan, *The Second Stage,* New York: Summit Books, 1981, p. 13.
10. Anuradha Roy, *Patterns of Feminist Consciousness in Indian Women Writers,* New Delhi: Prestige Books, 1991, p. 145.
11. K.R. Srinivasa Iyengar, *Indian Writing in English,* New Delhi: Sterling Publishers, 1972, p. 465.

16 K.S. Venkataramani as a Pioneer and the Seminal Themes of the Indo-Anglian Fiction

— Dr. R. Swaminathan

K.S. Venkataramani (1891-1951), "the first Hindu writer in Madras Presidency, who uses the medium of English...."(Brunton 117), was a true Gandhian in actual life. Hailing from Kaveripoompattinam in the fertile Tamil land of Thanjavur district, he could not bear that agriculture had gradually ceased to engage the landlord and peasant. He was unsparing in his criticism of the evils of the system of his days and he was too optimistic that his message alone would provide the solution. He established an ashram known as "Markandaya Ashrama" on the lines of Gandhian ideals.

Keen on observing the simple country folk, Venkataramani had an innate leaning towards the Indian village to hammer all his thoughts into shape. Chandrasekaran describes Venkataramani: "A little head bearing a tiny tuft on its top, an abrupt chin somewhat too small for the face, and a sly glance at the very corner of his spectacled eyes, goes to make or rather mar the personality of Mr. Venkataramani" (92).

> The sketch by Chandrasekaran (1932) says further: 'he is fundamentally generous. His sympathies are ever great for the poor and the needy. His insight into the workings of the human heart does him credit, when he is kind and considerate to all..: He is never harsh in his speech or fiery in his temper. He does not make much of uncompromising principles in life. He is supremely a man of the world.' (94-95).

He used to revise and prune his writings constantly before publication. He is said to have taken nearly seven years to revise his first collection of essays. The impression cited above throws light on the various aspects of Venkataramani's total personality. No doubt, "He is a fine representative of our thought revival and the first Indo-Anglian writer in South India to be crowned with laurels" (95) in his own lifetime. He was a lawyer, a poet, a short-story writer, a novelist, a philosopher, a thinker, a patriot, a true Gandhian and a friend of the needy—all rolled into one.

Venkataramani has written more than ten books in English. They present a wide spectrum of his genius and an impressive variety of his literary tastes. His works can broadly be classified into (a) non-fictional writings and (b) fictional writings. The non-fictional writings of Venkataramani include *Paper Boats* (1921), *On the Sand Dunes* (1923), *Renascent India* (1928), *The Next Rung* (1928), *A Day with Sambhu* (1929), and *After Gandhiji: On Problems* (1948). His fictional writings include the novels *Murugan, The Tiller* (1927), *Kandan, The Patriot* (1932) and a collection of short stories entitled *Jatadharan and Other Stories* (1937).

Non-fictional Writings of K. S. Venkataramani

His non-fictional writings constitute the growth and development of his intellect and sensibility. His first collection of essays *Paper Boats* is a delightful compilation of ten little essays, and each one of them presents some feature of the village life in South India. The first essay, "The Indian Beggar" reminds one of the essays of Lamb or of Lynd and it begins in this typical way: "The Indian Beggar is the most interesting of the world's ragged men. Of all the numerous progeny of poverty, he is the eldest born. Thus entitled to the virtue of the good law of primogeniture, he has inherited the vast estate of the world's wretchedness"(1). The essay is concluded with in defence of begging in a mock-seriousness vein: "If valiant begging disappears from our society, a picturesque side of human nature would be blotted out by unkind hands and a poetic pendant of society broken off by the prose of economic pedantry" (19).

The second essay on "Fisherman" is a notable instance of kindly description and truthful observation. The next essay "Village Cricket" begins with a hilariously overstated claim for the Indian village cricket, unknown to the sophisticated urban world. He says: "Indian village cricket is a picturesque cousin of the English game...It is a pre-historic survival"(41). To Venkataramani, "The Hindu Temple" is an architectural marvel as well as a celestial comfort. "It is ever the dream of his hopes and the hope of his dreams" (41). In the fifth essay "My Little Arunalam", Venkataramani gives a description of his pariah servant Arunachalam "with all sympathy, highlighting the noble qualities of the neglected race" (Gayatri 35).

The next sketch is that of "The Hindu Pilgrim." The Hindu pilgrims fall under two categories: the perpetual pilgrim in quest of the Supreme Being everywhere and the periodic pilgrim, a responsible householder, who always undertakes pilgrimages with his wife and progeny and some poor kindred souls. This sketch of the Hindu Pilgrim foreshadows the memorable character of Sundaram, the station master of Akkur, in Kandan, the Patriot.

"My Grandmother" is the seventh essay which is perhaps the most realistic and the most attractive of these little sketches of village life. As *The Times Literary Supplement reviews*, "A corner of the veil which is always down is lifted and we catch a glimpse of the real household life" (qtd. in *Murugan, the Tiller* 311). "The Grandmother" represents the "preservative power of every joint-Hindu family" and is "a benevolent despot"(Gayatri 41). "My Neighbour" humorously sketches the character and personality of Mr. Pichu Sastri, Venkataramani's neighbour. Pichu Sastri was the last born of thirteen children to his parents and the only surviving one. 'Pichu' in Tamil means 'alms' and he was the 'alms' to the family (Gayatri 45-46).

The next essay, "The Jagath Guru" is an account of the life and teachings of the great Adi Sankara. It also describes the Kamakoti Peetam meaning "Throne of the End of Desires" situated at Canjeewaram. The last essay, "Saraswati's Marriage" vividly gives pictorial account of a Brahmin wedding in South India in the early part of the century. Agree with what Annie Besant (xiv) has said in her Foreword to *The Paper Boats*: "It tells of the life of my village.... The booklet makes us live in the village, and share in its life. The writer is a complete master of English, simple, dainty, with a sense running through the living descriptions." *The New Pearson's* describes Venkataramani as "an artist within his genre, the interpretation of his own people" (qtd. in *Murugan* 312).

On the Sand Dunes, a collection of philosophical reflections on life, appeared in 1923. It is in this book that his reflective mind gets its full expression and "in which the serious philosophical reflections in free verse seldom attain the higher regions of felt thought (Naik 144)." The subtitle "Musings on Life in Free Verse" indicates that it is a long meditative essay on life in free verse. *The Birmingham Weekly* Post Review observes that they are "His snatches of reflection, and aphorism and small word-pictures in poetic prose ...." (qtd. in *Paper Boats*, 127).

On the Sand Dunes saw second edition in March 1933. Venkataramani himself spells out the main theme of these reflections in his Preface to the second edition: "Sand Dunes are never the same even for an hour.... But Sand-Dunes are Sand-Dunes for ever, ever-lasting, ever-changing, ever-fresh, wind-swept and smiling-welcome and pity—to all land-dwellers and to me." Thus, the essential theme of this work is the primordial theme of mutability. While everything changes and nothing is permanent, there is something that remains eternal and impervious in the midst of all these fluxes.

Renascent India was published in October 1928 and a second edition was brought out in December 1929. As *The Federated India* observes, "One feels in reading these pages, not merely the author's mastery of exquisite English, but also his renovating idealism. Venkataramani has done a splendid service by his ruthless discretion of the fundamental bases of modern society" (qtd. in *Murugan* 314).

He appears to give an address from a high pedestal like the ancient Greek orator about a federal government for the Renascent India. Venkataramani's vision of an ideal *Renascent India* depends upon an agenda of rural reconstruction and the creation of a new order of altruistic social workers.

The Next Rung (1928) brings out Venkataramani's interest in the evolution of humanity as a whole. He thinks that the historic encounter of the West and the East is only a rung in the ladder of human evolution. To proceed to the rung, the East must learn from the West, the philosophy of work, and the West must learn from the East, the philosophy of leisure. Iyengar (279) considers both *Renascent India* and *The Next Rung* "a critique of modern civilization from more or less Gandhian point of view."

A Day with Sambhu, first published in February 1929, ran to several editions and has been translated into several Indian languages including Tamil. The book is, in fact, a treatise on education, presented interestingly in the form of a lively conversation. A Sadhu, bound for Rameswaram, happens to be a guest of a young man called Sambhu.

Venkataramani, an ardent Gandhian, advises: "Ahimsa is the noblest rule of conduct that governs our relationships and actions, not only among all created beings" (57). This treatise echoes the philosophy of the thinkers of the 30's like Thoreau and Mahatma Gandhi. Venkataramani "glorifies the kind of education that teaches man to harmonize his life with the nature around him" (Gayatri 101). The need for cultivating the moral, the mental and the physical spheres in a balanced way is also strongly emphasized. Under the influence of Mahatma Gandhi, Venkataramani was one among the young intellectuals "who dreamt of reconstructing rural India into a veritable paradise on earth" (Ibid).

His work *After Gandhiji* (1948) is a realistic descriptive monument of our Indian civilisation—the Indian village life and its time-tested ideals. A rare charm, delicate insight and quaintly felicitous English mark Venkataramani's non-fictional writings. The image of Venkataramani that emerges from his non-fictional writings is that of an idealist whose main obsession in life is strict adherence to Gandhian teachings.

Venkataramani portrays faithfully and fascinatingly the social life of the Gandhian era in his works, idealism writ large on every page. His novels *Murugan, the Tiller* (1927) and *Kandan, the Patriot* (1932) throw light on various problems in India and bring to the knowledge of the West, a highly valuable philosophy of life. These novels deal with themes of typical interest in conjunction with the period in which they were written. However, the novels transcend time, space, and address certain perennial issues in life.

Ramachandran, known as Ramu, the hero of the novel *Murugan, the Tiller* (1927), is idealistic, compassionate and never hesitates to help people in distress. He fails twice in the B.A. examination, despite being industrious. He decides to take to agriculture on the advice of Murugan, the hereditary tiller of his land. However, unprecedented monsoon floods destroy the crops in his fields. At this juncture, his authoritative mother-in-law Meenakshi forces him to apply for a Government job. Before he joins duty as a camp-clerk to Mr. Cadell, the District Collector of Cuddapah, he takes it upon himself to reunite Sita with her wayward husband. Ramu executes his duty as a clerk efficiently. Owing to his mother-in-law's nagging, he has to sell all his land except the coconut grove to Periaswami Iyer, to clear the debts. Ramu makes Murugan the lessee of his coconut grove. In appreciation of his service as a clerk, Ramu is promoted as a Deputy Tahsildar, after three years of service and posted to Dusi, near Canjeevaram. With the cooperation of Mr. Cadell, now a Member of the Revenue Board at Madras, Ramu completes the Dusi-Mamundur Lake Project. This scheme, a brainchild of Ramus, eradicates not only the poverty of the people, but also many a social evil. His next assignment is to deal with the dacoits of the Nagalapuram hills. He firmly believes that the dacoits will lead an honest life, if the Government comes forward with a rehabilitation programme. With the permission of the Government, he appropriates the 'treasure' of the dacoits amounting to Rupees three lakhs, and embarks upon the Nagalapuram Settlement and Irrigation Project. He allots three acres of land to each dacoit family and helps each to turn a new leaf in his life.

Ramu's college-friend, Kedari, rises to the pinnacle of success in his career as a lawyer, but he falls due to his corrupt political activities and becomes bankrupt. He too joins Ramu in the rehabilitation of the dacoits and chooses to live with them. Sita, now a widow with a son, is the owner of every inch of the cultivable land in Alavanti. Inspired by Ramu's altruistic deeds, Sita decides to give three acres of land to each of the families in Alavanti. At the Nagalapuram Settlement, Ramu wants to impart natural education instead of the usual type of education. Forgoing his promotion as a District Collector, he decides to live with the rehabilitated dacoits.

Kandan, the Patriot (1932), as the title explicitly states, runs along the theme of patriotism. Kandan, an Oxford scholar, who is disappointed in love, vows to work for the freedom of his motherland. He gives up voluntarily the career of an Indian Civil Servant at the probation period. From Natal, he returns to his native village of Tillaiyadi. Leading an austere Gandhian life in his Ashram at Akkur, he tries to reform the untouchables and others, who are victims of social evils. Kandan wants to replace the toddy shop by a night school. Chockalinga Mudaliar, an extravagant landlord, a member of the District Board and a persecutor of the working-classes, causes many problems to Kandan.

Rajeswari Bai known as Rajee and Rangaswami called Rangan were Kandan's fellow-scholars at Oxford. Rajee is now a staunch freedom fighter and is willing to marry her lover Rangan, if only he gives up his present position as Assistant Collector and joins the struggle for freedom. Rangan is transferred to Tanjore from Guntur, because he is very lenient towards the freedom fighters there. Rajee and Rangan, who travel in the same train bound for Tranquebar, are held up at Akkur due to a train collision there the previous night and are pleasantly surprised to meet Kandan there. Under instructions from the Government, a C.I.D follows Rangan to spy on his movements.

Rangan's present association with Kandan kindles further his patriotic feelings. He camps at the Tranquebar fort with Kandan, Rajee and others. Reports about his affinity with and sympathy towards the patriots irk the Government. As a punishment, Rangaswami I.C.S. is transferred to Palani as Settlement Officer, which serves as the last straw in his emotional battle. He sends in his resignation and joins the freedom movement. A meeting is planned at Tranquebar Maidan in which he is to give an address. The police are unable to stop people coming from different places to Tranquebar. The speakers are not allowed to get on the dais. In the melee that follows, the police fire at the crowd and Kandan lays down his life for the country.

Gandhiji has said: "Non-violence is the first article of my faith. It is also the last article of my creed." 'Realization of Truth is not at all possible without Ahimsa' (Non-violence) (*A Thought for the Day 2*).

The novels of K. S. Venkataramani are punctuated with the article of non-violence. For instance, Kandan is "a saint, noble soul (13)." Gandhiji knew that drinking aggravates violence. So Kandan endeavours to eradicate in earnest, the evil of drinking among the downtrodden for it has been the unmaking of their family. He makes a fervent appeal to them: "Now is the time for you, O, Nanda, Irula and Nalla, to change your habits and make men of yourselves. Refuse to drink" (33-34). Chockalinga Mudaliar who is unkind and arrogant, ill-treats and deprives the pannaiyals (farm-labourers) of their legitimate rights. The pannaiyals plan to resort to violence to fight for justice. But Kandan warns them in time: "That way lies red ruin, ruin to all, ruin to my work. It would profit neither but only waste your own wealth, the food of people. Peace begets peace; war begets war." However, his advice falls on the deaf ears of the pannaiyals who, at last, in the absence of Kandan, burn down 2000 kalams of paddy and twenty haystacks.

In *Murugan the Tiller,* Ramu, the Revenue official is deputed to quell the violence of the dacoits at Nagalapuram hills. He goes straight to the den of the dacoits deep in the forest. The dacoits surround him and his party. They disarm the officials but are extremely hospitable. Incidentally, Murugan, the hereditary tiller of Ramu's land is the chieftain. Murugan faces a series of crises after Ramu left for Cuddapah and is forced to join the dacoits under the influence of Thoppai. Ramu understands that Murugan and others are basically good and are prepared to turn a new leaf, if a chance of rehabilitation is thrown at them. Ramu, eschewing violence, adopts the Gandhian ahimsa to win over the dacoits. This event echoes one such real episode encountered by Gandhi in life. Murugan says, "Violence is not the way to win in life anywhere...." (195).

Gandhian simplicity is proverbial. Gandhiji stands for simple life. Ramu of *Murugan, the Tiller* is a character that has been cast in the Gandhian mould of simplicity. While he stays with Kedari at Madras, he abhors pomp. Kedari is a spendthrift and refuses to emulate Ramu's ethics of simplicity. Ramu says, "But Kedari, pardon me, if I feel at times like an older brother, at least in age, as I am, and warn you against the costly habits you are now cultivating" (38). Murugan, the servant, is aware of the virtue of simplicity. When Ramu feels that hard work goes unrewarded in studies, Murugan consoles him: "This one veli will yield double, it its lord is here. It is enough to lead a simple and true life." Ramu happily responds: "I'll peacefully settle down in this village and toil with you, sans books, sans coffee club, sans friends, sans teachers, sans cribs .... Murugan, I will surely follow your advice.

I've now learned enough to know that virtue dwells only among the humblest folk of the land" (7). It is obvious that Venkataramani, influenced by Gandhi's ideal of simplicity, wishes to model Ramu's life on the lines of Gandhian simplicity.

Rajeswari Bai of *Kandan, the Patriot* is "the only daughter of a millionaire and the darling of an ancient house." She is above all a dedicated Congress worker. When she travels by train to Tranquebar with Rangaswami I.C.S., she is very particular to travel 'third' (69). When Rangan insists on first class travelling, she decisively says, "No, no, Ranga, I carry my own things - not very many. Besides I am travelling third."Travelling third", according to Rangan, is hell, "third class is worse than cattle-pen; it is hell; slime, spit and filth" (69-70). Here one can find that Gandhian simplicity has become part of Rajeswari's sensibility.

Gandhian Patriotism

The very title of Venkataramani's second novel *Kandan the Patriot* obviously spells out the main theme of the novel. Kandan is one of the patriots who attach great value to their country's freedom. He "threw up the assured and kingly career of an Indian Civil Servant at the probation period"(39). In the words of Rajeswari,: "Kandan's was a splendid sacrifice." In a letter to her, Kandan wrote in lyric prose about his resolution "to dedicate his life to the uplift of his mother country" (105).

When Chockalinga Mudaliar takes aggressive steps to ruin Kandan, he finds it no easy job to fight down the great cause of which Kandan is "but a servant or the spirit of freedom that stirs the life of New India"(31). Thus, the main characters embody the spirit of patriotism and feel happy to be willingly brought under the glorious influence of Mahatma Gandhi.

> Rajeswari is no less patriotic than Kandan. One can visualize the flame of patriotism burning through Rajeswari's words: "The love of my mother land has driven off my mind all thoughts of love of worldly things. The call of my country has changed all thoughts of selfish life into deeds of service and the love of home has changed to a love of the whole world. A vow of Bramhacharya has seized me till freedom's cause is won" (109)

She feels that Rangaswami must quit the British Service and join the freedom struggle because, "It's a sin for an Indian to toil at the desk in these critical days when the making of a New India is going on before our very eyes under the glorious leadership of the greatest living man in the world" (22).

Gandhian vision of India is the vision of Ram Raj wherein all are equal socially, economically and morally. To him, the means must justify the ends. He fought against so many social evils of the day—poverty, untouchability, communal hatred, religious intolerance, illiteracy, male- chauvinism and moral degradation. Like Gandhiji, Kandan realizes that India lives in its villages. He fights against rural backwardness. Drinking is a habit that spoils the rural poor and paves the way for many social problems. Gandhiji favoured prohibition as a starting point for his social transformation. Kandan "gathers all the idle fellows, knaves, and thieves together; with a view to making men of them", he advises them "to change your habits and make men of yourselves. Refuse to drink. Let us give up the toddy shop and in its place erect a night school and I'll be proud to become your pial teacher" (30).

Kandan's heart goes in sympathy with the untouchables who are the "Children of the soil, famished, and in rags, in dirt and poverty" (182). His zeal to improve the lot of the poor breathes through his words to Padma: "All I crave for is economic equality and no chance for one to exploit another" (Ibid). Kandan agrees with Gandhiji while he says: "The future government of man shall be carried on only by two agencies-the League of Nations and the Village Panchayat or the Urban Council. Decentralisation shall be complete and life-giving" (251).

"Woman", Gandhi says, "is more fitted than man to make explorations and take bolder action in ahimsa. For the courage of self-sacrifice, woman is any day superior to man". (1968, 1) Rajeswari is one such ideal woman. When her lover Rangaswami, an Assistant Collector, wants to serve his country by remaining within the Government. Rajeswari speaks assuredly and ideally: "All that you say, Ranga, is good when Swaraj is won and freedom for all is gained. You can never work for the poor, till the whole vicious system is changed" (28-29). She is prepared to risk her love for Ranga for the sake of her love for the motherland: "I'm going to work in the very district to which you now go out as Collector.

Let the very hand which should tie the marital knot sentence me to prison—it is a rare pleasure, if such be God's will" (Ibid).

Education is essential for a nation's progress; but according to Gandhiji, "education which does not mould character is absolutely worthless."(*A Thought for the Day* 414). Kedari, a first-class graduate and now a successful lawyer, makes a good example of a bad man. To him: "Civilized life is a game of skill in clothing" (164). He is a slave of human vanities and he cannot afford to go out without a hired car. In his opinion, the car owners too "must live and have their share of the common loot" (Ibid). Even with his high qualification, Kedari stoops very low in morality. Ramu of *Murugan, the Tiller* too has a vision of Gandhian India. He feels that the British, "Shaped our education to serve a definite end, clerkship in government. The higher aspects are ignored" (136). Mr. Cadell accepts Ramu's creed that "in an agricultural country like India rural reconstruction is the primary thing" (155). With this objective in view, Ramu begins his work: "Let me begin village reform with this chaste and loving wife" (60). This he does by restoring to Sita her husband. One can hear Gandhian echoes in Ramu's words: "Poverty is the parent of crime. The peasants of the last generation are turned dacoits now .... I can restore peace and prosperity in one year to something like twenty five villages to a quarter of a million souls" (160).

K. S. Venkataramani intends to draw a parallel between Gandhiji and Kandan. Gandhiji went to England for higher studies. Later, he went to South Africa to support the oppressed there. He returned to India to lead the freedom struggle. At last, he fell down to the bullets and attained martyrdom. Similarly, Kandan studied at Oxford and returned to his motherland to dedicate his life for Indian Freedom. He describes himself: "... I am but a servant or the spirit of freedom that stirs the life of New India" (31). Pavadai, a minor character at Akkur, speaks with feeling:

> Kandan is a saint, a noble soul, I saw him in his ashram this morning distributing charka and khaddar to the suffering poor. ... Kandan is the man to make men of us .... There is a magnet glow in his eyes, a purifying fire in his speech.

Nallan goes a step further and deifies Kandan: "... there comes Kandan,—yes, with the pure glow of kindness in his face, as you say. Let us all prostrate before him" (14).

Kandan voices Gandhiji's philosophy when he makes a fervent appeal to his followers: "Bramhacharya alone can lead us on to victory in the cause to which we are wedded. Till Swaraj is won, let us take this vow" (254). "Politics are wooden now.... The motives of action should be spiritualized" (248).

> Kandan too is shot dead ultimately like Gandhiji. In the words of Sarasvati: "Kandan had died a patriotic saint. Let his Samadhi rest by the side of the tank in the very coconut garden where the toddy-shop once stood. Let an ashram grow there for rural service, for the uplift and joy of the million poor. Kandan lives the deathless life of a Patriot, a martyr" (281).

In conclusion, Venkataramani is an immensely sincere writer, with deep sentiments and ideals. As a true patriot, under the influence of Gandhiji, the moral colossus, Venkataramani cannot but have the Indian village as the setting for his novels, Gandhi-type characters for his heroes, and his own fellowmen, both high and low, the good and evil for the other characters in his novels. While Murugan is a model practitioner of Gandhian economics, Kandan is a symbol of Gandhian politics. The scenes may shift from village to town and town to village in his novels and the characters may be caught in different situations, but the message is invariably the same—that of the Gandhian Philosophy of selfless sacrifice, patriotism and compassion. The Indian Freedom Struggle culminated in an epoch-making victory, thanks to the spontaneous participation of the vast multitude of the faceless Indians. As a fitting tribute to these unknown citizens, Venkataramani dedicates his novel *Kandan* to them: "To the unknown volunteer in India's fight for freedom."

As a committed writer, Venkataramani knew what ailed his society and his vision echoes the words of Tiruvalluvar (*Couplet* 948):

> Consider the disease and its root and the means to curing it, and then set about the cure with every precaution (Aiyar 232).

Works Cited

Aiyar, Sri V.V.S. Trans. *Tirukkural*. Tirupparaithurai: Sri Ramakrishna Tapovanam, 1989.

Brunton, Paul. *A Search in Secret India*. London: Arrow Books, 1965.

Gandhi, M.K. *A Thought for the Day*. Faridabad: Publications Division, Government of India, 1968.

______________ . *Thus Spake Bapu*. New Delhi: National Committee for Gandhi, Centenary, 1968.

Gayathri, R. "K. S. Venkataramani: A Study." M.Phil. Diss. Bharathidasan University, 1988.

Iyengar, Srinivasa, K. R. *Indian Writing in English*. New Delhi: Sterling Publishers Private Limited, 1983.

Mukherjee, Meenakshi. *The Twice Born Fiction*. New Delhi: Arnold Heinnomann Publishers (India) Private Ltd., 1974.

Naik, M. K. "Gandhiji and Indian Writing in English." *Critical Essays on Indian Writing in English*. eds. Naik, M.K. Desai, S.K. Amur, G. S. Madras: The Macmillan Co., of India Ltd., 1977.

Ramamurti, K.S., *Rise Of The Indian Novel In English*. New Delhi: Sterling Publishers Private Limited, 1987.

Venkataramani, K. S. *Paper Boats*. Madras: Ganesh & Co., 1925.

______________ . *On The Sand Dunes*. Madras: Ganesh & Co., 1923.

______________ . *Renascent India And The Next Rung*, Madras: Svetaranya Ashrama, 1928.

______________ . *A Day With Sambhu*. Madras: Svetaranya Ashrama, 1933.

______________ *Murugan, The Tiller*. Madras: Svetaranya Ashrama, 1927.

______________ *Kandan, The Patriot*. Madras: Svetaranya Ashrama, 1934.

17 An Appraisal of Salman Rushdie's *Midnight's Children*

— Rakhi Janghel

The term "Indo-Anglican" is used to denote original literary creation in the English language by Indians. Today there are a large number of educated Indians who use the English language as a medium of creative exploration and expression of their experience of life. Their writing has now developed into a substantial body of literature in its own right and it is this literature which is referred to as Indian English Literature.

Salman Rushdie is one of those Indo-Anglican writers who has given a wide picture of the awareness of Indian history and political changes in the nation from 1910 to 1977 which has an autobiographical touch also. Its ethos lies in the choice of subject which is very Indian.

Sentiments, feelings, thoughts and construction of the novel lies in the creative use of language which is incomparable. Salman Rushdie's *Midnight's Children,* is a novel on India that deals with Indian independence, partition and social problems. It is a political novel remarkably covering three generations of Adam Aziz, Saleem Sinai and Adam Sinai from 1910 to 1977.

Probably the most sensational event of the 1980s in colonial and post-colonial studies was the publication of Salman Rushdie's voluminous novel *Midnight's Children*. Indian novel in English was a quarter century after Independence actually going to lie down and die. But then came Rushdie and as he was able to proclaim within a decade Indo-Anglican Literature had come up in the 1980s.

Lets us all recall the famous midnight speech delivered by Jawaharlal Nehru on 15 August 1947 in the Central Hall of the Indian Parliament:

> At the stroke of the midnight hour, when the world sleeps. India will awake to life and freedom. A moment comes, which comes but rarely in history, when we step out from the old to the new, when an age ends, and when the soul of a nation long suppressed, finds utterance... We end today a period of ill fortune and India discovers herself again. (Ali 76).

Indians have at last tasted the most awaited sweetness of independence. At the very 'stroke of midnight' a child and the birth of a nation guides us towards. Salman Rushdie's Booker Prize (1981) as well as the James Tait Black Memorial Prize winning novel *Midnight's Children* (1980), a consummate masterpiece of its own kind. In this brilliant phantasmagoric saga, both child and nation go through the pangs of birth, the tantrums of childhood, the traumas of adolescence and the anomalies of adulthood, the novelist has woven dreams into reality, mystery into magic and truth into fantasy. The comic and highspirited novel about a fantastic protagonist whose birth coincided with the independence of India. *Midnight's Children* was gradually appropriated into a theoretical discourse about nation, history and their narrativity. According to Neil ten Kortenaar, *Midnight's Children* by opening out a range of possibilities, exposes the functionality, the contractedness of all the metaphors and narrative conventions implied in national history. Examples range form the central metaphors of the novel—the 'birth' of the nation and the 'body' of the nation to scores of minor tropes like 'freezing' of assets or sweeping something 'below the carpet', etc. history-as-shards of memory was the flavour of the decade and fantasy or to call it by its newer name, 'magic realism', became all the rage, thus given an new dimension by Rushdie in his novel.

In the annals of Indo-English writing, except Salman Rushdie no writer has been able to hug the limelight continuously forms the very first rise as a novelist of international repute. Yes, Rushdie achieved milestones in his literary career but has earned the disrepute of being the most controversial writer with the publication of each of his work ever since he was accorded world's acclaim for his oversized novel, *Midnight's Children*. The very first paragraph of *Midnight's Children* sets up three levels of narration-fairy tale ("once upon a time"), autobiography ("I was born in Doctor Nalikar's Ursing Home") and history ("India's arrival at independence"). The interplay among the generic conventions of each mode is sustained throughout the three parts and thirty chapters of the novel.

The life and experiences of three generations of a Sinai Family, staying in Srinagar, Amritsar, Agra, Bombay and Karachi is portrayed in the novel. The protagonist 'midnight child' Saleem Sinai works at a pickle factory and narrates the events and his experiences to his wife Padma. The narration of the major events like Quit India Movement, Cabinet Mission, Muslim League's activities, riots, Five Years plan, Pakistan war, liberation of Bangladesh and the sacred relic of Hazratbal Mosque ushers the dynamisms of the protagonist as well as the novelist. But does Saleem Sinai's character represent Salman Rushdie's own character? The novelist boldly affirms that as far as autobiography is concerned, Saleem and he shares certain things like they grew up in the same part of the same city and at the same time, but Saleem never really felt to him like a self-portrait. The novel deals with the multifaceted colours of India with ups and downs, films, mythology, politics, religion, marriage, friendship, enmity and so on. India is presented in variety of situations and moods right form Kashmir to Bombay and Karachi to Dacca. Every dimension of the story is different but the form remains intact, thus proving the artistic excellence of Rushide.

The great diversity of themes, narrative technique and stylistic devices that have gone into the making of *Midnight's Children,* and the intricacy of its formal arrangement, seem to defy and attempt at a comprehensive analysis of its structural pattern. This paper however attempts to draw out certain basic structural motifs and pattern of narrative design underlying the novel's close approximation to the variegated collective life of the Indian subcontinent during the turbulence of its modern history.

The first thing that strikes one about *Midnight's Children* is its sheer size and scope. For over four hundred crammed pages, the novel deploys a named cast of more than seventy, occupies a stage stretching from Kashmir, south to Bombay and from Karachi, east to Dacca, and encompasses the history of India from independence to the state of emergency decreed by Indira Gandhi. Rushdie himself has said of the novel:

> One reason the book is so long is... the idea of the novel being something that includes as much as possible. It seems to me

> really that there are only two kinds of novel. There are novels which proceed on the basis of excluding most of the world, of plucking that one strand out of the universe and writing about that. Or there are novels in which you try to include everything, what Henry James called 'the loose baggy monsters' of fiction. (2)

Saleem Sinai was born at midnight on August 15, 1947—the very instant that India attained her independence. Together in this brilliant, phantasmagoric saga, nation and child go though the pangs of birth, the tantrums of childhood, the traumas of adolescence, and the anomie of adulthood. Salman Rushdie has woven dreams into reality, mystery into magic, and truth into fantasy.

Rushdie's treatment of history form the 'underside', exposing the differential impact of events of different section of the population. The view of history which argues that rather than concentrate on 'the most capricious and delusive' 'short time span' which deals only with major events and frontline actors, historical study should move from surface to the depth, form event. In *Midnight's Children* India's hour of independence, for instance, is projected by snippets of Nehru's speech in the Parliament interspersed with Amina's labour pains, street celebration, ravaging fires, police hunts and desperate railway crowds. Such montage, representing the writer's multiple vision, dislodges history form chronometric time to expose the often contradictory realities hidden its official unlinear versions. Rushdie further believes that personal experience is the only representative of truth. Therefore the mercurochrome stains on Adam Aziz must represent India spilled by the British, and the compulsory sterilization of the Midnight's Children must certify the repressive nature of the emergency.

Midnight's Children runs into three parts. Part I concerns itself with the events that took place in India from 1915 to1947. All the major historical events from 1915 to1947 are beautifully interrelated... the Jallianwallah Bah Massacre, Muslim League and its communal policies, the role of the nationalist Muslim who opposed the idea of Pakistan, Quit India Movement the arrival of Mount Batten, the partition of the country and the consequent riots and the bloodshed. Saleem naively makes the dividing line between the old world and new. Saleem's autobiography is, in fact, the story of those children who are privileged to be both masters and victims of their time. His narrative is thus both a story of his own life and a mirror of the nation.

Part of the novel begins with the financial crisis faced by the family of Ahmed Sinai. After few trail and tribulation, the members of Ahamad Sinai's family migrate to Pakistan with a view to setting in Karachi permanently. They become victims of 1965-war. Part also deals with the childhood to adolescents who reflect the division of free India itself especially between 1947 and 1965. All the national events of consequence during this period of the countries of the post-colonial history are linked with Saleem's career. The assassination of Mahatma Gandhi, India's five year plans, reorganization of Indian states and language riots, the Chinese aggression, the theft of the holy relic in Srinagar's Hazartbal mosque, Nehru's death and the Indo-Pak war of 1965. At the autobiographical level, this section traces the ups and downs in the fortunes of Sinai's family, the birth of Saleem's sister the disintegration of Midnight's Children conference, the death of Adam Aziz and uncle Hamif and the revelation of Mary's crime which exposes saleem as an imposter and shatters his dream world. The Sinai's message to Pakistan, where Saleem reaches a stimulator's, adulthood and witnesses the removal of his family in the war of 1965. Saleem's narration of the evolution of India since independence is punctuated with many events which shook the nation, while his treatment of the history of Pakistan in full episodes of political nature. Rushdie noticed a downward slide in the past, independent India, particularly after the demise of Nehru. Progress of the country yielded to fanaticism and steamed growth and the political atmosphere. With the decay of the myth of the nation, Saleem was haunted by doubt and cynicism.

Part of the book, which runs like a fantasy, dwells upon politics directly, exaggerating the Emergency operations. Saleem grows along with India with all her excesses of emergency, her inner turbulence and the political suppression. Thus, Rushdie's *Midnight's Children* exhibits ironically the contemporary events that took place in India. Part, is primarily on emergency operations and brutalities in India during the seventies. Surprisingly, the fortunes of the protagonist are similar to those of the post-independent India. Rushdie weaves contemporary events—political and historical—into the main spectrum of the novel to produce the singleness of effect. As the narrator in the novel observes: "I must work fast, faster than Scheherazade, if I am to end up meaning—yes, meaning-something I admit it: above all things, I fear absurdity." (4)

These lines of the protagonist throw light on Rushdie's view of a novel. Saleem, the protagonist was born in the city of Bombay...once upon a time....on August 15, 1947. And the time....at the precise instant of India's arrival at independence. (3)

Saleem narrates the story of his grandfather, Adam Aziz, a young doctor who returns from Germany with a good medical degree. Adam is in search of his mooring like other Muslims of the times. One fine morning, he is taken to the house of Ghani Sahib, an affluent landlord. He bends his body and examines the patient thoroughly. Ironically, he marries her later with "A-1 fine dowry."

Soon Adam gets the job of a doctor at Agra University: While he is shifting his family to Agra, he witnesses the Jallianwala Bagh Massacre in Amritsar. The authorial voice runs thus: "I confess....I have noticed a thin crack, like a hair, appearing in may wrist, beneath the skin....No matter. We all owe death a life"(36). The narrative account here is in the shape of a selective recalling of the past from the vantage point of the present. The narrative in Part III becomes less digressive and the political satire more devastating. Saleem with his dream of saving the nation from her fate is drowned in politics which excels him and leaves him impotent. Dictatorial rule between 1975 and 1977 is damaged, because Indian reality betrayed the country's secular democratic ideals. The hopes of the nation generated at the moment of independence were drained with the castration of the Midnight's Children by Indira Gandhi. This disillusioned and impotent Saleem retires to the privacy of a pickle factory and decides to preserve his version of India's history for future generation before his demise. Saleem's progress from unlimited optimism to disillusionment which parallels the journey of independence from an optimistic nation to a despairing state, is a telling comment on the post-colonial history of the country. The title *Midnight's Children* drawn from the hour of India's independence on 15 August 1947, suggests both the promise of a new future that thousands of children symbolized and failure of the post-independence generation to fulfil that promise and realize their potential, the noble mansion of free India where all her children can dwell about which Nehru has famously said in his speech at that momentous hour. She freed children, betrayed the idea of a unified and secular India with their confusion and internal rivalry. Their story is in fact about these broken promises made to be broken. Another remarkable aspect of the book is its remarkable combination of the realist's background and fantasy. At once, a celebration and an elegy of India and her pluralistic culture, this remarkable novel remains a source of inspiration as well as a challenge to future novelists to emulate its success.

In this novel, the novelist ingeniously weaves the personal story of Saleem and his growth into the story of India and her development. Owing to the forces of circumstances, the parents of Saleem leave for Karachi with a view to settling down there permanently. Soon Saleem records the important events that led to the escalation in the relation between India and Pakistan.

> Entirely without my help, India conquered Goa.....I played no part in the acquisition of large-scale and for Pakistan, nor was I to blame for Sino-Indian border skirmishes in the Aksai-chin region of Ladakh: the Indian census of 1961 revealed a literacy level of 23.7 percent..and in the election of 1962, the All India Congress won 361 out of 494 seats in the Lok Sabha, and over 61 percent of all seats assembly seats (351).

Rushdie's *Midnight's Children* is a sort of comic epic genre, a form which is a fusion of Homeric, mythic and tragic connotations. This novel spreads through six decades and almost three generations of India's pre and post-independence history. It is an epic in the sense that it tries to describe or contain an India whose stories are too innumerable to be contained. Throughout the book, one finds the novelist stepping towards that involvement with mighty events and public lives from which 'I would never again be free....never, until the widow. In this novel surprising, ends are contained in the beginning, and beginnings in the ends. As each end is the beginning of a new story, the narrative is circular and neverending. Moreover, this is an epic that cannot contain all the untold stories that are waiting to be told. One finds the epic form becoming a strategy of liberation and the coming becoming painful to be expressed. There is the tragedy of Adam Aziz depicted in comic, mythic and so real terms.

Thus, Rushdie's *Midnight's Children* is an ironic commentary on the major political events that took place between 1947 and 1978. Like a historian, Rushdie records major historical events and like an artist, he recreates history also. The narrative and the theme go together presenting the personal as well as the untold story of the Indian subcontinent. It has to be admitted that *Midnight's Children* gives a fairly authentic history of contemporary India in the "matter of facts."

William Walsh rightly points out that the huge purpose of Salman Rushdie's Midnight's Children "is the personification and realization of Indian life. the novel is a piece of fiction faction by one born in India but settled in abroad who tries to recreate his homeland mixing memory and desire, fact and fantasy, reality and vision, time and timelessness." Rushdie suggestively remarks:

> And on such suspicious generalization may be that writers in my position exile or emigrants or expatriates are haunted by some sense of loss some wage to reclaim to look back even at the risk of being mutated into pillions of salt, but if we' do look back, we must also do in the knowledge...

As we may recall the three founding fathers of the Indian Novel in English R.K.Narayan, Mulk Raj Anand and Raja Rao had all risen simultaneously in the mid1930s, they seemed to have reached if not passed their peak by the 1960s and what may now in his sight be termed as the middle generation of novelists, Ruth Jhabvala, Anita Desai, Arun Joshi, etc. In the 1980s Rushdic was the best one.

The chief reason for the spectacular resurgence of the Indian novel in English since 1981 is undoubtedly Rushdie himself. Fantasy or to call it by its newer name, magic realism, became all the rage history as fiction was the flavour of the decade, down to a use of mercurochrome into a protagonist, belonging to a minority community and to valourize, generally the experience of minorities became the correct thing to do as it had hardly ever been before at least not since Dr. Aziz hosted those two English ladies at the Malabar caves to his own ruin. English became through the hype and the prizes and the astronomical advance payment on royalties, the literary language of India most keenly and covetously embraced by the ambitious young, for example, those studying at St. Stephen's College. What has followed Rushdie has been a literary stampede, demonstrating that in the matter of literary aspiration as much as in more mundane nothing succeeds like success.

In *Midnight's Children* Rushdie has presented the world with certainly the most talked about and probably the subcontinent since *A Passage to India*. He has also presented the academic world with what seems almost textbook examples of all that post-modernist criticism tells us should be found in any self-respecting contemporary novel.

The novel does expose the functionality of the nation and of its history, but the denial of the possibility of literal truth does not deny the nation; where there is no literal truth we must put our faith in fictions. All we have are fictions but fictions deserve our assent and others do not.

Thus on the one hand we have a novel held together by a pattern of similarity and contrast between the characters, by the single word of its title, and by a single minor character that becomes a metaphor for the theme announced history of an entire nation. It is driven relentlessly to its conclusion by one overriding message. It is, in a word, a Muslim novel. And on the other hand we have a novel, which, like Hinduism, tries to contain everything—a novel by a narrator who is turning his life into a piece of fiction and discussing the process as he does so.

In the last part of the novel saleem is enlisted in the Pakistani army as a 'man-dog' on account of his extraordinary sensitive sense of smell. Saleem's transmogrification into a man-dog suggests some deep self-loathing. In this episode the narrative slides almost completely into a dream. Another episode in which Saleem gets lost in the Sunderbans of the Ganges reveals 'absurd fantasy' and 'surrendered to the terrible phantasms of the dream of forest' (MC 363). He enters a magic world space and time disappears (MC 359).

Rushdie's narrative mode thus lies in the claims of realism and fantasy. An early articulation of this appears in *Midnight's Children* in the context of films, which make their presence felt because it is a novel steeped in the spirit of Bombay and it cannot escape the city's biggest cultural production. In fact, the very genesis of the novel has been described by the author in the film diction of the fifties. "I wanted to restore the past to myself, not in the faded greys of old family album snapshots, but whole in cinemascope and glorious Technicolor. 'Rushdie forwards a theme song from a famous film 'Shree 420' for Saleem: "Mera Joota hai-Japani" i.e., In Rushdie's own neat translation:

> O, my shoes are Japanese
> These trousers English, if you please
> On my head, red Russian hat
> My heart's Indian for all that.

In *Midnight's Children,* the Indian Independence is represented through refraction of the colours of the Indian flag onto national celebration (extravagant "saffron rockets" and "green sparkling rain") and the bodies of women giving birth: "green-skinned" "whites of eyes... shot with saffron."Significant juxtapositions and identitites; woman's plain with communal joy, human with nation birth woman's body as the national tricolour flag can be noted. In the Delhi sections of *Midnight's Children* the imagined India reappears in the visual space of the bioscope, the Dilli Dekho Machine that shows children the collage of a unified India:

> Inside the peepshow of Lifafa Dass were pictures of the Taj Mahal, and Meenakshi temple, and the holy Ganges... untouchables being touched; educated persons sleeping in large numbers on railway lines. (MC 84).

Every character in the novel has a morbid association. Saleem's aunt is 'lasicivious', his cousin 'were matresses'. There is also 'witch prvati', then there is also the incorribigle fascination of Rushdie for juggling with words like 'Chamcha' and 'ignoble ends.' Rushdie in an interview told Rani Dharker,' I have always thought of fantasy as only being useful as way of enriching realism and not as an end in itself. ("An Interview with Salman Rushdie," New Quest 35). 'The titular word 'midnight' in itself is the province of fantasy, a dreamlike recreation of the actual world. Fantasy is also an escape from the outside "midday" public world which threatens the quality of individual sensibility. The political leaders of India, Pakistan and Bangladesh acquired the quality of figures of fantasy in the novelist's creative hands:

> ....he engaged in political chitchat, and declared himself a firm admirer of Mrs. Gandhi, largely because of his hatred for her opponent Morarji Desai, who was intolerably ancient, drank his own urine, had skin which rustled like rice paper, and as Chief Minister of Bombay, had once been responsible for the banning of alcohol and prosecution of young goondas..... (MC 408).

This novel by Salman Rushdie is unparallelled and incomparable and will remain in the hearts of Indians forever, because it gives the real ethos of Indian writing in English which we can cherish in our memories forever. This novel represents a Muslim as a real Indian who has written the novel with reference to Indian ethos without being partial. Therefore this novel is loveable for every Indian. And to understand the Indian ethos of the novel, one has to go through it deeply—only then one could understand that how beautifully Rushdie has patched the various Indian concepts together and provides the real picture of post-independent India, how it was deprived of all types of facilitation, how after a great struggle got freedom. The pain of division of the nation into two parts inflicted on it is shown with great brilliance, intellect and Indianness.

True to fact, an ideal novel needs an excellent input for an outstanding output, and also to be unique we must tread the path not taken. To blame an author for his books arousing controversies is not at all justified. Along with the outraged readers, the media should be equally blamed for the same. Is it relevant to mark a creative writer like Rushdie as a controversial writer? The answer lies exceptionally on an individual's viewpoint, that how far they have understood the text. It is the genius of a prolific writer like Salman Rushdie to employ history for building the web of romance and fantasy. The narrator hero Saleem Sinai is handcuffed to the nation's history and also recounts his career by using events of history. The birth of the hero and the nation takes place at the same time, so their fate too is linked together. Actually in writing this novel, the novelist's aim was to relate private lives to public events and to explore the limits of individuality in a country as big, as populous and as culturally variegated as India.

Rushdie has sharply focused the space and time of the Indian subcontinent from 1915 to 1977.' There is a line in *Midnight's Children* (1980) thus, which demonstrates how epic fable, national events, family saga, advertisements, film, popular songs, newspaper clippings parody and gossip could all be gathered up in one comprehensive sweep that is comic, historic and mythic at the same time. Last but not least, Salman Rushdie ought to be ranked as a 'glittering novelist' with startling imaginative and intellectual resources, a master of perpetual story telling. His *Midnight's Children* has become 'a dazzlingly written novel, a fascinating history lesson, and an engrossing story.'

Works Cited

Mukherjee, Meenakshi, *Rushdie's Midnight's Children: A Book of Readings.* Delhi: Pencraft International,1999.

_______________, *Rushide's Midnight's Children,* Jain Anurag, New Delhi, 1999.

Pathak, R.S. *Modern Indian Novel in English.* New Delhi:Creative Books, 1999.

Rushdie, Salman. *Midnight's Children.* 1980. New York: Penguin, 1991.

Taneja, G.R., and R.K. Dhawan. *The Novels of Salman Rushdie.* New Delhi: Prestige Books, 1992.

18 Indo-Anglian Drama: Sources, Themes and Techniques

— Dr. Ketaki Goswami

In any discourse of Indo-Anglian drama, one must take into account the contributions of the contemporary playwrights writing in the vernacular medium. Indian drama in English translations have seen daring innovations and technical virtuosity. Among the established playwrights one may refer to with pride the names of Mohan Rakesh, Badal Sircar, Girish Karnad, Vijay Tendulkar and Mahesh Dattani. Sri Nirad Chaudhuri points out the contribution of Mohan Rakesh towards the fruition of Indian drama in the followings lines:

> With Mohan Rakesh Hindi drama makes a departure from pseudo-modernism and traditional symbolism to the drama of 'non-communication'—the modern man's failure to understand himself or to understand the other person and their mutual failure to understand each other, which is the real tragedy of modern life.[1]

The malaise is common to all the playwrights mentioned above in some degrees. Though they have been written in different languages like Hindi, Marathi, Bengali and Kannada, these powerful artists have enriched the direction of contemporary drama forwards a definite development. Their plays have been translated into English and staged in the theatres. Therefore any discussion on Indo-Anglian drama must take into account the thematic and technical virtuosities of these playwrights.

Section A

For Rakesh non-communication and a tragic sense of life verging on fatalism is detected. Some of his most remarkable plays are

Ashadh Ka Ek Din, Aaadhe Adhure, Shayad and *Leharon Ke Rajhans*. In *Enact,* a journal, Rakesh sums up his belief in the function of theatre as an effort to "help man know and discover himself in relation to his environment."[2] Badal Sircar claims to have initiated a newer direction to Indian theatre movement by explication of a peoples' theatre—popularly known as the Third Theatre. With the performance of *Nabanna* written by Bijan Bhattacharya, a parallel theatre movement taking into account, the impoverished mass started spreading its wings. The keynote was decidedly Marxist and the protagonists were the proletarian mass of agricultural and other labourers. To this trend, Sircar added the dimension of the psyche.

The radio play *Kamal,* Vimal Ebong Indrajit still rings in one's ears by its novel approach that touches the heart. The play was translated in several languages following its popularity. His other popular plays are *The Whole Night, Bhoma, Stale News, Procession* etc. *Ebong Indrajit* is a kind of shock therapy to the complacent belief of the fulness of life. There is no scope for such complacence in the modern days of cultural, social and ideological exploitations. The age-old tenets of morality and certainty have vanished from life. Random questions are asked in the persona of the characters about the supposed stability of values. Indrajit, the hero of the play, is a bizarre combination of Jimmy Porter, Prufrock, Vladimir and Estragon. Only he has shed off his anger unlike Jimmy. The writer, Indrajit's pair, asks himself meaningful questions unlike Becket's twin heroes. The questions relate to the nihility, the meaninglessness of existence. The established, conventional framework of living life is negated by the frustrated queries of a conscientious man. Amal, Bimal and Kamal are the regular traditional people happy with their destined lot as representatives to the society. The Writer and Indrajit do not fit in. Life is a jigsaw puzzle for them. Hence:

> No shrine for us
> No god for us
> But the road
> The endless road.[3]

The journey and the quest continue as ever. Written for the educated middle class people, the play created ripples in the theatre-loving people. A wave of shock as also an awakening to the newer avenues of thinking is demonstrated by the play. It raises innumerable questions about life shattering the romantic nostalgic illusion that man bears. The finesse, the brilliance of the play is in its technical novelty too. The playwright, present on the stage, chooses his characters from the audience. Therefore the act of writing itself is rebellious and against convention. There are as many as layers of interpretations as the audience can detect. Political, moral, social, relational and existential stratums of perceptions may be traced from the play.

Girish Karnad's stage effective plays include *Yayati, Hayavadana, Nagamandala, Tale-Danda, Tughlaq, The Fire and the Rain.* The immense contribution of these plays to the growth and development of Indian and Indo-Anglian drama has been assessed time and again. As his dramatic art cannot be discussed within the scope of the paper, only the salient features of his presentation of the reality of living and the anomalies thereof. One pointedout man is placed within the vicious cycle of innumerable contradictions, confusions and frustrations. Life is an enigma. Incomprehensibility of life's ways gives birth to impasse. Man has to opt for his chosen way according to his/her propensities. The opposition between tradition (man-made) and modernism, thus, forms a major part of the debate. Karnad's plays locate and offer a space for testing out the dichotomies and relative strength of the opposing forces working in the society. The polarities of fire and rain percolate in the man-made institutional bases like caste versus free society, (The sharanas), individual and community, myth and reality, secular and endorsed religion, etc. In all these dichotomies, definite political statements are issued forth from the playwright's end. To bring out the purport of these ideological contradictions, Karnad takes the help of the mythical and folk stories. The European Western modes, themes and styles are mixed and mingled with the Indian or Eastern modes and characters to focus basic human nature and the nature of the society. At the same time, the contemporary idioms of alienation, disillusionment and frustration are embedded within the mythical context. The problems are displayed in the 'space'—I talked about, for probable awareness and amelioration. But Utopic transformation is a distant possibility since equations of power is a much more complicated game. While Yayati takes away youth and therefore power from Puru his son, Sovideva snatches it from his father Bijjala. Therefore, power looks upon itself as the ultimate good. Asceticism and rituals like yagna may be looked upon alteratively as securing power though mesmerizing society. Rani's ultimate victory in conceiving, shocks Appanna into slavery of matriarchal power.

The multilevel structure and tone of Karnad's plays achieve success through symbolic innuendos, ironies that exist within the knowledge of the people. The primary level of story-telling and listening elicits appreciation. The inner level is to be realized by the conscious, educated public. It is, as if, characters in costume in *Miracle and Morality* plays speak of modern predicaments in hooded terms. While *Morality and Miracle* play characters carry a definite trait, Karnad's mythical characters often carry seeds of contrariety. Man finally sheds off his mask. The exploration of relationships and the vicissitudes of life is done in an undivined way by Karnad. Vijay Tendulkar's plays in Marathi are specimen of yet another avenue of criticizing the society and its ills. His remarkable plays include *Sakharam Binder, Ghasiram Kotwal, Silence! The Court is in Session, To Hell with Destiny and The Town.* Tendulkar's technique comprises the backdrop of history, the perpetuation of man's exploitation of another, rampant misuse of power by the rulers of the country, community and society, human degradation and loss of values. To authenticate the coercion and the societal ills, he incorporates macabre scenes of violence on the stage. Aggression, he feels, is innate to man. It is exposed at the wake of anguish and frustration. Tendulkar's plays also are a kind of shock therapy that helps in regaining the sense of reality of things by shattering complacence.

Ghasiram Kotwal demonstrates corruption in power structure. His butt of aspersion is the powerful Brahmin community here. Moroba Kanhoba's scholarly book written in 1863 is his source in this play. One such icon of inhuman torture was Nana Phadnavis who carried out his despotic rule under the umbrage of the Kotwali. In spite of his exploitative rule and clandestine, demoralized treatment of women, he was acclaimed as a good and just ruler by the posterior generation of Brahmins with the ulterior motive of perpetuating their supposed glory based on caste. Ghasiram, a Brahmin from Kanauj, cannot assimilate himself in the prudish society of Poona Brahmins for his poverty. He realizes the equation of power and uses his daughter Lalita Gouri as a bait to the all powerful womaniser Nana. Though he becomes a *kotwal* by Nana's recommendation, he fails to retain power as because within the short period of his demoniac power enjoyment Nana too loses his attraction for Lalita who ultimately commits suicide. Ghasiram is executed at the end. The play is a critique of the political misappropriation of power in the contemporary society apart from its powerful statement on caste and gender based discriminations of a particular space and time. Wives, concubines and whores are dictated by the patriarchal society to act in charted ways as reproductive machines, as weapons of illicit enjoyment through seductive mores and as licensed commodities of the market respectively. As history is a construct to conceal the nefarious self-interest, so also priesthood or brahminism is a construct based on arbitrary imposition of certain external symbols that can easily camouflage the dark, ugly interior.

Section B

Here the principal focus in the discourse of drama is on the plays of Mahesh Dattani who has proved himself to be one of the youngest pioneers of experimental theatre or the Third Theatre movement. It is common knowledge that drama is a performing art that finds fulfilment through equal and active participation of the writer, director, actor and the audience. A story or a situation, which is vital to literature of literary efforts, tends towards completion within the pages of that work, but in a play the same storyline or situation has to be transferred into action. Hence the story is retold in action and enactment is simultaneous with the growth, development and completion. Any discourse on drama, therefore needs to take into account the effective, simultaneous functioning of the four components. The actors and the audience relive the situation conceived of by the director and the writer. This complicated equation is actualised with judicious effort in Mahesh Dattani's plays. For the efficacy of discourse, the characteristic features of his plays are subdivided into broad segments. These may be insufficient given the newer dimensions and approaches of his pen in the recent years.

Society and Characters: Dattani's chosen subjects are the middle class men and women in urban cities. Urbanity tempts, enhances craving, restricts movement by overcrowding, generates alienation through confinement, breeds insensitivity to others' malaise and a mad utilitarian rush towards cash and comfort. In *Where There's a Will,* Hasmukh Mehta is a fastidious, suspicious and power hungry patriarch. Neither his wife Sonal not his mistress Kiran takes him to be a normal family man. His will is an absurd off-spring of his paranoid personality. An office secretary is commissioned to take over the charge of his immediate family after his death. The secretary works accordingly to prove herself no less bizarre though calculating. Sonal is dominated by her sister Minal and husband, Ajit by his wife Preety and Hasmukh (even after death), Kiran by Hasmukh—while he lived. Assimilation of Kiran in Mehta household and especially in the confidence of Sonal is unusual, though probable because each member of the family is cast in odd predicaments.

Urban centres are often susceptible to cultural colonization in which moral determinism of the tradition bound society loses stronghold. In *Bravely Fought the Queen* all the characters are like shooting stars living their lone, circumscribed lives in isolation to the society. Alka and Dolly's rebelliousness is non-functioning, devoid of 'isms' of any sort. All Alka can do is to turn insensate through intoxicating liquor. Dolly, the supposed queen fantasizes about an erotic relationship within the boundaries of her home. Baa thrives in the alternate spaces of the past and the present. Lalitha reaps satisfaction in tending bonsais and rarely in befriending people. Jiten is a sexual macho whereas Nitin—a sly homosexual under the façade of a heterosexual marriage.

Proportions rarely mark Dattani's characters. All suffer from aberrations they are not conscious of really. In his self-inflicted ostracization Chandan, one of the Siamese twins in Tara amputates his name and therefore identity as a possible amelioration of his guilt-ridden existence. He calls himself Dan in London. Rightful decision in the form of an axed limb stands outside the process of family consideration. Like Jonathan Swift, Dattani traces the inherent weakness of our fragile existence. A massive use of social irony thus pervades his choice of characters and situations. Ramnik's 'Gandhism' emits mixed reactions in his family in *The Final Solutions*. The shocking act of Javed in touching the Krishna idol thus falls within pace in *On A Muggy Night,*

Dipali and Kamalesh's ironic dialogue betray a childish prismatic play-conception of two adults regarding the conventional attitudes of marriage partners. Dipali says, "If you were a woman, we would be in love." Kamalesh answers, "If you were a man we would be in love." Dipali exhilarates at the prospect of their combined love by proclaiming, "If we were, hetero sexual we would be married ... Eeeck."[4] Dattani would not call such character perception as 'a definitive view of life'.

> "But several of the images that we carry around in our minds are politically generated images and we accept them to be as true. However, I don't think so and my characters are simply a personification of my perceptions."[5]

The characters who are seen on Dattani's stage are no newcomers from the outer space. They are the victims of a fast changing society. Their attitude towards life and society is shaped by their own perception that hang on a precarious balance since the power structure of the society has the final say about legitimacy or standard codes. The gay community thrives on a few wide-hearted patrons like Deepali and Kiran, though Kiran recoils in horror when it affects her personal life. The bone-chilling sort of criminal discrimination of Dr. Thakkar in active connivance of Tara's mother and grandfather is an abnormal effort of adherence to patriarchal norms. Hizras (trans-sexuals) and gay people cannot marry; Hindus and Muslims cannot live together peacefully; a son must follow meticulously the footsteps of his father in order to be in his good books, women must conform to the dictates of the male family members—all these imperatives describe the traditional society. Dattani has caught the glimpse of such stamped, registered codebooks. The society is ever resistant to changes that would bestow freedom to these small or perhaps widely located aberrant groups consisting of human beings not animals.

Dattani's subjects thus bring to the lime light complicity of a globalized post-modern existence and its angst. In an interview with Ranu Uniyal, Dattani points to the changing perspective of contemporary society. He says in answer to Ranu:

> '*RU:* Or is it all about the changing times?

> *MD:* I think it is all about reflecting the time which we are in and if those time are changing then I think that it needs to be reflected in the theatre.'[6]

Dattani calls his theatre "cutting edge theatre or radical theatre which questions existing values and challenges people what they consider the norm."[7] He owes his allegiance to Vijay Tendulkar and Tennessee Williams since both look forward to lay bare contemporary conflicts of the society on stage. 'Projecting a milieu' on stage presupposes drawing a large number of audience who live and is aware of the conflicts. So Dattani's subjects are gender inequality in violent society, the despair of the marginalized not economically but mentally and for that matter socially too, intolerance to each other, the inhuman social dictates, generation divide and reactionary resistance towards change of any kind.

Gender issues are the most important ingredients in a Dattani play. In almost all the dramas, the issue in question receives ample illustrations from different perspective. In *Tara* the leg that lives unattended would have been put to use in Tara's body so that she could use both the legs. The doctor finds in unnecessary in the context of the chances of a life time for a baby girl. This is a height of cruelty that unnerves the readers but not the social henchmen and conspirators from the family. The guilt envelops the household excepting the father of course. The father behaves in a normal way, but Tara's mother seeks to redeem her sin through theatrical over-attention to her needs. Chandan, exasperated by the family decision made long way back adds to his feeling of guilt arising out of his close mental proximity with Tara—his twin. This act of impiety on behalf of the family speaks blatantly about the vulnerability of being born as a woman.

In *Where There is a Will,* Sonal is a mute, passive sufferer incessantly striving to make her husband and son happy. She needs a counsel and Mrs. Javier proves fruitful for her malaise after Hasmukh's death. Here is a woman who is used to carrying out orders from almost everybody. She does not have an existence of her own. Preety is manoeuvring but not to the extent of being victorious in her plans. If she cannot propitiate the ego of her father-in-law, how can she stand a chance to receive his benevolence? A woman's success lies on the whims of her lord.

Smita, in The Final Solutions is an ineffectual rebel pottering under the directions of her mother Aruna. Aruna talks sense, for, she advises her daughter from the vantage point of a convert actualizing unconsciously the discriminating rules of patriarchy for women.

> "She hasn't spent any time with Baa. She must learn to be with elders."
> "Who were you talking to on the phone?"
> "Remember. Always be pure. Pure in your mind, in your deeds."[8]

What Aruna feels about purity may not hold good for the next generation, but she scarce by realizes it. Sensibility and therefore sensitivity often unnerves women in their cloistered lives. Daksha-Hardika alchemy reminds one of the fate of so many aspiring and conscientious women writers of the eighteenth century referred to by Virginia Woolf in her book *A Room of One's Own*. Daksha is the youth of Hardika sprinkling forth through remembrance of her past life. She is no 'mad women in the attic' but her traversing to and fro connects her present near vegetable life to the eventful history of her past when she tried frantically to dodge her likings and aversions to her immediate family. Women's life and painful evolution towards conformity are embedded in their psyche. So Daksha scribbled her heart into her diary. The pages of the diary here become metaphorically an instrument of mute protest and as an effort to understand the power equations in the society.

Bravely Fought the Queen exhibits an urban feminine world in the First Act. The interaction with the male world continues in the Second Act and reaches its peak in the Third Act. Women are not born but made like Lalitha's bonsai. Lack of nutrition stunts their growth, the branches of the pigmy tree in a shallow dish carry distorted curvatures. Baa—another grotesque bonsai personality—wields male hegemonic power on her daughters-in law—Alka and Dolly. Baa is a constant stage décor signifying the patriarchal power system. She revolves round her own orbit of past memories of depravity and the present position of relatively enhanced power as a mother-in-law. Alka and Dolly are stage pieces with the favourite pastime of looking good. Waiting is their lot but Dolly makes use of the zero hours by fantasizing about

Kanhaiya whereas Alka takes to indiscriminate drinking. Quite remarkably, the playwright would not allow them outside their cloistered home. Lalitha has that advantage being the wife of an inferior cleric. A painted exterior galvanized with distinction of wealth exposes a poor interior laced with depression and ennui. The absence of love, logic, peace and propriety haunt the over all atmosphere of the play.

Dattani poses a question, depicts a situation but abstains from prescription. He would let his readers think. But then, why do his female characters lack vocations of any kind? Most of them are housewives and students. Nobody seems to work for the sake of earning or for work outside the family arena. Dolly is the supposed queen in refuting and quarrelling with her husband on account of her spastic daughter but unfortunately from the worldly standard of an independent voice she is a miserable failure. Do women only crave for victory within the family? Some such questions will remain unanswered.

Stagecraft in Dattani's plays is unconventional and unique. Generally a multi-level set exhibiting the interior as well as the exterior of the house is in full view of the audience. *On A Muggy Night in Mumbai* contains a dark space or 'Shoonya' where innermost thoughts of the characters seem to be taking place. It is perhaps a free zone away from the interactive sessions of the living room and the bedroom. The window brings the characters in contact with the outside world. The outside world directly impinges upon the inside in *The Final Solutions*. The chorus or the mob is always present in the ramp like space on the fore while at the back, in lower and upper levels, the hall and kitchen including Hardika's room can be viewed by the audience. Through bits and pieces of Hardika's consciousness and memories of the past, 1940s infiltrate into the present. Nearly the same kind of a two-story painted house is set in the staging of *Bravely Fought the Queen*. Baa is 'visible through the screen wall when it is back lit.'[9]

In *Tara* the bedchamber of Chandan in London is in the middle level whereas Dr. Thakkar is above and the Patel house is on the stage level. These multi-dimensional stage spaces and their use serve the purpose of the playwright to rivet the attention of the audience throughout the performance. No major characters are out of sight and mind. Dr Thakkar, Hardika and Baa are constant presences reminding the audience about their importance in the scheme of things—Dr. Thakkar by his cruel decision, Hardika with the history of her aversion to Muslims and Baa through her dictatorial omnipresence in her sons' life. Public and private lives—their interaction bring in realism. From the beginning to the end, the audience is busy in following each dimension and segment. Technicalities in stage directions go hand in hand with over-lapping dialogues in Dattani's plays. From different dimensions characters speak out dialogues or pose questions while the answers ensue out of another level. At the same time, two levels of stage can act and inter-act taking irony as weapon. Hence Jiten's home and office are meaningfully connected through more or less stereotypical dialogues concerning depravity, disillusionment and anger over family and work. Again the chorus in *The Final Solutions* intensifies the atmosphere of a caste-based riot thereby exposing the mass—mindset on such sensitive issues. The curt dialogues of the mob—chorus help in conjuring up the bleak picture of a riot-ridden area in an effective way. The ghost of Hasmukh is also another remarkable addition that serves to foster the willing suspension of disbelief on the one hand and to focus and perpetuate the yawning gap between generations. Indeed a humorous approach to father son imbroglio is light heartedly dealt with herein.

As for language, it is once again a hybridised one like R.K. Narayan's 'Bharat Brand English'. Dattani approximates the spoken idioms of the contemporary generation of pizza eaters and coke drinkers—not to speak of the frequenters in abundantly available Hollywood movies. In *On a Muggy Night* the guard and Kamalesh speak Hindi: all other characters converse in a 'chutney' language. Sharad is 'as gay as a goose'. The innate qualities of a real man, i.e., a hetero are laid down by him in the lines:

> Look at all the kings ... all the male power they enjoy thrusting themselves on to the world, all that penis power! Power with sex, power with muscle, power with size... power, man! Power![10]

Power does overlook questions of sexuality. Hence the imagery of sex is brought in. Everyday use of English is the forte of the chorus.

> Of what use is this curfew? When there is unrest in our minds ! Have we to let them insult us? To close our eyes while they stab us.[11]

A mixed combination of masks advocated or suggested by Lalitha for the ball in Bravely Fought the Queen reads thus—

> The Shahs as astronauts, the Bedis as Laila-Majnu, The Mendens as Hansel and gretel. Mr. Kashikar as Shivaji, The Dutts as Raj Kapoor and Nargis.[12]

Cultural divide has evaporated from the dictionary of the contemporary, since the world is a globalized village. Jiten in Bravely Fought the Queen uses rampant abuses in Hindi and English both-like 'chooth', 'masti', 'gupshup', 'pukka' with 'smart ass', 'crazy bastard' etc. A playwright succeeds in making a spontaneous contact with his audience with the weapon of dialogue or vocabulary in which people of a particular space and time speak. This language again relates to the postcolonial condition and human identity. Dattani achieves this contemporaniety through a language that takes into account the real life idioms within closed circles and in real life situations. In a theatre, one cannot be pedagogic and therefore distant.

Symbols and their use are a veritable strength in Dattani. In Tara, an inherent symbolism is embedded within the tale itself. The question of a Siamese twin that Dattani uses with a fair amount of medical freedom (he says) is itself fraught with a deeper connotation. Society, especially in India is decidedly partisan when it comes to the choice of sexes. There is a clear divide between options of a newly born daughter or a son. Every other day, sex determination tests and aborted female foetus stories come up in the news lines. The conception of a Siamese twin—a boy and a girl covertly points to the undeniable fact that both are equals and should be treated as equals. Society forgets that, patriarchy encourages neglect of the female. Truth lies neglected like the third leg and it rots. Taras of this society are 'twinkle Taras' to be extinguished soon. Chandan would receive higher education, would frequent his father's office during vacations, but not so Tara. Priorities in the family are categorized according to sexes. But both come to the world from the same womb. Dattani impresses upon his audience the truth of equality of sexes with the induction of an emotional story. Hasmukh's ghost may as well as be treated as the ever dominating voice of patriarchs, the money-mindedness of the urban families and of course the lack of communication between human beings—even the inmates of a family. While living Hasmukh was a lonely man, even after death he continues his lone journey till he is dislodged from his arboreal branch of a neem tree. The story continues as Ajit learns the rope of being another bullying father to his would-be born son.

Perhaps the finest example of symbolic dealing with the happenings in a Dattani play can be found in *Bravely Fought the Queen*. Without much deliberations, one can easily lift a finger and point towards the bonsai Lalitha presents to Dolly and proclaim its implications as a dominant motif of the play. The dwarfed fruit-bearing tree has its compatible companion in Dolly, Alka, Baa and Daksha—the all-female world. The first three have faced repeated humiliations at their husbands' custody. At the fag end of her life, Baa has become a nagging, complaining woman alternating between her past and present. It is a state of seasonal lunacy, therefore abnormality like the grotesque figure of the pigmy tree. Alka is a dipsomaniac, Dolly—a sex freak. Daksha has a deformed body created by the virulence of her macho father. The beggar woman with a tarpauline covering is a mirror image of Jiten's nasty overtures with pimps. The sense of guilt is concretised in the figure of the beggar woman. Very significantly the record player plays Naina Devi's *thumri* creating an ambience of passion in loneliness. The ball and the bell are the other important metaphors of the play. Dolly wears a peel off mask; the mask cracks; the ball would contain masked men and women and the model would ultimately strip off for exhibiting Ree Va Tee undergarments. When the masks will be shed, real faces will come into the light of day as Dolly's cracked mask. Baa's bell is the voice of patriarchy cautioning housewives to maintain status quo. Through the incessant ringing of the bell Baa, as if, transfers her vulnerability to her daughters-in-law. Examples of such metaphoric presentations are abundant in the pages of Dattani.

The overall pattern of a Dattani play cannot be singled out since he deals with gnawing problems of the contemporary generation from different angles and connotations. In that case, each play should come under discourse to do justice to his art.

Critics have by and large, categorized his plays as tragedy, comedy or tragic-comedy. I beg to differ from such simplistic notions because each of his play contains a myriad of tones depending on the situation. I hope I may not be wrong calling his plays situational with a focus to modern man's malaise. He betrays a black humour of a rare kind. Dattani's plays are serious plays depicting tight rope situations fraught with complicity. If the total pattern poses to be humorous, the humour is blackened with irony. Again when the pattern betrays sorrow, it is inevitably laced with ludicrous elements. Shock-absorbing elements are impregnated into the body of the script. Dattani takes us towards shock and bewilderment, but then he would not leave the theatre-goers disillusioned for silver lined clouds form here and now there.

Section C—*Bravely Fought the Queen*: An Assessment

The play basically deals with the plight of woman in the Indian sub-continent garnished with innovative techniques of the modernist theatre of India. It is generally said that Dattani never draws conclusions or offers judgments. But then, his plays contain the nuances of the labyrinthine ways along which his characters and situations move. His dramas offer visions of disillusionment, nihility and for that matter the angst of living—living in the wasteland of deteriorating values, morals and the meaning of existence. As such, his plays may as well be treated in existential terms. Human relationship in a family ambience can take bizarre destinations. He goes on to portray them graphically through stage properties, technicalities and meaningful interactions of characters on stage. The plays can also be discussed in terms of the post colonial condition, post modern views of the society, progressing toward a lifeless economy based utilitarian life people called globalization. There is a visible tension between the hegemonic coercion of the male world with the fast advancing spirit of independence of the women in the family and the society. The development of this inherent antagonism finds an apt treatment in his plays.

The evocation of the atmosphere speaks largely of a hybrid culture nourished by the principal characters of the play. As per the stage direction, the play opens in a middle class household of Dolly and Jiten in a suburb of Bangalore. The house is expensively furnished, though badly maintained with a well-stocked bar—so very modern and unusual in such a family. A stereo system goes on playing the scintillating thumris of Naina Devi. The juxtaposition of a bar and a classical backdrop of music confuse the audience as to the basic ambivalence of choices and tastes of the inhabitants of the house. Dolly, understandably the 'Queen' of the play wears a dressing gown and a mask. She is after proving herself to be an immaculate beauty with the aids and accessories of nail file and mud mask.

The First Act introduces an intruder Lalitha in Dolly's house. Dattani has entitled the act as The Women and so it is a woman's world. The various topics that get preference in this world comprise tips on beauty, meditation, yoga, parties and on top of all these impassioned discussions on their respective husbands and in-law's family. In between the leisurely talks, there is a constant and forceful presence of Baa, the mother-in-law. She calls Dolly intermittently, so Dolly is caught between her duty and desire of going out for a party. Her daughter Daksha though not seen on stage, is a great presence. One learns about her from the delirious talks of Alka under the intoxicating spell of rum. Dolly would never like to speak of her daughter as there is an association of pain in her social existence as a mother. Her reticence is thoroughly corroded by the thoughtless comments of her sister Alka. Lalitha is embarrassingly caught between the intricate web of difficult relationship of the two families. Lalitha feels responsible for shattering the sisters' hopes of dining out with their husbands. She is the more uneasy as she is more knowledgeable than the family members of the programmes of Nitin and Jiten.

The sisters' desire to escape temporarily from their claustrophobic existence is foiled by the information followed by subsequent phone calls. This ineffective bid epitomizes the basic question of servility in a middle class Indian family. Excepting Dolly both the young women drink and indulge in loose talks that range from the pain of a mother having a disabled child to notorious family scandals like Dolly's homo-erotic relationship with Kanhaiya—the replacement of the old cook and also a positive hint on the unseemly relationship between Alka's brother and husband. By the process of construction and deconstruction, Dattani presents the antiquated tradition of a middle class family myth. He chooses his location in the pre-existing pattern of a contemporary urban Indian family and simultaneously impregnates the seed of corrosion within it. By bits and pieces he crumbles the edifice of the myth of the family and exposes the fractured reality behind the glittering façade. The grotesque image of a nagging mother Baa, the macabre presence of the old, nasty beggar woman, the tranced alcoholic dance of Alka in the rain, the meaningfully suggestive closing /opening of the kitchen door, the switching of the light—all help to peel off the mask from the established institution of marriage. More so in the Second Act where in the men's world virtually naked men are seen quarrelling like cats and dogs in the office.

The men's world proves to be more violent and deceitful. Jiten often copulates with whores in the office. He induces Sridhar, an accounts employee, to bring a pimp for him. Nitin eschews with such naked situations, for, he too has driven away qualms of morality for the sake of his homosexual promiscuity with Praful. It is a world of betrayal, of cunning, of practising deceit with untrampled hearts and clean consciences. Sridhar stays out of the vicious cycle perhaps for his ulterior motive of sticking to the job and buying a flat in near future. Praful's benevolence in lending money for the hapless business of his brothers-in-law is taken with contempt. They would 'insult him and treat him like a scrap'. He is a 'bastard', a 'sentimental fool' to the brothers though they need a bastard's money without the knowledge of the sisters. Sridhar is a'chooth' as he cannot secure the client's agreement on the advertisement of the lingerie. Eve after the melodramatic III Act, Nitin is not abashed at the poor sight of his sleeping wife in a muddy, distressed condition. He is seen spelling out deceptively soothing words of supposed love and care at his sleeping wife. Alka should always sleep, so that he can continue with his nefarious task of enticing Praful to bed. He would not deflect from his path of homosexual enjoyment. Jiten, however, after a fervent attack on Lalitha and a nasty altercation with Dolly, suffers a visible humiliation and for that matter a change from his former invincibility. With moist eyes and an overwhelmed heart he drives off smashing the beggar woman or perhaps the haunting feeling of guilt. There is a sinister yet metaphoric suggestion of disowning the sin of torturing his pregnant wife, of neglecting his own child by not acknowledging her fatherhood and of innumerable other misdeeds.

Much has already been said about the overt feminine view points from the symbolic motifs as also the unfolding of the stories of humiliation narrated by the sisters in the previous discourse. Now one ponders over the title of the play. Who is the queen that fights bravely? Alka is obviously vulnerable in her forced assimilation in the role of a devoted wife. Dolly poses to be nonchalant in her daring rendezvous with Kanhaiya. She even enthuses Alka to initiate in such extra-marital affairs. Alka recoils and indulges in her masochistic overtures. Taking drastic actions is not her forte. Her future, she knows, is at stake while Dolly can do that being a little more victorious in her motherhood. Hence it is Jiten who goes out of the house while Dolly stays back. Nitin is inflamed into throwing Alka out, but he abstains from the act since he needs the camouflage of Alka for his obscene desire. Lalitha has little identity apart from being Mrs. Sridhar. But she can keep to herself in the common dream of making her married life a peace haven. Her male chauvinistic husband is no hindrance to her feeling of belonging. It is Dolly who fights all along—with her sister, with her husband and above all with the society that has forbidden the privilege of freedom in women. The play ends on stage but her fight does not. She asserts her selfhood within the short span. It is significant to notice that Baa in her physical and mental infirmity takes a solid decision regarding her ancestral house. She would bequeath it to Daksha under the guardianship of Praful and not let her sons to devour it. This perhaps goes back to her cruel instigation to Jiten to kick Dolly on the womb during the latter's pregnancy. Thus Dolly wins through a middle class sentiment of giving birth to an heir to the family unlike Alka.

Post-modern artists portray mutilated, fractured reality along with the vivisection and distortion of the mind. A thin curtain of the façade often flutters in the wind to expose the obscenities, aberrations and guilt of the mind. Values are not permanent, so also a sense of certainty of life. A cosmopolitan angle of transculturalism combined with a residual local, traditional rootedness portrayed in the play signals a change of perception and therefore a transition that is painful. The said change breeds restlessness, vacillation and frustration. The sisters in the First Act float between hope and despair. One takes to drink, the other has a rambling discussion on the proposed ball with masks. They cannot advance much due to Baa's intermittent calls to Dolly. Uncertainty of the family dinner is paired with a heated badinage between the brothers in the office. They decide and undecide over the issue of Praful's motive in lending them money, of divulging or keeping the matter secret to the sisters, of the selection of models or advertising strategies. A highly synthetic frame of relationship prevails in the interactions of the characters in the play. The interplay between the world of reality and the world of fantasy accounts for the vacillation embedded in all the major characters. Dolly fantasizes about the strong embrace of Kanhaiya, Nitin about the black arms of the auto driver and the enticing body of Praful. Women are in perpetual quest for their husbands' attention while men are engrossed in profit and carnal satisfaction away from home. Meanwhile a slow cultural deterioration or perhaps transition takes place. On one side, there is the fixed principle—the background in Baa round whom the peripheral characters oscillate, on the other, the preoccupations of the public world where every other day new mutations take place. In absence of the traditional principle, the private world would go to shreds, so it seems at the end.

References

1. Quoted in R.K. Dhawan and Tanu Paunted, *The Plays of Mahesh Dattani: A Critical Study*, Prestige Books: New Delhi, 2005, p. 15.
2. Quoted in K. Venkata Reddy and R.K. Dhawan. ed. *Flowering of Indian Drama: Growth and Development*, Prestige Books: New Delhi, 204, p. 109.
3. *Ibid*, p. 65.
4. *Mahesh Dattani Collected Plays*. Penguin Book: New Delhi, 2000, p. 65.
5. Quoted in Asha Kuthari Chaudhuri. *Mahesh Dattani*, Foundation Books: New Delhi, 2005, p. 48.
6. R.K. Dhawan etc. p. 179.
7. *Ibid*, p. 178.
8. *Collected Plays*, pp. 172-3.
9. *Ibid*, p. 233.
10. *Ibid*, p.101
11. *Ibid.*, p. 188.
12. *Ibid*, p. 254.

19 The Element of Immediate and Enduring Delight in Vijay Tendulkar's *His Fifth Woman*—An Analysis

— V. Anbarasi

Vijay Tendulkar, the most celebrated avant-garde Marathi playwright, has a vast realm of literary output to his credit. His creative genius has prompted him to write full length plays, one-act plays, children's dramas, essays, novel, social criticism, biographies and screen plays. Though he has tried his hand in his own mother tongue, namely, Marathi, a regional language in India, the very fact that his major works are being translated into English, stands as a solid proof ascertaining his merit and uniqueness as a great writer.

Exposure to the world of drama right from his childhood has lured Tendulkar greatly and his amazement towards this literary genre has never subsided or decreased. His deep immersion in this world of fantasy has resulted in the creation of outstanding literary works, which would be preserved by posterity. As a playwright, he constantly and continuously shocks and surprises his audience. His keen observation of life with all its minutest details, his reaction to violence in all forms, his helplessness at the atrocities meted out to hapless women in a patriarchal society and his restlessness at the sense of alienation experienced by the modern man, make him experiment with the form of drama. He has felt the need of focusing his attention on the neglected aspects of life thereby creating an awareness regarding the various ills of the society. His aim is to probe deep into the inner workings of the human psyche and to project what he has deducted there. His focus is not on the ordinary but on the extraordinary and the eccentric. "Reading his plays", says Tom Alter, "leaves one spellbound and shell-shocked."[1] The various issues, that he has dealt with in his dramas, do deeply affect the sentiments of the lookers-on, because they have universal significance and timeless quality. In appreciation of his meritorious contribution to literature, he has been honoured with many prestigious awards. His *Silence! The Court is in Session* has raised his status as one of the leading playwrights of India and won him the Kamaladevi Chatopadhyay Award in 1970 and Sangeet Natak Akadami Award for playwriting in 1971. His dance drama, *Ghashiram Kotwal* has earned him international reputation. He has been awarded with the Padma Bhushan, the Vishnudas Bhave Memorial Award, the Katha Chudamini Award and Saraswati Samman Award for his effective presentation.

Tendulkar has written thirty full-length plays out of which, ten dramas are available in English. All these ten plays expose his eagerness to introduce neglected aspects of life through innovative forms. Dhyaneshwar Nadkarni feels:

> Vijay Tendulkar leads the vanguard of the avant-garde theatre that developed as a movement separate from the main stream. Tendulkar and his colleagues were dissatisfied with the decadent professional theatre that characterized the Thirties and Forties. They wanted to give theatre a new form and therefore experimented with all aspects of it including content, acting, décor and audience communication.[2]

His keenness to experiment is clearly obvious right from his *Silence! The Court is in Session* to his latest play, *His Fifth Woman.*

Tendulkar, though has not proclaimed himself as a spokesman for the women's emancipation, has brought out the struggles and plights of women in his plays. Besides that he, in all his plays, has been making a thorough analysis of the various vital issues prevalent in the society. In *Kamala,* Jaisingh Jadav, a young journalist, aspires to enthrall the mass through exposing the various inconceivable atrocities happening around the country. In his anxiety to reveal the existence of flesh trade, where women are sold and bought, he turns out to be as heartless as the masters of those slaves. He cares neither for the sentiments of Sarita, his educated soul mate, nor for the fear and anxiety of Kamala, the slave. The play ends with Sarita's firm determination to assert herself. But she waits for time to ripen and comes forward to assuage and mollify the afflicted Jaisingh.

Silence! The Court is in Session has enabled Tendulkar to establish himself as a promising playwright. In this play, under the guise of a mock trial, the co-actors of Leela Benare, a schoolteacher, successfully bring out the carefully hidden private affairs of Benare to public scrutiny. The boisterous and confident young woman is cornered with the charge of infanticide and forced to be silent when the various charges are leveled against her. These malicious attempts of the gang against this individual transform her from an agile and brave woman into a hapless and dumbstruck victim.

The Vultures, Tendulkar's next play, where in vultures are accursed to lead the life of human beings, exhibits their heartlessness. It is about the family of Hari Pitale. His daughter and sons are after money and are shamelessly ready to go to any extent, employ any means or stoop down to any level in order to materialise their schemes into deeds. They are, in fact, worse than King Lear's ungrateful daughters and inflict great violence on each other and pave way for their downfall.

Tendulkar has written two political plays also. *Ghashiram Kotwal* has made an indelible mark in the annals of literature because of its form, action and innovative technique. The effective employment of the human curtain and its various functions captivates the attention of the audience. This play is about Ghashiram Savaldas, a Kanoj Brahmin. He goes to Poona in search of fortune and becomes its kotwal (a person officially designated to guard the city) at the cost of his dearest daughter's honour. His tyrannical ways and barbarous punishments make people shiver in fear. In the power hierarchy, even this cruel Kotwal has to submit himself to the will of his higher authority and is tactfully removed from the world by Nana Phadnavis, the chief minister.

The other political play, *Encounter in Umbugland,* reveals the gradual but steady metamorphosis of Vijaya, the Princess of Umbugland, from being a half-witted girl to a diplomatic queen. Her ceaseless efforts to rule her country in earnestness, her sincere strivings to uplift the Kadamba tribe from its pitiable condition, her incessant struggles to outwit the cunning schemes of her ministers and her victorious emergence and assertion are effectively delineated.

A Friend's Story discusses the problems of a lesbian, Sumitra Dev. In addition to that, the playwright, through his portrayal of Bapu, has sung the glory of friendship and its power to concrete the bond between individuals as well as to undo their associations with the world.

Kanyadaan, which won Tendulkar the Saraswati Samman Award, reveals out the problems encountered due to an inter caste marriage between a dalit boy and a brahmin girl. The inability of the dalit youth to acclimatize with his brahmin wife, her miserable attempts to transform him and the ultimate bitter consequences are very effectively portrayed by the playwright.

The Cyclist is another noteworthy creation of Tendulkar, in which he explores into the psyche of a slightly mentally deranged adult and captures a few rare sequences. Though this play is designed in the form of a travelogue, through the various encounters of Main Character (that is the name of the protagonist) with a variety of personages, Tendulkar has brought out the selfishness and cunningness of people.

In *Sakharam Binder,* he has exposed the masochistic tendencies of men. Sakharam, a Brahmin by birth but a binder, does not conform to the general or common norms of the society. He formulates his own rules and regulations and strongly advocates them to his subordinates. Sakharam wants to lead a free life and does not want to be bound by anything. He does not agree to marry a woman because that would legally bind him to her. He prefers "contractual co-existence", which allows him as well as his companion to free himself or herself the moment they do not feel the need for the other. He goes in for "drop-outs" and brings home a destitute and lives with her. Though he strongly condemns the inhuman attitude of heartless husbands, he conducts himself in no way better than them. As per the agreement, the woman he brings home, is entitled to have two meals a day, shelter and two saris per year. In the play *Sakharam Binder,* to the enquiries of the latest entrant Laxmi, he sums up his experiences with the previous woman. It was just a month since she started living with him and all of a sudden, she fell sick and died and he had a tough time with the crows, which refused to eat the food offered as part of the funeral rites. It is this little episode, which has been elaborated in *His Fifth Woman.*

Tendulkar wrote *His Fifth Woman* (2004) in English, as part of the celebration of the New York Tendulkar festival. *His Fifth Woman* is a prequel to his popular *Sakharam Binder* written in 1972. As is the case with his other plays, this play too entertains, enthralls, surprises and amuses the reader and audience greatly, constantly and continuously. Unlike in his previous plays, in *His Fifth Woman*, Tendulkar has not developed a gripping story. Since, his *Sakharam Binder* is a very well known play, which has already disclosed the nature of the protagonist as a megalomaniac, who considers himself to be a saviour of destitutes, the reader's and audience's curiosity is greatly kindled to see what is to be exposed of this cocksure male. Though *Sakharam Binder* had been very strongly denounced because it seems to propagate against the established customs of the society, it cannot be denied that it has brought to the limelight the sufferings that the dropouts of family and society undergo to stay alive and come to terms with life. Frank Thakurdas and Rajinder Paul earnestly aspire to create awareness among the readers and audience with their following exclamation:

> Here indeed is a sample of the 'slice of life' of a section—the majority, alas - who everyone takes for granted and turns a blind complacent eye on their individual trials, sorrows and sufferings and who look upto fate or fortune for succour or redemption ... This play demonstrates powerfully a disturbing problem of social pathology in our midst and as such should be translated into all the Indian languages and played everywhere. Perhaps it might disturb the slumbering social conscience of our prudish state officials and stir our countless social reformers and workers to greater concern and activity.[3]

Such an analysis stimulates the curiosity of the reader and audience, and Tendulkar, known as a social critic of traditional India, does not disappoint his avid audience with his latest creation.

In *His Fifth Woman*, there is no unfolding of an absorbing tale of revelatory facts but it is highly dramatic and arresting from the beginning to the end. It is a play with five scenes and each scene has its own surprising element. When the curtain rises, the audience find themselves taken to the lobby of a government hospital. It is late night and the weather is very cold. When everyone is trying to escape from the biting cold, two men, Sakharam Binder and his friend Dawood, bring a woman patient in a handcart and get her admitted. While Sakharam sends Dawood home, he waits in the hospital for the doctor's arrival but falls asleep. He has a strange dream, in which the sick woman ascertains that her husband is her saviour and everything happens as per his will. Sakharam is greatly annoyed and agitated and at that point the nurse calls for his presence as the patient has regained her consciousness. Sakharam is dazed and puzzled about his dream and the scene ends with his following the nurse.

The ambience for the II scene is Sakharam's humble house. He is found to be playing on the mrudanga (an Indian percussion instrument). His conversation with Dawood reveals the fact that the sick woman is dead. He narrates her last moments. Before she bade farewell to the mundane world, she recognized Sakaram but she was talking about her husband. She expressed her indebtedness for all that Sakaram had done for her. She was sure that she would meet her husband soon and beg excuse for giving herself to Sakaram. She would plead him to pardon Sakaram too. She went into delirium with those words and went on conversing with her husband as if he were sitting by her side. Holding Sakaram's hand, talking semi-consciously to her husband, she breathed her last. Since she is not related to Sakharam, he has left her dead body in the hospital and the cadaver would meet the same fate as that of the unclaimed ones. Dawood is unable to digest that notion and he makes it dawn on Sakharam that if her dead body is not buried or cremated with due funeral rites then her soul will not get deliverance. Though Sakharam does not have unshakable faith in all these customs and rites, he, at last, consents to abide by Dawood's request.

The III scene takes place in a burning ghat for the Hindu dead. Groups of men are waiting for their turn to perform the funeral rites of their dead relative. Sakharam carries out his work as per the instructions of the Brahmin. When the priest is conducting the ceremony, Sakharam finds it difficult to concur with him many times, which are very easily resolved by Dawood by bribing the priest with money. Though they surmount such difficulties easily, they become hapless with regard to the unwillingness of the crows to accept the food offered by them. According to Hindu custom, the non-acceptance of food by the crow is an indication of the displeasure of the soul of the dead. It is believed that the soul has an unfulfilled wish. Hence it becomes a tiresome task to Dawood to coax and cajole Sakharam to make an earnest appeal to the crows, which are the representatives of the soul. Sakharam, though grumbles and grudges, holds his temper under control and ultimately succeeds in feeding the crows.

Scene IV has certain unique revelations. Tendulkar's *sui generis* exploration into the nether world and its features are not merely astounding or amusing but highly thought-provoking. The common standpoint about the other world is exemplified here too but with a difference. The souls, once they take leave of their temporary abodes. Namely the bodies, are completely freed from their earthly ties. The woman, who had been strongly hoping to meet the soul of her husband and to live happily in unison with him in heaven after her death, is unable to recognise the soul of her husband. She seems to retain her gender consciousness though she is devoid of the feminine features. She feels very light and free. This woman comes across a man, who vehemently searches for something. He is haunted with the fear of loss but refuses to admit the loss. The omniscient crow discloses the fact. "It happens to all men when they arrive here. They miss their dick" (*His Fifth Woman* 72).

Chitragupta, Director of the department of heavenly affairs, comes in search of the lost two and takes them with him. The crow divulges a few more points about the nether world and turns its focus on Sakharam. The V scene is a very short one, which ends with Sakharam's entry into the house with the next woman.

Tendulkar's plays deeply affect the society because of their delineation of stark realities of life. He has declared once, "Sometimes my plays jolted the society out of its stupor and I was punished. I faced this without regret...,My plays contain my perceptions of society and its value and I cannot write what I do not perceive."[4] It is this strenous effort to portray life as is perceived by him that has contributed to the uniqueness of his plays and his place as a playwright. Even this latest play, *His Fifth Woman,* has enjoyed the kudos of the western audience when a stage reading of it was done in New York. If his plays are scrutinized, it can be easily analysed that there is a "marriage of words and visual images", which according to Dr. Garcia,"is the cornerstone of effective communication of ideas"[5] (He chooses to call this WED-Writing-Editing-Design).

Angus Bowmer, in his Foreword to *Drama: A Critical Collection* has stressed on the need to devote one's scrutiny on six elements in a literary work of art, especially in a play, to deduct how successful or impressive is the artist in combining the intellectual with the emotional. He suggests Aristotle's six components of a play namely "plot, character, thought, diction, music and spectacle."[6] Every play is expected to contain the first four elements and only the handling of the last two elements exhibits the creative genius, uniqueness and originality of the playwright. A script is not the ultimate form of the artefact because it is a means to the end, that is, the performance of the play on the stage.

Tendulkar has established his individuality as an effective playwright through his efficient employment of the required sounds and spectacle. The techniques introduced to portray the theme deserve a special mention. In his latest literary tour de force, *His Fifth Woman,* there are various elements that account for its immediate and enduring delight. Even the episodic plot structure further kindles the curiosity of the reader and the lookers-on as it continually surprises them with its revelations which are inconceivable and peculiar.

As a committed dramatist, Tendulkar has been striving to unmask the various ills prevalent in society and reveal the truth. *His Fifth Woman* is no exception. The first and foremost reason for the everlasting appeal of his plays is that his plays deal with problems vital not only in the past but also in the present. These are the problems common to humanity and by being exposed they attain universal significance and appreciation.

Tendulkar's portrayal of women reveals his deep understanding of their problems and feelings. The woman in *His Fifth Woman,* is a destitute who lives in harmony with Sakharam who is not her husband, because she nurtures certain strong sentiments which are revealed through Sakharam's dream. She firmly entertains the thought that everything, that happens in her life, happens according to her late husband's will. She further believes that her husband is her protector and discloses that she serves Sakharam having only her husband in her mind. Women, with such concepts, who revere and deem their husbands not only as soulmates but also as their Gods, do live till date.

Women, though despite their reverential attitude towards their husbands, never receive the same importance or recognition they actually deserve. The apparent unconcern and negligence with which women's lives are designed in the patriarchal society are exemplified through the following utterance of Dawood.

> What a life! Sold in marriage to a man older to her by thirty years and who already had a wife of her mother's age. Then not even six months have passed and he dies in an accident. The first wife throws the unfortunate girl out with only the clothes she is wearing and nothing else. Her parents refuse to take her back, mother fuckers (51).

Though, she has undergone such hardship, she does not blame her husband but argues with anxiety, "His soul lives on. A soul cannot be burnt. And his soul decides for me. I live because his soul wills so" (53). These remarks cannot be ignored as mere revelations in a fantasy, which are unreal because Sakharam, in his report about her death, delineates her eagerness to meet her husband's soul and seek his pardon. Tendulkar wrote this play in 2004, and the condition and status of women in the urban parts of India might have improved to a noticeable degree but their rural counterparts mostly do undergo the same treatment as is portrayed by him.

Though this play seems to wear the look of a collage, that does not constitute a unified plot, even through this Tendulkar reveals the eluding nature of human beings. Habits and customs are mechanically formulated and the customs and rituals have lost their significance and meaning in life. The scene in the cremation ground casually reveals the matter-of-fact attitude developed among humanity. The death of a person does not evoke any feeling of sorrow or fate. The relatives of the dead are bothered about the additional expenses due to the rise in the kerosene rates. One man, in fact, envies another because the other man's uncle died a day earlier thereby sparing him the additional expenses of costlier kerosene. The cremation ground does not give room for any contemplation on the illusory nature of life but has become a breeding ground for rumours and scandals.

The attempts of Dawood to pacify the Brahmin are other episodes, where Tendulkar, with a smile on his cheek, hints at the disloyalty and non-commitment of the so called "holy" priests. The Brahmin accepts the money offered by Dawood and conveniently ignores many vital points while performing the funeral rites. When Sakharam has been making an appeal to the crows to eat the food offered, lest her soul would be hanging in a condition without a body, the Brahmin urges him, "Be quick, Sir, I have to attend to another dead person. His relations are waiting there" (65). This episode ironically discloses how the materialistic aspirations of people cannot be cowed down even when they are in a cremation ground.

The crows, despite the numerous efforts and promises do not touch the food. Sakharam raises a doubt, "Can it be that those crows here are playing foul? Can it be that they don't represent her?" (68). He further criticises in an aside, "Or can it be that these Brahmins here train those crows to earn more bucks from people like us?" (69). Through this scene, Tendulkar, one of the prominent social critics, has vividly portrayed the customs and traditional beliefs of Indians with regard to their attitude to the souls and their deliverance as well as their hypocritical stands.

Another noteworthy aspect of the play is the depiction of the dramatic personages. These personalities are drawn from the human, animal and nether world. What makes them more sensational and exciting is the inextricable human element in all the three types. Sakharam's megalomaniac attitude has not been vehemently exposed in this play since it deals with a crucial situation in his life. He cannot be ruled by any sentiments and remains steadfast in his principles of life. His uncaring and undiscerning attitude towards his dependent woman is brought out through his own statement. He is highly self-centred and the woman, according to him, is meant merely to gratify his urges and needs. Sakaram utters, "I could not even know her name. Never had the time to ask for it. She called me Aho and I called her Ay. She remained Ay to me. An anonymity. But forget it, Yaar. Forget her... Gone is gone. We must live in the present, Dawood, Present is true" (57). He feels that he does not owe her anything. He does not bewail or bemoan over her death and he believes that the deal has ended.

Though Sakaram appears to be incorrigible in connection with his style of life, which is almost animalistic and impudent, his humane side cannot be ignored. His deep understanding of Dawood's inconvenience is reflected when he requests him to go home and rest soon after the sick woman is admitted in the hospital. He insists that Dawood should go home. He convinces him, "I can sleep through the day tomorrow you have your shop to look after. Go, have some sleep. Bye" (52). In another place, though he adamantly refuses to perform the funeral rites, at last he consents to the proposal of Dawood, because, declares he, "I do them not for her who is a cadaver in the morgue at the hospital but for you who is living and happen to be my only pal" (59). Neither the cremation ground nor the untimely and unforeseen demise of his close associate results in making any visible change in his outlook of or attitude towards life. This unwavering and uncompromising quality accounts for his popularity.

Dawood, his Muslim friend, is given a prominent role to play in this play than in *Sakharam Binder*. He seems to exercise great influence on Sakharam. Tendulkar harmonizes the Hindu-Muslim tie and their religions never stand on their way in extending a helping hand or in exchanging an understanding glance between each other. He seems to be filled with full of the milk of human kindness. Like Antigone in Sophocles's *Antigone,* he vigorously strives to do the required honour to the body of the dead woman. Unlike his Brahmin counterpart, he entertains great belief in the deliverance of the soul. His attitude towards women is also quite sympathetic. He is a sharp contrast to Sakharam. While Sakharam leads his life with women, based on their agreement without developing any legal or personal ties with them, Dawood identifies them as his 'bhabhies' (sister in law). He nostalgically expresses, "...who was I to her except just a frequent visitor to your house? But every woman you bring and keep in this house becomes a bhabhi to me. I call her *bhabhi*. She too was my *bhabhi*" (58).

Dawood is kind, practical and highly adaptable. He is not curt or adamant as Sakharam is. His dealings with the Brahmin in the cremation ground reveal his profound understanding of human nature. His unselfishness is also brought to the limelight through his efforts to perform the funeral rites for Sakharam's woman at his own expense. Thus the portrayal of Sakharam, his friend

Dawood, the Brahmin, the crowd in the cremation ground, the ward boy and the nurse as ordinary human beings, with common merits and weaknesses makes them real and life like in their speech, habit and behaviour.

The crows, in this play, are endowed with human qualities. One crow calls itself the "creative crow" which has the power to observe, assess and foretell happenings in the human world and the nether world. Its views regarding heaven and hell are quite novel. It describes that all souls, after being freed from all earthly desires, go to the same place. The crow depicts, "Some call it heaven. The other name for the same place is hell" (71).

Its further disclosure is only highly amusing. Says it, "Those who leave for there in poverty find it heavenly while those who leave with fat bank accounts in Switzerland get an attack of acute depression when they reach the same place. You know the place does not have a free market economy, yet. And no credit cards" (71). Tendulkar has, thus, insisted on the pivotal role played by money and its impact over the living and the dead. He has used the crows as symbols too. As a chorus, the crow exposes the nature of humanity. They are the crows of "the burning ghats of the humans" and "human desires." These crows are able to grasp the inner and interior thoughts of man and vehemently comment on them.

Tendulkar's portrayal of the nether world deserves a special mention. He presents the feelings, anxiety and reactions of the souls of a male and a female to the amusement of the audience. The soul of the fifth woman exclaims in ecstasy over the loss of her feminine graces. She happily heaves a sigh of relief, "At last here is freedom from being a woman! Came late, but life being what it is, you always come to know of better things late. Worse is easily available..." (72). This utterance is both sentimental and philosophical. This soul is freed from her bothering body but not from her gender consciousness or awareness.

Tendulkar, through his portrayal of the soul of a man, digs at the "manly vanity" which is uppermost in a person even after his death. Tendulkar has been revealing the self-centered and egotistic nature of men in his plays. But in *His Fifth Woman*, he makes a direct attack on them. Through the crows, he is trying to dispel many superstitious notions held dear by humanity, and makes a strong declamation against men's superiority complex. Chitragupta's presence and verbal expressions also are highly human. He has come in search of the two missing souls and charges them, "You would have made me lose my job! And after such a specklessly clean service record with only a few years left to retire" (74).

Death is mysterious because experience of death and after life has not been brought to the limelight. The various existing concepts regarding death and soul are the most difficult puzzle that remains unsolved. The crow reveals to the audience, "AND THEY DID NOT RECOGNIZE EACH OTHER! But that is precisely the fun of being dead. All relationships and obligations die" (74) and further makes an apt observation by saying with a sigh, "It happens in life too sometimes. Relationships die" (75). As the crow continues to worry regarding the fate of these 'bodiless, dickless, bumless and bustless human souls who were once a couple' the reader and audience would feel sure that Tendulkar is likely to offer some valuable suggestions or solutions and look eagerly forward at the crow. Tendulkar, who has already very diplomatically utilized the reversal device in *Silence! The Court is in Session*, adapts the same technique here too. The crow admits that it feels worried but diverts the attention of the viewers by drawing it upon Sakharam, who enters with a new woman.

Tendulkar has, with his wings of imagination, fused these three worlds. The animal world is devoid of its beastiality. The human world has been endowed with all its inevitable pangs and problems. The nether world is neither gruesome nor awesome nor fearsome. The human element in all the three worlds makes them look more realistic and appealing.

The various directions given in brackets provide adequate information about the action, voice modulation, sound sequence, light effect and movements thereby enabling even the readers to envision the happenings and enjoy them. This play is the first play attempted in English by the playwright. Feelings and emotions are succinctly presented. There is a judicious combination of facts and fantasy. As this play deals with life and after life, expressions suffuse with philosophical and spiritual undertones.

The episodic structure, in fact, is the binding element in the play, which makes it more interesting and impressive. The playwright achieves the same effect through the dream scene, as is done by the modern novelist through the interior monologue. He enlightens the audience regarding many facts that took place off stage through 'reports', the last moments of the sick woman, for instance, are reported by Sakharam. The crows serve the purpose of the chorus and the omniscient narrator. Thus the matter and the manner in *His Fifth Woman* quite enthrall the audience and they willingly allow themselves to be lured by his world of semblance of reality.

The status of Tendulkar, as one of the most celebrated skilful playwrights of India, has been affirmed because of his portrayals of life, its various problems and ills. Even the controversial responses received from the critics only confirm the influential impact of his plays. A playwright should strive not merely to entertain but also to affect and if possible alter the notions of the public. Tendulkar's plays constantly surprise due to their novelty in their subject matter, style and techniques. Arundhati Banerjee affirms this notion with her glorious tribute. "Tendulkar's multifaceted creative genius continues to experiment and explore the potentials of the dramatic genre-his primary area of creation."[7] While his other plays won the admiration of the spectators because of his unique treatment of the problems of life, *His Fifth Woman* is widely applauded, for, as a mature artist, Vijay Tendulkar has taken not merely the mundane world but also the nether world to task and divulged certain rare revelations regarding death and after-life. "Tendulkar's iconic status as the playwright who shattered barriers of conservatism in Marathi theatre and triggered a cascade of outrage needs no reiteration"[8] is the observation of *Times of India*. Tendulkar's efforts, to bring in innovations in matter and manner, have opened many fresh avenues, which remained unexplored thereby creating an awareness with regard to the need for change in order to make life an endearing experience.

References

1. Tom Alter's view quoted from the blurb of *Two Plays* by Vijay Tendulkar. New Delhi: OUP, 2006.
2. Dhyaneshwar Nadkarni, "Contemporary Marathi Theatre," *Contemporary Indian Drama*. Ed., Sudhakar Pandey and Freya Taraporewala. New Delhi: Prestige, 1990. p.9.

3. Frank Thakurdas and Rajinder Paul, "'Sakharam Binder': Two Views," *Enact*, No.68-69, Aug. – Sep. 1972, p.55.
4. Vijay Tendulkar, *Kanyadaan*. Translated by Gowri Ramnarayan, New Delhi: OUP, 2002. p.71.
5. Mario Garcia. "The Story Teller: Art of Being Simple and Brief", *The Hindu*, July 19, 2005, p.22.
6. Angus Bowmer, "Foreword" *Drama: A Critical Collection*. Ed., James K. Bowen and Richard Vander Beets. New York: Harper and Row, 1971. p. ix.
7. Arundhati Banerjee, "Introduction" *Five Plays* by Vijay Tendulkar. New Delhi: OUP, 2002. p. xix.
8. Rev. of *Times of India* quoted from the blurb of *Two Plays* by Vijay Tendulkar New Delhi: OUP, 2006.

20 Basavaraj Naikar's *A Dreamer of Freedom*: A Post-colonial Magic Realism Play

— Prof. Kh. Kunjo Singh

It is not an easy thing to define the term "magic realism" in an ordinary and normal literary formulation. But we should know that the term was originally applied in the 1920's to a school of painters and is used to describe the prose fiction of Jorge Luis Borges in Argentina, as well as the work of writers such as Gabriel Garcia Marquez in Columbia, Ginter Grass in Germany, and John Fowles in England. M.H. Abrams attempts to define the term in connection with the above writers: "These writers interweave, in an ever-shifting pattern, a sharply etched realism in representing ordinary events and descriptive details together with fantastic and dreamlike elements, as well as with materials derived from myth and fairy tales."[1]

Observing the above definition we may construct a form of "magic realism" to be a combination of sharply etched realism, fantastic and dreamlike elements and materials derived from myth and fairy tales. Originally the term connotes a kind of structure of novel. But in the postcolonial space where writers are concerned with the reconstruction of history, refinding of roots and belongingness, recovery and revival of lost culture, restructuring of identity and setting pace in the global race, the technical contents of the term "magic realism" have been employed in play also. Many post-colonial playwrights have adopted colonial and native history as a proper and significant theme of their plays successfully. In doing so, they have mingled ordinary details of life with historical realities, fantastic and dreamlike elements of society and materials derived from myth and fairy tales.

In the light of the above hypothesis we may interprete B.S. Naikar's *A Dreamer of Freedom* as a post-colonial magic realism play, despite its being a historical play about 1857 Indian War of Independence. The play vividly reflects Indian history of the time of 1857 Indian War of Independence popularly known as the Sepoy Mutiny. It was the time when Lord Dalhousie was the Governor General of India. Apart from a total of about 650 princely kingdoms of India, 63 kingdoms were in South India. The East India Company government popularly known as Company Sarkar ruled over the native princes and kings. As a policy of subjugation of Native Kings and annexation of their kingdoms to the British Empire, Lord Dalhousie introduced "The Disarmament Bill:" "According to this law, all the arms and ammunitions in the native kingdoms should be surrendered to the Company Sarkar." It is just to reduce the strength of the *native armies. Next* Dalhousie introduced "The Doctrine of Lapse." "According to this law all the kings of the Princely States who have no children of their own, cannot adopt anybody without the permission of the authorities of the Company Sarkar. In case the Company Sarkar 'refuses permission to the kings, they have to lose their kingdoms. The Company Sarkar will annex them."[2] The British Company Sarkar appointed Mr. Manson as the Political Agent of the 63 kingdoms of South India while.

Mr. Malcolm was made the Collector at Dharwad

For such subversive and subjugating laws of the Company Sarkar, the North Indian kings have already rebelled against the British authority. Important kings were the Badshah of Delhi, Tantya Tope, Queen of Jhansi, etc. Bahadur Shah of Delhi was the leader but all of them were defeated by the British authorities. But Nanasaheb Peshwa invited the South Indian kings to join the rebellion against the British Company Sarkar. Accordingly, the South Indian kings were holding a meeting in which Bhaskararao Bhabe gives an encouraging speech:

> .... we must fight for our freedom until our last breath or attain heroic Heaven on the battlefield There is no rest for us until we reach our target. We have sounded the clarion call itself Victory to Hindustan! Jai Hindustan!
>
> [Act III, Sc. III, p. 69]

The play presents the patriotic actions of Bhaskararao Bhabe of Naragund kingdom of Karnataka. He was childless and according to the Doctrine of Lapse, he applied to the British authorities for permission to adopt a boy for continuity of his royal family. But the British authorities represented by Manson rejected his request. So he was angry with the British and prepared for a war with them. He also hoped that he would get the support of the other South Indian kings. But as there were pro-British people among his subjects, his plan was sabotaged. Anyhow, his men killed Mr. Manson in a night attack while Manson camped at Ramdurg, very near to Naragund palace. Manson's head was severed.

The diplomatic British officer Manson, before his death, conspired with the native betrayers Banyabapu and Ktishnajipant to destroy the gunpowder in all the magazines of all the cannons of Naragund kingdom. Manson asked them to mix oil and millet with the gunpowder with the promise of giving half the share of Naragund kingdom after its capture by the British authorities. Now, the two betrayers did what they were told to do and came to Kolhapur to take shelter there in the camp of Malcolm saheb. The scene which shows how these two betrayers destroyed the gunpowder is presented as follows:

> *Banyabapu:* (Looks around him suspiciously. Then in low pitch)
> Saheb, both of us went to the hilltop at midnight, opened the gunpowder-magazine and mixed oil and millet in it and rendered it dysfunctional.
>
> *Krishnajipant:* So that the cannons may not explode even if Babsaheb Sarkar ordered them to be fired. This time he is sure to be defeated by your Company Sarkar.
>
> *Malcolm:* Wonderful! You have helped us very systematically and solidly. We are very thankful to you.
>
> [Act V, Sc. VI, p. 131.]

On Tuesday the historic day of June 2, 1858, Bhaskararao's palace is guarded by Virabhadranayaka's battalion while four other battalions are guarding the four City gates. The war has already started. At first, the native soldiers kill many Company soldiers in the sword fighting. But the Company soldiers begin to shoot guns and kill native soldiers. Moreover, the Company soldiers are approaching the palace gate. The native soldiers cannot defend the palace as their cannons are not exploding. The scene of the helplessness of the Naragund soldiers is presented by the playwright through the dialogue between Commander Vishnupant and King Bhaskararao as:

> *Vishnupant:* We are in great danger, Sarkar!
>
> *Bhaskararao:* Why? What happened?
>
> *Vishnupant:* Sarkar, I ordered the cannons to be fired. But unfortunately our cannons are not exploding.
>
> *Bhaskararao:* What do you mean by that, Vishnupant? What is the reason for that?
>
> *Vishnupant:* Sarkar, our gunpowder seems to have been adulterated. Our own people have stabbed us in the back!
>
> *Bhaskararao:* What is this? Should our people betray us like this? Who are those traitors?
>
> *Vishnupant:* Those scoundrels Banyabapu and Krishnajipant have done this treacherous thing.
>
> [Act V, Sc. VIII, pp. 136-137]

In the meanwhile Vishnupant is requesting Bhaskararao to escape from the palace through the underground tunnel. He says so because Babasaheb's life is more precious *than the kingdom at* the present moment. At first, Bhaskararao (Z is not willing to escape alone. But on being pursued vehemently he decides to escape. Then he comes to meet his mother and his wife for the last time. He also asks them to escape from the palace to protect their honour from the enemies. They don't like to do so. But when he earnestly requests his mother to convince Savitri the gravity of the situation, his mother consoles Savitri and lets her son escape instantly. They also follow suit. They are accompanied by Ramachandra, their attendant.

Very soon the Company Sarkar captured Naragund palace. They removed the native Bhagava Zenda flag and hoisted their own British flag, Union lack. Virabhadranayaka and his battalion guarding the palace have been defeated and they shot Virabhadranayaka and many of his soldiers to death.

On the one hand, Yamunabayi and Savitri after walking a fairly long distance accompanied by Ramachandra, decided to get a permanent solution of their problem. They decided to drown themselves in the Malaprabha river after giving all their golden ornaments to Ramachandra. Actually, they did it. Ramachandra came back home with the ornaments. On the other hand, Bhaskararao and Sahasrabuddhe were going on the road while Company soldiers surrounded them. They arrested Sahasrabuddhe and tried and sentenced to death by hanging. Bhaskararao escaped and took shelter in the Mantralaya Monastery for about three months. Unfortunately, he was arrested while eating mango in the house of the Gowda of Toragal. He was tried and sentenced to death by hanging. But through a strange quirk of Fate, he was saved when a brahmin cook in the Belgaum jail surrogated for him and died by hanging.

History records that Bhaskararao proceeded up to Nepal where he met Nanasaheb Peshwa. He enjoyed the appreciation of his revolt by Nanasaheb. After sometime there he came to Kashi where he met a Naragund woman, Kashibayi. Kashibayi requested Bhaskararao to many her only niece Savini, a girl who was also from Naragund. Bhaskararao was in the guise of a Sanyasi. Buthe was compelled to disclose his identity. He really married the girl and got a son named Ganeshpant. Now, he had nothing to pay his son as legacy except leaving a dream of freedom which his son and others might enjoy. The plot of the play does not go beyond this point.

Apart from constructing a historical plot, the playwright has also fictionalised the historical tradition of paying a visit to Lord Venkateshwara of Tirupati by the father of Bhaskararao, popularly known as Appasaheb. The play reflects the situation how the temple of Venkateshwara was constructed at Naragund. Appasaheb's grandfather, King Ramaraya-I, visited Lord Venkateshwara of Tirupati every year. Once the king and his party suffered a lot because they could not cross the flooded river Tungabhadra. Anyhow a shepherd came there and helped them crossing the river over a ford by taking the lead of them himself.

For which the King gave him a necklace as his fee. But the shepherd whose name was Venka did not accept the necklace. He asked the King to distribute alms of two paise each to the poor devotees gathered in the temple on that day.

When the puja was going on Ramaraya fainted to see the face of Lord Venkateshwara as the face of the shepherd boy who helped them crossing the river the previous day. He regained his conscience and also realised that the shepherd was none other than Lord Venkateshwara, Himself. This is a mythical belief. Then in their return journey the soldiers of Ramaraya destroyed the cropp fields of Tirupati. So the farmers of Tirupati area got angry and prayed to Lord Venkateshwara to ward off such torture. Therefore, Lord Venkateshwara appeared in the dream of Ramaraya one night. The Lord asked him not to come to Tirupati anymore. Because the Lord Himself would be at Naragund for which the King should build a temple. Very soon Ramaraya built Lord Venkateshwara temple at Naragund. The presentation of scenes with such flashback details in the form of dialogue between Appasaheb and Babasaheb is really the mythisisation of history. And this very technique is an ingredient to the magic realism structure of the play.

Another ingredient of magic realism in the play is seen in Bhaskararao's romance with the temple dancer, Bhimsani. It is really a fantasised story apart from the actual tract of history. The playwright has tactfully handled fantasy as a strand in the plot of the play. In the play, history runs as the plot while patriotism and sacrifice are the dominating themes. To provoke the admirations of the readers and audience and maintain their curiosity all through, the dramatist has fantasized this episode. Actually a great king and virtuous devotee of God would not behave like this of keeping a mistress illegally and immorally.

One aspect of magic realism is seen in the playwright's handling of the situation under which the King and his courtiers are presented as staunch believers in horoscope reading and fortune telling. In that age of scientific civilization and sophisticated weapons like cannons and guns, Bhaskararao Bhabe believed in the reading of horoscope. He thought if unwanted happenings are predicted, they would try to ward off them by worshipping Gods or by performing some pujas, etc. Once again fortune telling and astrology are employed as ingredients of magic realism. These things are semi-metaphysical and semi-mythical in nature. Though astrologers are a kind of scientists/hey also possess some qualities of mendicants sometimes telling false or exaggerated statements. In the play, Bhaskararao is projected as a character expecting a hopeful future as predicted by the astrologers and fortune tellers. The nature and profession of an astrologer are vividly shown by the following dialogue:

> *Astrologer*: Sarkar, I scrutinised the lines on your palm carefully. Likewise I examined, your horoscope also minutely. Sarkar you have Rahu-tunga-yoga in your horoscope. Similarly, there are many planets with rajayoga status. Hence you are lolling in happiness and abundance.
>
> *Bhaskararao*: Punditji, what you say is indeed true. But I have a big worry in my life.
>
> *Astrologer*: (Growing serious.) An astrologer's life is indeed very dilemmatic!
>
> *Bhaskararao*: Punditji, in my opinion the astrologer should follow the path of Truth only.
>
> *Astrologer*: Well said, Sarkar' I like your partiality to Truth. Then it means that I must tell you the truth. Shall hope that you have the courage to bear my words of truth?
>
> [Act II, Sc. I, pp. 28-29.]

Another aspect of the play that contributes to the formation of magic realism play is the strange way of saving the life of Bhaskararao. The playwright has set the very situation as if in a fairy world. In a fairy tale everything is made available when needed by the protagonist. Because there is always fairy-godmother by his side to provide whatever is necessary by him. The dramatist has tactfully tackled the situation by projecting the character of Shankarabhatta and making room for his meeting with the King as his temporary cook in the jail of Belgaum. It is strange and unexpected that Shankarabhatta willingly surrogated Bhaskararao and allowed himself to be hanged. Such happenings are found only in fairy tales where the controlling spirit of the plot is the omnipresent, omniscient and omnipotent fairy-godmother.

Bhaskararao dreamt a dream on the previous night of the night on which he was saved by Shankarabhatta. In the dream, Lord Venkateshwara came to him as Shankarabhatta and saved him. The playwright has skillfully mixed up such dream elements prevailing in our society and culture with real situations to form his play a magic realism play. Very unexpectedly and in a strange manner Bhaskararao himself could not believe what he experienced in real life situations. The strangeness and dream likeness of the situation is justified by the very speech of Bhaskararao:

> *Bhaskararao:* How strange and mysterious is God's lila! I was waiting for leaving this mortal world and attaining mukti. But God's will seems to be altogether different. In the last moment it seems Lord Venkateshwara Himself came to me in the guise of Shankarabhatta and saved me.
>
> [Act VIII, Sc. I, p. 195.]

The playwright has technically fictionalised some facts of history. The story of Kashibayi and Savitri II's migration from Naragund to Kashi (Varanasi) is fantastic and fictional. It is hard to believe that such a frail and fragile woman Kashibayi could easily cover the long distance from Naragund to Kashi along with a small baby girl during those days of hackneyed road journey. But for making continuity of the plot and to enliven the dream of freedom of the country, the playwright has to fictionalize and fantasize a portion of history. So on the ardent request of Kashibayi Bhaskararao married Savitri II. It is deliberately made so to beget a son to Bhaskararao in his 60s to wallow in the dream of freedom.

The fictional and fantastic nature of Kashibayi's migration to Kashi is proved by the following dialogue:

> *Kashibayi:* Swamiji, there is a city called Naragund in South India. We come from that city.
>
> *Sanyasi:* (Surprised and happy at the same time, but trying to hide his real feelings.) To which family in Naragund do you belong, amma? And what is your name?

Kashibayi: Swamiji, my name is Kashibayi Mane. But I used to stay in my brother Tadmiri' s house at Naragund.

Sanyasi: (Aside) What a surprise! These people belong to my kingdom.

[Act IX, Sc. II, p. 209].

At the end of the play, Bhaskararao in the guise of a Sanyasi gets a son by his young wife Savitri II. The son is named Ganeshpant. The protagonist father has nothing to give his son as legacy except leaving a sweet dream to be wallowed in by him. The condition of the dreamer and the nature of his dream are vividly shown by the following speech of the Sanyasi father:

> *Sanyasi:* Don't cry, my dear Ganeshpant. Don't cry. (He snaps his middle finger and thumb and produces a sound. The baby laughs.) How unlucky are you, my dear Ganeshpant ! You were born after I lost my entire kingdom. Now I have nothing to give you as legacy. Let it be. But I hope that the fire of mutiny that many patriots like me have kindled, will one day burn bright like the Light of Freedom. My life is over. 1 only hope that you will live as a subject of free India. May my dream of freedom come hue in your time at least!
>
> [Act IX, Sc. II, pp. 217-218.]

To conclude, it can be said that Basavaraj Naiker's play *A Dreamer of Freedom,* despite its being a historical play about 1857 Indian War of Independence, has a strong claim for a play of magic realism in its structure, technique and style.

References

1. Abrams M. H.. *A Glossary of Literary Term,* Bangalore: Prism Books Pvt. Ltd., 1993, p. 133.
2. Basavaraj Naikar. *A Dreamer of Freedom,* Delhi: Authorpress, 201[illegible] p. 36.

21 Social Problems as Portrayed in Sri Lankan Poetry

— Dr. K. Balachandran

"There cannot be peace in Sri Lanka" (p. 80), wrote L. Piyadasa in his book *Sri Lanka: The Unfinished Quest for Peace* after seeing the 1983 Holocaust. After the traumas of 1983, "Most exciting material emerged." The ethnic crisis dominated Sri Lankan society during this period. Spontaneous emotions found their expressions in powerful writings.

Wijesinha writes that in 1971 New Ceylon writing and in 1973 some more volumes came. In 1979 Yasmine Gooneratne emigrated to Australia. The English Association of Sri Lanka brought out *Navasilu-I* (1976). 7 more volumes came till 1987. Since young writers couldn't find their place in this one, *New Lankan Review* was started in 1983. Magazines like *Kaduwa* published by the English Students' Association of Peradeniya University and *Blink* by Kelaniya University came into existence in 1983. The Arts Council conducted annual competition for writing in English. The British Council launched new publications and book exhibitions of Sri Lankan writing. Sri Lankan Broadcasting Corporation did its best by featuring Lankan Anthology. As in India, mostly established writers dominated the anthologies. It was disappointing to note that the new writing dealing with the traumas of Sri Lanka was not comprehensively available in any anthology. Hence Wijesinha brought out *An Anthology of Contemporary Sri Lankan Poetry in English* in 1988. This book is devoted to the ethnic crisis in Sri Lanka.

Jean Arasanayagam, Patrick Fernando, Yasmine Gooneratne, Anne Ranasinghe, Kamala Wijeratne, Lakdasa Wikkramasinha are some of the significant writers in English. For the Sri Lankan Poetry, they have set the canon. The poetry of the younger generation like Suresh Canagarajah, Angela de Silva, Richard de Zoysa, Angelo Fernando, Ianthe de Silva, Wilhelm Ephraums, Sumathy Sivamohan, Angie Singham and Hans Wijayasuriya is provocative and perceptive.

Roots give life to a tree, plant or creeper and without which life is not possible for any vegetation. So it is for a citizen or a writer. One can migrate to any country and settle there. It can be done—it may be successful or unsuccessful, both depend upon very many factors. To have one's root in one's own country is easy; but in an alien country, it may be difficult. Alienation is one of the social problems. This may detract one's progress and well-being.

Jean Arasanayagam in his poem 'Roots' (p. 43-44 in *An Anthology of Contemporary Sri Lankan Poetry in English*) speaks of alienation. It is important to have roots; if it is eroded and washed away by rain water or drought, one cannot belong anywhere. He asks:

> how can my roots grow deep
> seed planted in drought desiccated by heat—
> my eyes looking into yours t1ell me that I
> cannot belong... (p. 44)

Even the buffaloes and snakes have roots in this land (Sri Lanka) and if he can't have any, then what is the use of being a human being?

Yasmine Gooneratne is at her best when she defends the English Language. The Sinhala writers were continually attacking the English Language. Unable to bear their unjustifiable attack on a language, she wrote this poem 'This Language, This Woman' as a kind of reply to them. So, problems exist even at the level of languages. One need not praise a foreign language but one should not denigrate another language. She even warns fellow writers:

> Beware how you insult her
> in your ignorance. (p. 72)

One should not be jealous of another language, if she is very prosperous for the loveliness of that language will be otherwise missed. English is no more an "Empress's daughter" but the language is used not only by the rulers but also by the ordinary people in the cadre of clerks and merchants.

> No more an Empress's daughter with a
> bribe locked in her purse,
> the clerks, the merchants, and their hireling tribe
> long since dispersed. (p. 72)

Yasmine beautifully and sympathetically narrates the story of English thus:

> She wanders here alone and unbefriended
> She has known greatness, borne illustrious sons,
> her mind's well - stored....
> fit her to be your mistress and my Muse. (p. 72)

One need not be told about the greatness of the English Language or the illustrious writers she (the language) had produced. As a beautiful girl can be a handsome youth's partner, English can be wedded by any poet (i.e., English Language can be used for writing poetry) and for the poetess, the English Language is the Muse.

Death is inevitable in everyone's life. But it can be digestible to people, if it comes at a later stage say, for example, after 60 years of life. If the God of death snatches one's life in one's prime years who will take it easily, for, grief will be thousand fold. Patrick Fernando's poem, 'The Fisherman Mourned, by His Wife' (pp. 64-65) is a classic example of the problem of fear and unexpected death. The fisherman who was unlucky and washed away by the sea waves even before he was thirty, is mourned by his wife who has become pregnant. Their other children weep and their youngest child thinks that his father is fast asleep.

> our children weep, the youngest thinks you're fast asleep:
> theirs is fear and wonderment
> ....I cannot with simple grief
> assuage dismemberment. (p. 64)

She hasn't understood that fishers are always 'riders to the sea'.

Bravery is an ornament to men as shyness is to women. Once 'Soldiery' was compulsory to every house—every house should send a youth to the army for a minimum period of service. When soldiers return victoriously from the battlefront, they will be wearing olive leaves around their foreheads and garlands on their necks. A Hero's welcome will be there for a soldier. Many times this may be the scene; sometimes the scene may change to that of a sad occasion when a soldier's dead body comes in a coffin to his native place. One such scene is word-painted dexterously by Kamala Wijeratne in her poem, 'A Soldier's Wife Weeps' (pp. 37-38). In nine stanzas, the dead soldier's wife recalls her past life. It is the problem of death in the battlefield. The previous Saturday when he went back from leave, she even prayed to Lord Buddha after lighting a lamp. On Wednesday when the crow cried, she had no fears about her husband in the war front; she had his horoscope reread and "there were no malefics." But on Thursday when people bore him away, she says,

> I did not know what to believe, what to think it was as if I had slept a long sleep and saw things in a haze between life and death.

She recalls how both bathed together at the village well on Saturday; and he, like a boy threw stones at the sneering frogs. She recalls how he used to touch her hair, and she sobs with much attachment.

> They gave you a hero's burial with all military honours the band played and your body passed from hand to hand. (p. 38)

Now on weekends, to preoccupy herself she spreads her white wedding saree on the floor and contemplates how she stood on the marriage day with him, "shyly tying the piece of white cloth around her waist."

> The end of the poem is very apt and satirical.
> How wrong the horoscope readers were....

Very artistically and realistically, the poetess has ended this poem. So it is not only the problem of death for soldiers in the war front, but also the problem of the unsuitability of the horoscopes which has brought her hubby's unexpected death in the war front.

Mahagama Sekara's poem, 'Forgotten Village' (in *Gestures: An Anthology of South Asian Poetry*) (pp. 288-89) celebrates the preciousness of a village. Bundling up his belongings, inherited from his village, he made a trip to the city.

> There is nothing that I have earned here
> Except the false pride that weighs so heavily upon me.
> (p. 288)

He complains that he has earned nothing but false pride. Now he longs to return to his village:

> I must return to my village, of dear mother, wave your hand
> And show me the way home.

It is not only his complaint but many right thinking people also feel like him. He requests his mother to show him the path home:

> To bathe in the holy river,
> To dispel the body's heat,
> To wash away my impurities; (p. 288)

Can we find a holy river in any metropolitan city? Any river which runs in a city is invariably polluted, all the unwanted dirt and the garbage will be there; the sewage water also will be there; all the cowdung and industrial wastes will be there. One cannot take a bath in it; instead of washing away one's impurities, one will get all the impurities from the river water! But it is the contrary in the rural side. Hence when he yearns to return to his village, there is no surprise in it.

> To weed my plot of land, To tighten the fences,
> To sow new seeds
> And to reap the golden harvest. (p. 289)

Life in a city nowadays is problematic. Hence his wish to return to his village to do agricultural work will fetch him the happiness, peace of mind and contentment which he lost during his sojourn in the city.

Vimalaratna Kumaragama in the poem, 'The Prison' (pp. 295-96) describes the struggles of an elephant and its calf which were trapped in a rocky pothole.

But it was difficult to believe
That even a mighty elephant could not scale
Those walls. Again and again she battled to the edge,
Terrible her struggles, but of no avail. (p. 295)

This is the problem to the people who live near the forest areas. Especially when the elephants trumpet cruelly, it is terrorising to the people who live in that surrounding.

Even distant villages heard her trumpeting
As though she mourned the passing of her might.

All the efforts taken to bring up the elephant above were of no avail. After a sevenday's drama, the animal died leaving everyone to feel for its absence. It is a loss no doubt to its young one, its relatives and to the forest wealth!

In his book *New Verse* Guy Amirthanayagam writes in his poem, 'To My Austic Son, Revantha' (pp. 42-43) that even heredity is a problem.

Early childhood autism, my psychiatrist rist beckoned,
Heredity's the problem, the biologists believed,
Mother was cruel, the maid-servant proclaimed:
The servant was vile, his mother declaimed. (p. 42)

In his poem, 'Age and Age's Evils' (From *The Face and the Dream and Other Poems*) he says what he would meditate-about the problem of evil.

When I was convalescing at a nursing home With a broken
hip, I would meditate
On age and age's evils. (p. 17)

Indran Amirthanayagam (from Ceylon, R.I.P. *Selected Poems of Indran Amirthanayagam)* in his poem, 'There are Many Things I want to tell You' speaks of the caste system in Ceylon.

how in the churches the lower castes sat on the floor, the high
on benches. (p. 6)

This is the case generally in our country too; instead of saying lower caste and higher caste, here it is the poor and the rich—the poor sit on the floor and the rich on the benches!

In the poem, 'Not much Art' Amirthanayagam speaks of the problem of guerillas hiding in bush empires (p. 10 and

> When each minute Sons and daughters
> raped and murdered. (p. 11)

This is really an unbearable situation for any country. Guerillas' and terrorists' problems have to be tackled; if allowed they would be big problems to the safety of the people and security of the country. Raping of women and murdering of men should not take place in an ideal country.

In his poem, 'Elegy for Neelan Thiruchelvam' (pp. 3-14) he speaks of peacemakers who try to live with dignity and

> .....that letters.......... that letter
> Written in laws had the power to absorb
> A bullet, to convert its powder into a flower. (p. 13)

> .....boys and girls study nerves at home, watch television,
> or listen to the radio, or sleep, or smoke
> ganja while the afternoon rolls into evening' (p. 17)

It is the problem of school-going students about which he narrates here. They become addicts to ganja smoking and other bad habits. This should not happen, for, it would affect their bright future. If they are spoiled once, they can never be useful to themselves, to the family, and to the country.

In his poem, 'The Last Question' (pp. 21-22) he speaks of the problem of pirates who set five to the Colombo port

> Of the poor port of Colombo, in flames, lit by your hands
> after the visit of pirates who sacked Tamil from your tongue?
> Where have the ruffians gone? (p. 22)

In his poem, 'The City, with Elephants' (pp. 30-31) he writes about the freedom loving people who do underground work.

> while in some houses freedom-bound lovers embrace late
> and read Tagore about the people working underneath the
> falling of empires. (p. 31)

In the poem, 'Yamoussoukro, with Cathedral' (pp. 41-43) he writes about a very practical problem which one can find in any country.

> Every monument in the modem world requires a parking lot.
> Here you may leave your horses, tents, motor cars. (p. 43)

In the poem, 'Elephant Meditation' (pp. 55-56), he writes about the problem of digging up even the graves by anti-social elements.

> ..... how even graves
> are sometimes defiled, the bodies removed by vandals
> and thieves. (p. 55)

In the poem, 'Advice to Young Poets' he advises like, 'Stay away from delusion. Welcome illusion... ' (p.72)

> ... ...
> encourage all such attempts to return the poet to the
> city, to bring him back as king. (p.72)
> ... ...

"As I've said to the mirror, do not believe your own press, Fight to keep a space open in your heart, ears, brain in you." (p.73)

How true they sound to us! Practical and useful pieces of advice, they are. Press (Newspaper) don't publish the truth; often they give false news and because of pressure from higher ups or those who are in power.

In the poem, 'The Death of Allen Ginsberg', (pp. 87-88), he speaks about the problem of forgetting Tamil.

> Like forgetting Tamil which insecured The anchor of my nostalgia, shipped Me out to write and make my home on the sea. (p. 88)

Conclusion

1. If studied carefully it can be learnt that all social problems are situations which have injurious consequences for a society.
2. The social problems occur because of the deviations from the ideal situations.

3. The social problems have some common basis of origin - in poverty, ignorance, illiteracy, etc.
4. The social problems occur in all the continents irrespective of the caste, colour and country.

Works Cited

Amirthanayagam, Guy, *New Verse,* Harris Hulugalle, Colombo-2, Sri Lanka, 1990.

______________, *The Face and the Dream and Other Poems,* Marga Institute, Colombo-6, Sri Lanka, 1999.

Amirthanayagam, Indran, Ceylon, R.I.P. *Selected Poems of Indran Amirthanayagam,* International Centre for Ethnic Studies, Colomboo8, Sri Lanka, 2001.

Piyadasa, L., *Sri Lanka: The Unfinished Quest for Peace, Marram Books,* London, 1988.

Satchidanandan, Ed. K., *Gestures: An Anthology of South Asian Poetry,* New Delhi: Sahitya Akademi, 2001.

Wijesinha, Ed. Rajiva, *An Anthology of Contemporary Sri Lankan Poetry in English.* The British Council, Sri Lanka, 1988.

22 Naipaul's India: A Million Mutinies Now—A Post-modern Travelogue

— Dr. Basavaraj Naikar

Although Naipaul has written many novels, he is also known for his four travelogues about India, like *An Area of Darkness, Overcrowded Baracoon, India: A Wounded Civilization and India: A Million Mutinies Now*. These travelogues are, obviously, records of his four travels in India undertaken at different times. Hence he, who studies all the four travelogues, will be able to have a chronological picture of India as perceived by Naipaul. As Martin Amis rightly points out, "Naipaul remains our most exhilarating explorer with a corpus of travel writing that now surpasses that of D.H. Lawrence and Graham Greene."[1] But in the present paper an attempt is made to analyze only one i.e., the latest (perhaps his last) travelogue on India.

He has visited India four times with an intention of understanding and writing about it. Although he has visited the same country, there is some difference among them. There happens to be a repetition and a variation in each of his travelogues. Every time he meets some new people and a few old people, who, he had already met during his earlier visits. But there is one striking difference between his latest travelogue and the earlier ones i.e., *India: A Million Mutinies Now* happens to be the biggest one, almost more than double the size of each one of his earlier travelogues. Its canvas is epical. Another distinct quality of *India: A Million Mutinies* happens to be Naipaul's patient hearing of the Indian voice and his control over his own. In other words, he observes more than he comments upon them.

> In his first visit, India was An Area of Darkness, in the second, he visualized India as layers and layers of wounds inflicted on Indian Civilization. During his third visit, he

> finds himself in Post-Independence India, where life is stirring energetically. He interacts with numerous people and let the voices speak for themselves. Abundant energies of the Indian subcontinent are revealed through the post-modern technique of projecting pluralistic voices.[2]

A travelogue presupposes a lot of physical as well as mental energy on the part of the traveler, sufficient money to spend, a willingness to understand the people of different cultures, photographic observation and absorption of experience and an ability to analyze the observed phenomena from his subjective point of view. Obviously, V.S. Naipaul has all these qualities combined in him. In Nirad Chaudhuri's opinion, India is far too big a country to be understood by anyone. Even Indians cannot boast of understanding the diverse life of India totally. But Naipaul has attempted to accomplish such a formidable task mainly because of his quest for knowledge of the country where his ancestors' roots lie. He seems to have a sort of nostalgic attachment to India, which makes him undertake the journey to this country many times. Secondarily, the travel is also a kind of investment for the future gain—of writing a travel, thereby, earning international recognition and huge royalty.

Although Naipaul is a brahmin by birth, his long stay in England seems to have anglicized and de-brahmanized him to a great extent. He believes in the British values of reason, order and measure. That explains why he has developed a broad humanist vision instead of a parochial brahmanical outlook towards life. Happily free from a sense of superiority or separatism, Naipaul has exhibited his ability to meet all kinds of people and understand them sympathetically. He has shown godlike compassion for all types of characters whom he meets in course of his travel across the length and breadth of the country.

Unlike the early travelers like Nuniz and Paes, who visited India and wandered in the country by themselves and observed things, beings and events of the contemporary times, Naipaul follows a different method. Far from visiting the people and places alone, he takes the local Indian friends (like journalists, officers and laymen, etc.) who act as his guides and take him to the people and places suggested by him. These friends act as translators or interpreters for the native Indians, who do not know

English, but who are engaged in conversation with Naipaul. While going to different places of India, Naipaul observes all the striking geographical details and contemporary events that are happening at the moment. After meeting the people of his choice, Naipaul poses a number of questions to them thereby eliciting maximum possible information from them. One of the conspicuous differences between his earlier travelogues (*like India: A Wounded Civilization*) and the present one (*India: A Million Mutinies Now)* is that in the earlier ones, he not only observes and records the Indian phenomena, but also comments upon them very incisively whereas in the present one, he has developed the patience to listen to the voices of Indians without making his own harsh comments elaborately. That is why the critics have perceived a note of reconciliation here instead of that of conflict; a note of affirmation instead of that of negation or interrogation. One may see in Naipaul, the presence of greater sympathy for India now, than the one he has shown in his earlier travelogues.

India: A Million Mutinies Now is quite a bulky travelogue running into 520 pages of small print and to be read only at leisurely intervals. The reader is not bored but exhausted by the seemingly interminable narrative and abundant details that go on piling up and offer a cumulative picture of the Indian society. Another feature to be noted in this work is that the author does not follow a discursive method of narration, but adopts a fictional mode. When a travelogue is written in the fictional mode, it tends to become very minute, photographic and microscopic and helps the non-Indian reader to visualize the whole scene. But the Indian reader is likely to be rather bored with the fictional mode of narration and the abundance of detail because of his familiarity with the Indian scenario.

In the present travelogue, Naipaul visits a number of places and individuals in India and records a bewildering multiplicity of voices. There is almost 'God's plenty' here. That is exactly, why, it becomes very difficult for the reader or critic to discern a knowledgeable pattern of ideas. (Naipaul has confessed that he also felt the same difficulty in imposing some order on his amorphous experience of travelling in India for two full years.)

Naipaul has travelled all the important centres of India like Bombay, Bangalore, Chennai, Amritsar and Srinagar representing the local cultures of those areas. We may have a rapid survey of his experiences in these parts one by one.

The first thing that catches Naipaul's attention in Bombay is its huge crowd. Then he notices the awakening of Dalits and their respect for Dr. Ambedkar. Then he meets a Jain businessman called Papu, who says some important things about Jains. For example, according to him, Jains are strict vegetarians, lovers of non-violence and traders but they are not involved in industry because "The killer-instinct is required in industry, not in trading."[3] (p. 11). The modern Jains show their philanthropic instinct by building orphanages and hospitals, whereas the earlier generations of Jains used to build marble temples. Papu, the young Jain stockbroker, believes in rituals, as they are harmless, in purity and charity. They have to feed a cow every day with certain things. Then Papu takes Naipaul to the famous Dharavi slum and shows it to him. Naipaul observes the squalid conditions of life there.

Then Naipaul meets Mr. Patil, who is an active worker for Shiv Sena. The Shiv Sena is named after Sovereign Shivaji and pleads for the protection of Hinduism from the onslaught of other cultures, especially the Muslims.

When Naipaul meets a Muslim called Anwar, he learns some details of life from the Muslim's point of view. For example, Muslims are the enemies of Shiv Sena and its anti-Muslim philosophy. Anwar points out some contradictions in his community. For example, the uneducated Muslims indulge in criminal activities but still read the *Quoran* and do the namaz five times a day. They watch the TV, though it is forbidden by their religion. Muslims believe in brotherhood.

Naipaul meets Mr. Raote, who belongs to the carpenter's family specialized in making coffins. He is proud of Maharashtrian culture because "Maharashtra is a land of saints" (p. 45) and "The Gymnasium is a Maharashtrian institution" (p. 44). He speaks about his poverty, his specialization in furniture making, his belief in his guru and his six pilgrimages to the cave of Amarnath in Kashmir.

In Bombay, Naipaul meets Namdev Dhasal, an important member of Dalit Panthers. The idea of Indian Dalit Panthers is borrowed from that of Black Panthers of USA. Namdev Dhasal is not only a Dalit activist, but also a poet, who lived in a brothel area and expressed the agonies and dilemma of the downtrodden classes and castes of India. Naipaul discovers that Namdev Dhasal married Mallika after falling in love with her; that Mallika wrote her autobiography in Marathi entitled *I Want to Destroy Myself*, which was "a story not only of love, but also of disillusion and pain" (p. 99). Although Mallika knew that her husband had venereal disease and went with the women from the brothel area, she did not disdain him because she loved him. Naipaul attends the demonstration of prostitutes organized by Namdev Dhasal. Mallika tells Naipaul, "Dalits will sacrifice anything and everything for Ambedkar. He is not an extra god for them. He is God" (p. 108). Referring to the contrast between the past and the present, Namdev Dhasal tells Naipaul, "There was a time when we were treated like animals. Now we live like human beings. It is all because of Ambedkar" (p. 119). Namdev Dhasal extended the definition of Dalits to include all the oppressed people and not just the scheduled castes and struggled hard for this noble cause. But unfortunately, there came about a split in the organization. "When the Dalit Panthers split, I used to drink heavily. I started the Panthers and then they put me in a minority. It was a great blow. It saddens me still" (p. 118).

Then Naipaul meets Mr. Ghate, a high official of Shiv Sena and observes his life and learns many things about his family. A tiger emblem is the characteristic Shiv Sena emblem. Mr. Ghate speaks about the chawl life, which is the communal life. "The chawl is like a bigger family. The area is even bigger family."

A common feature noticed by Naipaul is the criminalization of Indian society. "Crime now paid well. The gangs fought like politicians for territory, and the gang wars of Bombay were in the news." Underworld activities are very common in India like the 'biscuit' work and black money. Even in the gangs there is a communal split. "Vithal said he didn't trust the Muslims in his own gang and preferred not to work with them" (p. 74).

Next, Naipaul meets a pujari, belonging to the priestly group of the Chitrapur Saraswat Brahmins. He has migrated to Bombay, "an unwelcoming city" (p. 76). He earns Rs. 1,000 per month. As he tapes his mantras and sells them to clients, he is nicknamed as 'The Electric Pujari.'

Subrato is another man with whom Naipaul comes into contact. He has come to Bombay from Bengal and entered the film world by becoming a scriptwriter. He tells Naipaul some details about the production of Hindi films, like scriptwriting, shooting, editing, etc. He also recounts his poverty and struggle for survival. Then Naipaul is taken by Nikhil to Rajan, who had met Naipaul in 1962. Rajan tells him about his father, brother, and his suffering and late marriage.

After completing his travel in Bombay, Naipaul flies to Goa, where he sees the famous cathedral of St. Francis Xavier. He refers to Vasco da Gama, who had discovered India in the fifteenth/ sixteenth century and to Camoens's epic *Lusiads*. He notices, "the Portuguese had created in Goa something of a New World emptiness like the Spaniards in Mexico" (p. 142). He thinks that the British rule had given some direction to Indian history. "Just as Portuguese rule had given a great simplicity to the history of Goa, so the British rule gave a direction to later Indian history and made it easier to grasp" (p. 143).

While traveling from Goa to Karnataka, Naipaul notices the devotees of Swami Ayyappa and describes the myth as recounted as Devaiah. When he enters the Karnataka region, he notices the Indian poverty, "Indian poverty was still visible, the middens, the broken-down aspect of houses and lanes" (p. 149). But still he notices some change there, "There were none of the walking skeletons, with their deranged eyes. The agricultural revolution was a reality here; the increased supply of food showed" (p. 149). Like every foreign visitor Naipaul observes, "No corner of this land was without its connection with the gods" (p. 149). "The land was almost beautiful, almost without pain for the beholder. It was a kind of regeneration that could have come only slowly" (p. 149). In Bangalore, Naipaul meets the scientist Dr. Srinivasan's Father. Then he meets another scientist Mr. Subramanian. One conspicuous thing about these two scientists was that they came from priestly families. The Brahmins try to combine the traditional learning with modern English education. Naipaul learns that the brahmanical domination in administration has been replaced by the non-brahmin one due to the general social awareness. Naipaul notices the 'Hindu awakening' and says, "If Subramaniam was right, there was a hidden irony in that awakening: that the group, or caste who had contributed so much to that awakening should now find itself under threat" (p. 161). Then Naipaul meets some other Brahmins like Pravas (an engineer) and Kala, who tell him about the ritualized families and their problems.

When Naipaul meets Minister M.P.Prakash, he notices the importance attached to politics in India, "As in old Rome, so in modern Bangalore; the more important the man, the greater the crowd at his door" (p. 181). Mr. M. P. Prakash tells Naipaul how caste is of great importance in Indian political scene and how individuals enjoy greater power when elected and nowhere to go after the fall, unless he is involved with some socio-political movement. Mr. Prakash tells him how the political power gives so much of comfort, perks and status to individuals.

Naipaul then goes from Bangalore to Mysore, where he happens to meet a Brahmin pundit, who was appointed as a vaidika by the Maharaja of Mysore. Through the pundit Naipaul learns many details about His Highness Sri Jayachamarajendra Wodeyar—like his loss of power as a Maharaja, his appointment as Governor of Karnataka, his special love of books, temples, pilgrimages and his untimely death by ulcer at the age of fiftyeight. Naipaul observes the architecture of the palace, its garishness, mixture of styles and paintings in it, etc.

After covering the south-western part of India consisting of Bombay, Goa and Karnataka, Naipaul moves to the south-eastern part consisting of Tamil Nadu, especially Madras (or the present Chennai) and meets a variety of people, observes a variety of events and sees a number of things, which show the conflict between tradition and modernity, Aryans and Dravidians and Brahmins and non-brahmins indirectly showing the motion of the wheel of Indian history. Tamil Nadu represented by Chennai happens to be a stronghold of traditional brahmanical culture. Naipaul meets Mr. Sugar in Chennai at his Mylapore house and gathers some information with his help. The South Indian food consists mainly of rice in its various guises and never gives the satisfaction of a filled belly. Naipaul records his feeling very honestly and frankly, "This vegetarian food of the South—which drew the crowds to the Woodlands—was too subtle, too light; it made no impression on my stomach; it never left me feeling fed" (p. 208). Madras City is known for its religious orthodoxy symbolized by a variety of temples. Mr. Sugar takes Naipaul to the Mylapore temple. "The sculptured pyramidal towers, the palm trees, the bare-backed brahmins among the old stone-pillars, the big and beautiful water-tank at Mylapore, with internal stone-steps all around—they were like things in old European prints" (p. 209). Naipaul perceives a change between the present Madras and the old Madras that he had seen in 1962.

> After my introduction to the brahmin culture of the South, this was my introduction to the revolt of the South; the revolt of South against North, non-brahmin again Brahmin, the racial revolt of dark against fair, Dravidian against Aryan. The revolt had begun long before; the Brahmin world, I had come upon in 1962 was one that had already been undermined. (p. 210)

Naipaul notices the conspicuous conflict between Brahmins and non-brahmins in the philosophy of the DMK Party established by the dynamic political prophet called Periyar. 'Periyar' is a Tamil word meaning a sage or a wise man. The emblem of the party is the rising sun above the hills. Periyar was an atheist and a rationalist. "And what Periyar offered, with his 'rationalism' and his rejection of God, was his rejection of the Brahmins and their language, his rejection of the North; his rejection of caste; his rejection of the disregard the fair people of the North had for the dark people of the South" (pp. 217-218). Periyar ridiculed the Hindu gods. He cruelly mocked at the caste-Hindus, comparing the poverty of their scientific achievements with the great achievements of Europe. He also said that the Hindus had copies of their gods from the gods of ancient Egypt, Greece, Persia and Chaldea. One of Periyar's sayings, virtually an incantation, was very famous: "There is no God. There is no God. There is no God at all. He who invented God is a fool. He who propagates God is a scoundrel. He who worships God is a barbarian." 'This was how Periyar began all his discourses' (p. 217).

Naipaul points out some similarities and dissimilarities between Periyar and Gandhi. Periyar finally became anti-Gandhi. Whereas Gandhi was a vegetarian, Periyar was a glutton and made a point of eating beef, pork, and mutton in his *biriyani*. Like Gandhi, Periyar came from a Hindu merchant class, but he was not as well educated as Gandhi. Although initially Periyar joined the Indian National Congress, later he broke away from it, because of the ideological differences he had with the party.

> It had to do with the caste prejudices of the Brahmins in the South. Non-brahmins were not allowed free entry to temples. They were absolutely barred from the inner sanctum where the temple deity was; they had to be content with a view from a distance. Sometimes non-brahmins were not even allowed to walk on the lane in front of a temple. (p. 219) Thus Periyar broke from Gandhi and the Congress.

Naipaul offers a few more details about Periyar's political mission. In 1925, Periyar founded the Self-Respect Movement and symbolized his cause by wearing a black shirt. He offered a Utopian vision of future bright with the fruits of science. "Communications will mostly be by air and of great speed.... Radios may be fixed in man's hats.... Food enriched with vitamins will be encased in pills or capsules sufficient for a day's or week's sustenance. The average life may stand at 100 years or more.... Motorcars may weigh about one hundred weight and will run without petrol... Electricity will be everywhere and in every hut serving the people for all purposes.... No industry or factory will run for the private profits of individuals. They will all be owned by the community at large, and all inventions will cater for the needs and pleasures of all people.... When the world itself has been converted into a paradise, the need to picture a paradise in the clouds will not arise. Where there is no want, there is no god. Where there is scientific knowledge, there is no need for speculation and imagination.... The struggle for existence needs to be changed into a life of happiness" (p. 220). His utopian vision easily corresponds to Marx's idea of a classless society. Periyar was an iconoclast and the white-bearded king of Tamil Nadu. After Periyar's death, his mission was continued by Mr. Veeramani and Mr. Annadurai.

Naipaul meets a number of people like Sadanand Menon, Gopalakrishnan, Palani and others, who subscribe to Periyar's philosophy and plead for reservation for non-brahmins in educational institutes and for employment.

Naipaul has a number of experiences of meeting different kinds of people with mutually contradictory philosophies and beliefs. For example, after meeting the non-brahmins of DMK party, he meets a number of Brahmins like Kakusthan and others. Kakusthan is a poor Brahmin, who takes Naipaul to the

Parthasarathy temple and tells him a number of things about brahmanical Puritanism, separatism and the inevitable need for adaptation of modernity in their life.

After travelling in South India, Naipaul goes to Calcutta in the north-eastern part of India where he notices certain contrastive features of British and Indian architecture. According to him, the British bungalows "were well suited to the climate. But they seemed too grand for the poverty of the Indian countryside" (p. 280). By contrast the architecture of post-colonial India is a mechanical and surface imitations of the international style. "What is not easy to understand is that, unlike the British, Indians have not really built for the Indian climate" (p. 280). He continues to comment "much of the architecture of free India has become part of the ugliness and crowd and increasing physical oppression of India" (p. 281). But the British Indian architecture "is the finest secular architecture in the sub-continent" (p. 281).

In Calcutta, once known as the City of palaces, Naipaul notices that it has lost its charm due to overcrowding and become an ugly city with its broken roads, dust, "the day-long cicada like screech, rising and falling, of the horns of the world's shabbiest buses and motor-cars" (p. 282). He notices the very big movement of refugees and "Decay within, decay without" (p. 282).He sees the contrast between the grandeur of British India and the ugliness of post-colonial India, "The British built city could still be seen, even in this ghostly way, because so little had been added since independence; so little had been added since 1962" (p. 282).

After making his observations on the City of Calcutta, Naipaul meets a few important persons, who acquaint him with Bengali life and culture. First, he meets Chidananda Das Gupta, who is a filmmaker and who takes Naipaul to Shantiniketan and shows him the house in which Rabindranath Tagore lived. He tells Naipaul that his father had been a preacher for the Brahmo Samaj all his life. Naipaul comments on Brahmo Samaj as follows: "The Brahmo Samaj was a kind of purified or reformed Hinduism, which the father of Rabindranath had elaborated in the 19th century. It was an attempt to synthesize the New Learning of Britain and Europe with the old speculative Hindu faith of the Vedas and the Upanishads. It was a direct development of the ideas of Raja Ram Mohan Roy of Bengal (1772-1833), the first modern Indian reformer and educationist" (p. 286). Then

Chidananda Das Gupta tells Naipaul about Vishwa Bharati University, Satyajit Ray and CPI(M).

Dipanjan tells Naipaul, "In Calcutta minor scientists are quite common. This is the city of M.N. Saha, S.N. Saha, J.C. Bose and P.C. Roy" (p. 301). Naipaul comments that "In the South, science had grown over two or three generations out of the brahmanical tradition of abstract learning. In Bengal, in the British built city of Calcutta, science had come with the New Learning, scientific achievement had come out of colonial competitiveness and the wish of Indians to prove themselves" (p. 301). Further, Dipanjan tells Naipaul some details of his own family life. Then he acquaints Naipaul with the problem of destitutes in Calcutta and shows him the place where Mother Teresa built her home for such destitutes later. Naipaul learns from Dipanjan some details about the soaring prices, the crisis, the food riots, and the failure of the government, the police firing and about how the movement was always called the Food Movement. Likewise, he learns some details about the Naxalite Movement in Bengal, Marxism, slums, peasant uprising against landlords and the problems of tribal people.

Naipaul meets another man, Ashok, who comes from a South Indian Brahmin family and who tells him about his personal problems of adjustment. Then Naipaul meets Debu, who tells him about his involvement with the Naxalite Movement and his admiration for Charu Mazumdar. After gathering information from such people living in Calcutta, Naipaul makes his own frank observation about the city. He deplores the private and public squalor, the shoddiness of industrial goods, the ugliness and unsuitability of post-independence architecture and the suffering of everybody, etc.

After travelling in Calcutta, Naipaul goes to Lucknow and sees the Residency built by the Nawabs. He observes, "Lucknow was the end of the line for Muslim India" (p. 231). Naipaul meets a Muslim young man Rashid, who takes him around in Lucknow. Naipaul watches the bazaar, the mosques, Koran shops, children, and eunuchs with curiosity. Rashid tells Naipaul about the Muslims' illiteracy, Shia-Sunni clash, and the split of Muslim families after partition, etc. Naipaul sees the Great Imambara, the Butler Palace etc. Rashid tells him how he belongs to Lucknow and how he did not feel like staying in Pakistan after partition, "After my two months I was glad to leave. I felt relief to be back in India, after the claustrophobia of an Islamic society" (p. 387). Naipaul learns many details of Muslim life and culture of Lucknow.

Before going to Delhi, Naipaul pauses for a while to comment on a book entitled *My Diary in India* in the 1958-9 written by a British correspondent, William Howard Russell. He says, "I found the book hard to read" (p. 389). In that book Russell has recorded his experiences in India during 1857-Mutiny period. Russell has described the 'Plunder of the Kaiserbag' - the sight of dead bodies of Sepoys, looting, plundering and burning, etc, being infernal—in photographic detail. Naipaul "found Russell's book 'Victorian and wordy'" (p. 393) and "It is hard for an Indian not to feel humiliated by Russell's book" (p. 395). Then Naipaul comments upon how Sir William Jones, a judge of the Bengal Supreme Court, had come to India to make his fortune and actually amassed nearly 50,000 Pounds and how he translated Sakuntala from Sanskrit into English. Then he ruminates about the cultural destitution of Indian history.

Naipaul uses some of the ideas contained in Russell's book to understand the present India contrastively. He finds that caste-system is very powerful in India as compared with the society in Trinidad, where he was brought up. "...I had no easy idea of an enemy. Growing up in far-off Trinidad, I had no idea of clan or region, none of the supports and cushions of people in India" (p. 399). The seventy-year-old man and publisher, Vishwa Nath tells Naipaul, "The main reason why we are slaves" (p. 399) is the caste and that "The Brahmins let the country down", during all those dreadful invasions by the Mohammadans. All through, they went on chanting their prayers, their *havans*: 'Gods will protect us' (p. 400). Naipaul understands Vishwa Nath's anger, "And he had what I never had: a clear idea of the enemy. The Brahmins were the enemy—yet again, and more than 1000 miles north of the anti-brahmin politics of the South" (p. 400).

Naipaul's attention is turned from Vishwanath's anti-brahmin rage to the women's magazines that he edited in four languages. He comments on *Women's Era* and its simple contents like bride viewing, how to behave, personal hygiene, bathing and washing the undergarments etc. Naipaul is very frank in his opinion when he says, "Simple instruction- it made for dullness, if you were on the outside" (p. 404). He deplores the 'unglamorous subjects' and says, "There was nothing here to exercise the fantasy, to encourage longing. Who would ever have thought that this was the formula for a best-selling women's magazine?" (p. 404). The same is the case with other magazines like *Eve's Weekly, Femina* and *Savvy,* which publish sleek stories and articles on women's personal problems and trivia.

After commenting on women's magazines, Naipaul returns to Vishwa Nath's rage about the Indian history. His views are very realistic,

> The Hindu religion is a conglomeration of faiths, 500 religions or faiths. We've had reformist movements from the very beginning. From the dawn of civilization, we've had reformist movements against orthodoxy. What happens is that every reform movement degenerates into a sect-the Lingayats, the Arya Samajists, everybody. Buddha rebelled. Mahavir, the founder of the Jains, rebelled. Guru Nanak, the founder of the Sikhs, rebelled. It's long list. They rebelled and degenerated into sects, and became as orthodox as the previous orthodox people. So I didn't put on those saffron robes and start going about to those conferences, or preaching in public. I published my magazines. (p. 416)
>
> Vishwa Nath's summing up of his philosophy on Indian life is as frank as realistic, 'I think religion is the greatest curse of mankind. It has killed more people, destroyed more property, than any other thing. Even today - Northern Island, the Middle East. The Hindus, Muslims, Sikhs, all fighting each other in India. The oldest profession is not prostitution. It is the priesthood. (p. 418).

Naipaul goes from Delhi to the Punjab, where he sees some kind of awakening. He notices this awakening and anger as a common feature of contemporary Indian life. "To awaken to history was to cease to live instinctively. It was to begin to see oneself and one's group the way the outside world saw one, and it was to know a kind of rage. India was now full of this rage. There had been a general awakening; and every group sought to separate its rage from the rage of other groups" (p. 420). The Punjab was associated with terrorism during Naipaul's visit there. He notices it specially, "Everyday the newspapers carried plain official accounts of events in the Punjab: so many killed by Sikh terrorists; so many people arrested for harbouring terrorists; so many terrorists killed by police; so many 'intruders' from across the Pakistan border killed" (p. 420). The Sikh terrorism was part of the barbarity of the country or simply the barbarity of war, according to Naipaul. "People within the Hindu fold had always been rebelling against Brahmin orthodoxy, Vishwa Nath had said; and everyone, who had rebelled, had started a sect with its own rigidities" (p. 421).

Guru Nanak, who rebelled against Brahmin orthodoxy, belonged to the Punjab. The Sikhs had undergone humiliation at the hands of the British, but they were also influenced by the New Learning that had come to India. Naipaul collects several details about the Sikhs, their religion, their gurus and their attitude to life. He learns a lot about Bhindranwale, who was a poor villager, who tasted political power, organized his people, occupied the Golden Temple of Amritsar and declared war on the Hindus. But the Indian Government could not keep quiet. Mrs. Indira Gandhi ordered the army to attack the Golden Temple, to control Bhindranwale's terrorist activities. But later by way of wild justice, Mrs. Indira Gandhi was murdered by one of her Sikh bodyguards (i.e. Satwant Singh).

> Then Naipaul goes to Chandigarh and meets a few men like Gurtej Singh and Kapur Singh and learns a few details about the Sikh life and culture—like their persecution mania, passionate view of their religion, Hindu versus Sikh hatred and memories of Sikh glory. As Gurtej Singh tells Naipaul, "The great enemy of Sikhism and the Sikh empire of Ranjit Singh had been-again-Brahmanism... The brahmanically oriented forces within and without the Punjab cooperated in destroying the Sikhs, who alone held out a promise of the early redemption of India" (p. 444). A general feature that Naipaul notices in the Punjab is their search for identity. "The establishing of a Sikh identity was a recurring Sikh need. Religion was the basis of this identity; religion provided the emotional charge" (p. 448). Bhindranwale was a symbol of the quest for Sikh identity. Naipaul meets a number of Sikhs like Ram Singh, Joga Singh, Avinash Singh and learns many details about the close relationship between Bhindranwale and Buta Singh.

> When Naipaul travels to Amritsar, he meets Mr. Amarinder Singh, the Maharaja of Paitala, who tells him about his family, which has been blessed twice by the Guru. Amrinder Singh takes Naipaul to the new Patiala palace and shows the photographs of rulers hung on the wall there. Naipaul sees them as symbols of a changing India. "In its various reception rooms were signed photographs, such as the visitor sees on open days in grand houses in other countries. But here the photographs—of rulers—marked a changing world, a changing vision, an emerging India: the Kaiser, Victor Emmanuel, the Belgian royal family, Tito, Nehru, Indira Gandhi" (p. 464).

Amarinder Singh tells Naipaul that "My grandfather was an autocrat through and through" (p. 464) and that "the old Patiala palace had 1000 rooms and 400 acres" (p. 465) and that "In our family archives there is a letter from the last Moghul Emperor, Bahadur Shah" (p. 467). On the whole, Amarinder Singh gives a positive picture of the glory of their past life and the present degeneration. For example, when his father lost his kingdom to the Punjab, "my father became a nobody" (p. 469). He is very proud of his people and their history. He tells Naipaul, "When the chips were down I couldn't let 300 years of history go. It was the Sikhs, who made Patiala. The two Gurus have blessed us. I had to stand with our people" (p. 470). Then Naipaul meets other Sikhs in the Punjab and learns more details about Bhindranwale and terrorist activities there.

After completing his tour in the Punjab, Naipaul goes to the vale of Kashmir and stays in the same hotel, i.e., Palace Hotel in which he had stayed in 1962. The hotel was the summer palace of the Maharaja of Kashmir. Naipaul had met Maharaj Karan Singh, who was the Governor of the State then. He meets the hotel servants that he had met earlier in 1962—like Mr. Butt and remembers the past meetings. Naipaul remembers the Shankaracharya Hill and the Hindu temple on it. In Kashmir, Naipaul buys an expensive shawl for Rs. 7,500. Then he visits the cave of Amarnath. He observes the slow change that has come over Kashmir between his 1962 trip and the present one. He says, "Much money had come to the valley; many people had risen; there was a whole new educated generation. But a good deal of that improvement had been swallowed up by the growth in the population" (p. 513).

After his visit to the vale of Kashmir, Naipaul winds up his journey in India and flies back to London. He feels some difficulty in writing his travelogue on two counts: one, the content of his experience and two, the technique of organizing the amorphous experience.

> The next year, in an oppressive furnished flat in South London, I began to write my book about India. I had intended to write one, but after my early weeks I had begun to give up the idea. Travel writing was new to me, and I didn't see how I could find a narrative for a book about India: I was too overwhelmed by the distress I saw. I had kept no journal, made few connected notes. But money had been spent, and book had to be written... After the book was written, order given to memories, a narrative found, Indian emotions faced and written out—the details began to fade. The time came when I no longer read the book. (p. 493)

Thus Naipaul succeeds in giving an artistic shape to his travelling experience in India. Having perceived a conspicuous change in Indian life from his 1962 visit to the present one in 1988, he sums up his observation. He notices that India has been remade and restored to itself after its own Dark Age; that India has been lucky to have leaders like Ram Mohan Roy and Gandhi that India has a new kind of intellectual life and spirit of liberation. He is happy to see the spirit of liberation writ large on Indian life:

> In the 130 years or so since the Mutiny—the last 90 years of the British Raj and the first 40 years of independence begin increasingly to appear as part of the same historical period—the idea of freedom has gone everywhere in India. Independence was worked for by people more or less at the top; the freedom it brought has worked its way down. People everywhere have ideas now of who they are and what they are themselves. The process quickened with the economic development that came after independence; what was hidden in 1962, or not easy to see, what perhaps was only in a state of becoming, has become clearer. The liberation of spirit that has come to India could not come as release alone. In India, with its layer below layer of distress and cruelty, it had to come as disturbance. It had to come as rage and revolt. India was now a country of a million little mutinies.

> A million mutinies, supported by twenty kinds of group excess, sectarian excess, religious excess, regional excess: the beginnings of self-awareness, it would seem, the beginnings of an intellectual life, already negated by old anarchy and disorder. But there was in India now what didn't exist 200 years before: a central will, a central intellect, a national idea. The Indian Union was greater than the sum of its parts, and many of these movements of excess strengthened the Indian state, defining it as the source of law and civility and reasonableness...
>
> Excess was now felt to be excess in India. What the mutinies were also helping to define was the strength of the general intellectual life, and the wholeness and humanism of the values to which all Indians now felt they could appeal. And—strange irony -- the mutineers were not to be wished away. They were part of the beginning of a new way for many millions, part of India's growth, part of its restoration.
>
> (p. 518).

In this travelogue, unlike in his earlier ones, Naipaul becomes a greater listener than a commenter. He has exercised his self-control and conquered his righteous anger and disgust and tried to stimulate Indians to speak for themselves so that he may understand their life, problems and predicaments from their point of view. He seems to have cultivated the fine habit of anthropologists, who believe in the view that the best way to understand a culture other than your own is to achieve a kind of empathy with it. To show sympathy to somebody is to understand him or her. It is this affirmative approach that he has adopted in this travelogue and kept his rational ego under check.

One might ask the question as to what kind of vision of India that emerges out of Naipaul's latest travelogue. Certain things become explicit in it which may be summed up briefly as follows: India has been growing into a more and more overcrowded country, partly due to the general explosion of population and partly due to internal migration of people from the country side to the metropolitan cities. One might remember here that Naipaul had described India as an overcrowded baracoon. That impression continues here also.

Another conspicuous thing about the Indian socio-political reality is that there has been going on a cold war between brahmins and non-brahmins. The democratic way of thinking has made the people of all communities and religions of India to reject the hierarchical varna-system propounded by Manu in his Dharmashastra. The transition from the feudal and hierarchical system to modern democratic system has been a painful one, though it is most welcome at the same time. But one of the ironies of Indian society is that the people, far from becoming secular, have become more communal. What was said about America may be said about India now. Far from becoming a melting pot of cultures, India has become a pot of salad, wherein all the communities and cultures have to live together with their separate identities. The non-brahmins like Dalits, Sikhs, Jains, Lingayats and Sikhs want to solidarize their own groups and fight against the Brahmins for equal opportunities and privileges in all walks of life, especially education, officialdom and politics. Due to this general non-brahmanical awareness, the brahmanical hegemony is threatened. We have already seen how Periyar and Namdev Dhasal have given voice to the non-brahmanical point of view. The conflict between brahmins and sudras expresses itself in various forms, especially in the conflict between Aryan and Dravidian consciousness.

At the same time, the modern brahmanical life is also characterized by internal contradictions and attempts of adjustment and reconciliation. Though they are proud of their Vedic knowledge, rituals and purity-mania, yet they are shy about their churkis, separatism and priestly habits and wish to modernize themselves by learning English and science and doing non-priestly jobs and entering politics.

Whereas there is one kind of conflict between Brahmins and non-brahmins, there is another kind of conflict between Hindus and Muslims in India, which is noticed by Naipaul. The Hindu fundamentalism represented by Shiv Sena provides a parallel and a balance to the Muslim fundamentalism. Naipaul cannot find fault with them as both have their own logic of historical action and reaction. But he cannot understand the criminalization of society, which goes hand in hand with fundamentalism.

Naipaul's vision of India corresponds to Nirad Chaudhuri's. The Chaudhurian view that India is a land of many contradictions—geographical, cultural, social, political and religious and so on—is amply confirmed by Naipaul's observation. For example, the central Government is trying to evoke the feeling of nationalism in the minds of its citizens. But this nationalism provides a contrast to regionalism and parochialism. Naipaul mentions Mr. Rao, who is proud of being a Maharashtrian. Naipaul's observation easily corresponds to Chaudhuri's view that it is difficult to find Indians in India, but it is easy to find Maharashtrians, Gujaratis, Bengalis and so on.

Contradictions are found in India in terms of religion and culture also. The non-violence of Jains provides a good contrast to the violence and terrorism of Sikhs and Muslims. Similarly vegetarians and non-vegetarians practise their philosophy with equal force of conviction. Likewise superstitious religiosity goes hand in hand with science and technology (especially technology). Most of the Indian scientists happen to hail from priestly Brahmin castes. The non-brahmin scientists complain that science in India has not developed because of its association with Brahmins.

Since India is a multi-lingual and multi-cultural country, each community has to follow its own ideal or dharma. Since there is no single or uniform dharma (Lord Krishna preached in the BhagavadGita that it is better to die in one's own dharma than follow others'.) to be commonly followed by all the Indians, nay, Hindus, contradictions are bound to be there, resulting in countless conflicts and million mutinies. Although Naipaul is himself a brahmin, his diasporic status and westernized way of thinking have prevented him from taking sides with the brahmanical point of view and from looking down upon the non-brahmanical one. What is admirable in Naipaul is his maintenance of psychic distance and objectivity.

One broad theme that emerges in his travelogue is that in spite of all these countless contradictions, conflicts and million mutinies, there is a change (though it is very slow) in the Indian society in terms of education, agriculture, economics and, of course, politics. The general awakening that is taking place in the Indian psyche is appreciated and admired by Naipaul. "In his classic travelogue Naipaul reveals his new vision of India. It is the voice of optimism; and with all the awareness of the paradoxes of freedom, there is in it, a postmodern acceptance of its vital energies and conflicting claims."[4] Although Indian readers may not be fascinated by the abundant details of Indian life offered by Naipaul (due to their familiarity with them) *India: A Million Mutinies Now* is sure to attract the attention of the non-Indian readers. Auberton Waugh says, "Brilliantly enjoyable... I loved the old Naipaul for his sardonic wit. The new one is to be loved for his sweetness of nature, amounting almost to sanctity."[5] Paul Theroux writes, "It is literally the last word on India today, witness within witness, a chain of voices that illustrates every phase of Indian life...with a truthfulness and a subtlety that are a joy to read. Something like love enters the narrative—a real feeling for the land and its people."[6] Obviously *India: A Million Mutinies Now* is a postmodernist travelogue with its characteristic polyphony.[7]

References

1. Quoted by Rob Nixon, *London Calling*, London: Oxford University Press, 1992. p.25.
2. Yashoda Bhat, *V.S.Naipaul: An Introduction*, Delhi: B.R.Publishing Corporation, 2000, p.131.
3. V.S.Naipaul, *India: A Million Mutinies Now*, London: Vintage, 1998. p.11. (All the subsequent page references are to this edition.)
4. *Ibid*, p. 133.
5. Auberton Waugh, *Sunday Telegraph*, quoted on the blurb of *India: A Million Mutinies Now.*
6. Paul Theroux, *Literary Review*, quoted on the blurb of *India: A Million Mutinies Now*
7. *Ibid*, Quoted on the blurb.

Index